Far Enough Away

Everyone's life is full of stories to be told. The art comes from sharing those life experiences in a way that makes people care, that offers insight and wisdom, that entertains and humors. David McGrath is just such a storyteller. His memories are rich. His writing is brisk, lucid and purposeful.
—Kerry Temple, Editor in Chief, *Notre Dame Magazine*

McGrath captures not only the nuances of his own life in these stories, but the life of a city.
— Tom Fate, author of *The Long Way Home* and *Cabin Fever.*

David McGrath keenly understands how family and place profoundly shape us. His reminiscences about growing up in suburban Chicago don't just entertain with sprightly prose, which in itself is a gift to readers. Beyond that, his stories illuminate essential aspects of what it means to be human.
—Colleen Kujawa, *Chicago Tribune* Opinion Editor

Reading David McGrath's stories from Chicago to Wisconsin's north woods is a chance to consider our own stories. Of growing up. Of the people we love. Of all those things that make us, us. His memories spark so many of our own memories, reminding us how we can be our best selves and see the best in others.
—Chuck Frederick, Editorial Page Editor, *Duluth News Tribune*

Dave McGrath's intelligence, humor and humanity shine brightly through each of these thought-provoking essays. What's more, his compelling writerly voice creates the feeling that you're communing with a friend.
—Robert Georgalas, author of *Deep Focus, All That Remains,* and *Nothing Lost*

Far Enough Away

David McGrath

Essays originally published in slightly different forms in the *Chicago Tribune, Notre Dame Magazine, Chicago Sun Times, Naperville Sun, Daily Southtown, Elgin Courier, Florida Sportsman Magazine, Minneapolis Star Tribune, St. Paul Pioneer Press, Duluth News Tribune, Angling International Magazine, Madison Capital Times, Sawyer County Record, Wisconsin State Journal, Orlando Sentinel, Fort Myers News Press, Sarasota Herald Tribune, Naples Daily News, Charlotte Sun.*

Kindle Direct Publishing
Copyright © David McGrath 2023

For Marianne

Cover Photo of Author and Granddaughter, Summer Allen
Courtesy of Jacqueline McGrath

Contents

Introduction	5
Family	7
Romance	26
Fatherhood	44
Motherhood	56
Friendship	66
Education	82
Race	118
Conservation	136
Holidays	154
Journeys	175

Introduction

My daughter asked me to give a toast at her wedding reception.

Traditionally, remarks by the father of the bride are a combination of marital advice ("always listen to each other... never go to bed angry") and good wishes for the future ("may even your rainy days have rainbows").

But trying to avoid reruns and cliches, I focused, instead, on Jackie's character, combing through memories for something unique and true.

How, for example, she was a precocious and affectionate child. And how when she would hug her mother, she would wrap her arms around her neck, squeeze her eyes shut, and pat my wife's back with her little hand.

Later, at age 5, she announced that she would marry Freddie Papke. Her mother and I were not ecstatic. Like any other father, I did not think that the boy next door was good enough for a daughter of mine.

Between them, Jackie usually did most of the talking with the vocabulary of a miniature adult. Whereas, Freddie was content to listen, responding chiefly with eyebrows, his mouth preoccupied with cookies or licorice whips.

But the little dude did possess one attribute attractive to my daughter: he was oppressed.

His parents never let Freddie out of their sight or voice range, so that he might remain attentive to their non-stop instructions to wipe his nose, get up out of the dirt, or pull up his pants. And the most serious prohibition imposed on Freddie was that he was not allowed to enter the steep alleyway behind the garage.

As far as his parents were concerned, Piggy Toe Mountain, as the alley was locally known, was a no man's land where wandered raccoon, stray dogs, and reckless kids who plunged down Piggy Toe on their sleds in winter, and on bicycles in the summertime.

Jackie, of course, became obsessed with Freddie's liberation. And on a fateful day in spring, she led him through the back gate and onto Piggy Toe Mountain.

It wasn't for very long, and it's not known what transpired. Just that they returned breathless and with dirt stains on their knees. Yet as soon as Freddie returned home, he ratted Jackie out to his parents, who were outraged that our little "hussy" took him where it was forbidden.

More significantly, Freddie's betrayal was Jackie's first lesson about men. Not only did she change her mind about marrying Freddie, but she swore she would never marry at all.

The story was a hit at the wedding banquet, garnering some laughs and a round of applause when I concluded that it took a man as kind, honest, and both as interesting and as adventurous as the groom, to get Jackie to rescind her oath.

A concrete and enduring feature of the story, of course, is Piggy Toe Mountain. In the 1950's, municipal engineers in Evergreen Park decided that rather than level what was likely the peak of a glacial moraine, they would terrace 96th Place and 96th Street on both sides, thus leaving a steep and unnavigable hill, and what would turn out to be a shangri la for swarms of children.

It was close enough to the security of our homes and parents, yet far enough away for freedom, risk, and creativity, rather like a tree bough jutting into the sky from which baby birds try out their wings.

From my first sled ride, my first fist fight, my first cigarette, and my first kiss, Piggy Toe was our arena for danger and for dreams. Neither as long nor as wide as Huck and Tom's Mississippi playground, it was, nonetheless, far enough away for launching life's journey toward independence and self knowledge and who we are today.

***

Family

-My family's Irish heritage made me proud. Then my sister got a DNA test.

I have a confession to make. I have been living a lie.

The fraud has persisted for over a half a century, although it has only come to light this past year. And I need to come clean about it before March 17. That is, of course, St. Patrick's Day, which for my birth family has been a holiday on par with Christmas in importance and veneration.

It was the only day when my five brothers, two sisters and I felt entitlement because of our last name. My parents, who sometimes struggled to procure enough milk, bread and cornflakes for a family of 10, always managed to purchase plenty of green derbies, neck ties, carnations and four-leaf clover pins for us to wear to school to show off our ethnicity.

Uncle Don McGrath, for whom my father worked as a salesperson, permitted his employees and their families to watch the annual South Side parade from behind the store's display windows as the marching bands and floats with leprechauns made their way down Ashland Avenue. This was a heady perk, especially when March in Chicago came in "like a lion," and everyone else lined the sidewalks in the frosty outdoors.

When St. Paddy's fell on a school day, my mother, Gert, whom we could never fool by faking bellyaches to ditch school, had no hesitation when it came to writing notes to eight different teachers to excuse our absences for the celebration.

And in our teens, when we joined other South Side Irish youth in chugging quart bottles of beer on summer nights at Kennedy Park, even the police seemed sympathetic to the tradition, issuing warnings, confiscating our Blatz and Old Style, but never calling parents or hauling us in.

My father, Charlie, the head of our clan, was the life of

every party, telling stories and prompting laughter with his twinkling eyes and charm. He was elected president of our neighborhood association, trustee of Evergreen Park and offered a job on radio, all thanks to his gift of blarney.

He bequeathed his powers, and my siblings and I became the eulogists, speechmakers and toastmasters at funerals, anniversaries and other social functions. I was repeatedly drafted as master of ceremonies for retirement parties at both schools where I worked, and I hosted the campaign kickoff event for our school administrator when he ran for Congress.

I was even asked to do "stand-up" at the Christmas gala my friend threw for his employees. I flopped, having overestimated the open mindedness of the audience which wanted to run me out of the banquet hall on a rail — all in jest, of course.

In the tradition of world heavyweight champion James J. Braddock, Charlie Jr. was our Irish strongman and brawler. Kenneth and Kevin inherited Dad's tart wit. And following the lead of legendary troubadours, from Irish tenor John McCormack, to rockers Bono, Sinead O'Connor and Van Morrison, my older brother, James, entertained U.S. troops with his band, "The Unclassified Three," at Army bases all over Europe during his military service.

Predictably, I had Marianne's father, Tom, paged at a parish St. Patrick's Day party to ask for her hand, proposing marriage to her later that night at a romantic dinner at the Italian Village. The next day we learned that Tom and his wife, Ruth, won a trip to Ireland in the parish raffle. I've chronicled it all here, and I've published half a dozen other stories about the Irish bloodline and the stereotypes manifest in our family history.

Most of which I must now retract, for I fear it's all a lie.

Last spring, on a whim, Nancy treated herself to a DNA test from Ancestry.com, just for fun. Instead, it felled our family tree: 35% German; 33% Russian, Pomeranian; 13% Baltic; 9% English (and northwestern European); 5% Greek, Albanian, Peloponnesian; 3% Balkan; and 2% Swedish and Danish.

For the first time in our lives, we were speechless. My

desperate hope was that the 9% portion that included northwestern Europe, indicated, at the very least, a smidgen of Irish blood. But the shaded portion of the DNA map which included the United Kingdom and Scotland, steered totally clear of the Emerald Isle.

James thought that there may be an explanation and is researching the possibility either that our father was adopted, or that there was a mix-up at the hospital at birth. But photos of Grandpa Ray, all but indistinguishable from photos of Dad at the same age, call his theory into question.

Subsequently, James had his own DNA tested with findings similar to Nancy's.

What does it all mean? Is it a definitive resolution of the age-old debate of nature vs. nurture? Does the power of suggestion trump chemical and genetic composition? Did our presumption of Irishness hypnotize us into cultural assimilation? Even worse, cultural theft?

Can we McGraths no longer do what we do? Be who we are?

As for me, well, I don't know. As a former Irishman who tends to believe in a pot of gold at the end of every rainbow, I read up on the Pomeranians and found they were especially fond of folk dancing.

And lately, and especially after both of my hips were replaced last year, I've been feeling a mysterious urge to shuffle and shimmy.

Chicago Tribune, March 4, 2022

-Summer and Grampy

Summer is 5, and she addresses me as "Grampy," especially when teaching me things.

Like when we went swimming last week, and she taught me how our fingers get wrinkly from the water. But she assured me they'll get better after a while.

Mostly, she teaches me about animals, as with the important lesson after I incorrectly identified her stuffed unicorn as a horse.

"Focus on the horn, Grampy," she said.

She knows a lot for a kindergartener because she's always reading. Her mother is an English teacher and her father a writer, and reading preceded even potty training in their household.

There's not much a plain grandpa can teach her, though I did buy her a fishing pole and have been showing her how to cast. It's a Zebco reel, and you have to push the button to release the line an instant after the apex of your overhand motion. She learned quickly, not an easy feat of hand and eye coordination for a 5-year-old.

Summer stays overnight some weekends, and upon awakening, usually says she dreamed about elephants, though I think it's partly because she likes when I press my lips together to blow out their trumpeting sound.

Some mornings she asks for a story, of which I have many, since I am old. I recount adventures with playmates Robert and Joseph when we were nearly her same age. Summer listens hard and is a vigilant fact checker, and I've been more careful ever since she asked me to show her some "vampire gold" from one tale, and I could not oblige.

After another story about the Michigan cabin we stayed in 50 years ago, where my brothers Jimmy, using a pillow case, and Kenneth, his cowboy hat, and myself, a bow and suction-up arrow, failed to catch the plump gray mouse running circles in the kitchen, she asked if we could revisit that cabin.

"We need to catch that mouse, Grampy."

I'd be remiss if I didn't mention that Summer's favorite person here is my wife Marianne, whom she calls Mimi, who is not silly, whom she loves to cuddle with, and is the person in charge.

We have fun, though, when Mimi goes for her walk and announces that "Grampy is in charge," and Summer's eyes get big, and Grampy winks.

Before leaving, Mimi warns, "And no Bugs Bunny on TV," and Grampy makes a funny face behind Mimi's back. Summer stifles a giggle but immediately rats me out: "Mimi, Grampy made a baby face."

For her parents told her it is good to be a tattle tale, and she should never hesitate to snitch on the other boys and girls at school, her cousins, or any grownups.

As soon as Mimi's gone, we find the yoga ball and play soccer in the living room. It's so fun because the ball, says Summer, is "ginormous," and also "humorous" (she has named it Bella), though somebody once kicked it high, cracking a miniature vase.

And since Summer is a good girl, she's upset when something's broken or spilled and starts to cry, but not too long, since nearly all grampas have fix-it shops in their garages, and I repaired it with a fast-drying marine epoxy so that Mimi would never know.

Occasionally, on cloudy days, after perhaps dreaming of something not as joyous as elephants, Summer nestles in Mimi's lap for a long time, once or twice peeking over Mimi's arm at Grampy, reading the paper across the room. It may take until the sun comes out, or until lunch time, before she warms up and is ready to play again.

Summer's back home, and I have asked her parents' permission to write all this down on the occasion of National Children's Day on June 12, which is freighted with more significance this year after the horrifying school shooting in Uvalde, Texas exposed our failure at keeping them safe.

Since kids can't vote, it's up to us in the upcoming midterm election to cast ballots for those who prioritize the lives of children.

Not only supporting sensible gun control measures to prevent schoolhouse atrocities, but also regarding legislation mitigating childhood poverty, hunger, and homelessness, and supporting universal pre-school education, health care coverage and child care.

Nothing has more value than our children. And I've never been more acutely aware of that fact than when I was christened 'Grampy,' and inspired, loved, and awed by my amazing granddaughter.

Chicago Sun Times & Duluth News Tribune, June 10, 2022

-Eight authentic ways of knowing you're Irish

Though it has taken nearly a year, a resolution is finally within reach after last year's shocking news that my birth family is not Irish.

Readers may recall my op-ed prior to St. Patrick's Day in 2022 about my sister Nancy's jarring discovery that the heritage we had been claiming, celebrating and actualizing with our beliefs and practices for the previous 50 years, was apparently a big fat lie. Ancestry.com broke the news to Sis that there wasn't a single chromosomal strand of Irish in her DNA.

Understandably, my seven siblings succumbed to various states of pique and dissension. Kevin questioned Ancestry's accuracy. James questioned our parentage. Kenneth questioned Nancy's reason for getting tested. And they all questioned my reason for blabbing it to the world.

OK, maybe not quite the world, but a whole bunch of people in places where the story was reprinted, from the St. Paul Pioneer Press to the Pittsburgh Post-Gazette, among others.

Emails poured in from all over. Readers commiserated, corroborated or thought I was joking. (Would I?)

The messages fell into one of three categories: readers with stories of their own DNA test nightmares; readers venturing hypotheticals about our family's lineage, such as a secret adoption in a branch of the family tree; and readers assuring me that the Irish "spirit" is what's important, not DNA, though I could not always tell whether they were referring to culture or whiskey.

In the wake of the conflicting advice and misdirected sibling anger (toward me), the good news is that I have seized upon a solution to propose to my kin:
My Dear Brothers and Sisters,

In keeping with a great American tradition, let's "sue the bastards."

How better to redress our grievances than in a court of law, where we can hold somebody responsible and make them pay. "Somebody," of course, does not mean your loving baby brother, who was only the messenger.

Instead, let's hold Ancestry.com's feet to the fire. Who, after all, caused the pain and suffering you all endured? The public embarrassment. Defamation of your character.

Not to mention the collateral damage to others, such as my wingman, Ron O'Jerak, heartbroken that I can't, in good conscience, join him on St. Paddy's Day.

The thornier question, you're probably thinking, is what's the basis for the lawsuit? How, exactly, is Ancestry in the wrong? Doesn't a defendant have to have "malice of forethought" or be negligent in some way? After all, every source consulted says its DNA testing is more than 99% accurate.

Won't such an indisputable statistic daunt our legal team? Ha! About as much as sparrows frighten eagles, or a hare intimidates a lion, to paraphrase the Bard.

That's because DNA, my sweet and kind siblings, is at the very heart of our case. Think of the historic Scopes monkey trial, in which famed attorney Clarence Darrow and evolutionary science were pitted against William Jennings Bryan and the Bible. And we all know how that turned out.

But instead of monkeys versus good Christians, it will be Ancestry.com versus the beleaguered McGraths.

I can see it all now: Ancestry's lawyers calling to the stand dozens of experts on chromosomes and recessive genes and such.

Meanwhile, we McGraths challenge the core of Ancestry's claim that deoxyribonucleic acid is the determining factor for ethnicity by calling our blood witnesses who embody ancient and universally accepted markers of Irish identity:

"If it pleases the court, your honor, plaintiffs would like to enter into evidence Exhibit A, the grand Irish tenor singing voice of brother James, frontman for a rock band that toured Europe in the 1960s; Exhibit B, the positive spirit of youngest sister Nancy, so vivacious that she'd smile and wish the devil himself a good morning if he happened by; Exhibit C, the legendary Irish talent for humor and storytelling of McGrath middle child Patrick; Exhibit D, the famed "Irish goodbye," or first son Charlie's self-assured way of vanishing from a party or happy hour, sparing everyone the prolonged farewells; Exhibit E, the gift of gab of brother Kenneth, whether at a wedding, the golf links or at graveside; Exhibit F, the personal warmth of elder sister Rose, at whose home you must always stay for dinner; Exhibit G, the unfiltered sharp wit of brother Kevin, inspiring brawls in which he delighted to engage; and Exhibit H, David's affection for Irish lagers and ales, primarily for medicinal purposes, of course."

And just as we are about to rest our case, Nancy and Rosemary promenade up the aisle of the courtroom to the organist's strains of "Tura, Lura, Lura," while cradling a lacy pillow on which sits our late dad's green derby hat!

Just like "Miracle on 34th Street," there won't be a dry eye in the place.

Victory is assured, so long as teetotalers are excluded from the jury pool.

Chicago Tribune, March 16, 2023

-Evergreen Park science teacher Monica Fudacz shared gifts with students, friends and family

Monica had beautiful hands.

Her older sister, Marianne, my wife, and I thought it remarkable, in consideration of everything she put them through as a seamstress, a chef, phlebotomist, gardener, occasional carpenter and science teacher.

Yet even in her 60s, her hands looked like Barbara

Streisand's in "A Star is Born." Strong, sculpted fingers, smooth skin, neat and polished nails accentuated by a stunning diamond ring given to her 41 years ago by her husband, Joe.

Monica Fudacz, a science teacher at Central Junior High School in Evergreen Park, died June 17 at age 63. Besides her husband, she left three children, Eddie, Laura and David, two grandchildren and a life long legacy of service to the community and of generosity and love to family and friends.

As a science teacher, she believed in tactile learning for individuals and small groups, assiduously crafting experiments and projects which she would model with those hands, guiding her students to follow suit. They responded positively, grateful for a teacher who spoke to them like adults.

After school, Monica resumed work on gifts with which to surprise a neighbor, a friend or a relative, such as draperies for the living room in her sister's new home and a quilt for her niece's new baby. She taught herself to sew and found it to be one of the more edifying outlets for her creativity, along with her garden and her kitchen, which like her classroom were a playground for discovery of daring recipes she shared on Pinterest.

A memorable example of her resourcefulness was in the mid-1980s, when the Cabbage Patch doll became the must-have Christmas gift for little girls, including for our daughter Jackie. The manufacturer issued naming and adoption papers with each "baby," a gimmick helping to create a huge demand for the toys. It also created shortages in stores, fights in shopping malls over the meager supply and a price close to $100 for each toy, an amount we could not afford to spend on a single Christmas gift.

Aunt Monica came to the rescue, sewing a replica Cabbage Patch doll for Jackie with $20 worth of material. Jackie loved the "knock-off" and named her after former first lady Abigail Adams. Monica, like any self-respecting Fairy Godmother, loved being able to provide that joy.

Years ago, when I first started dating Marianne, we drove to Michigan to visit with her parents in their rental lakeside cottage. Monica was just a youngster, and I still remember how she loved jumping off the dock and paddling around in a floatie. Her ecstatic expression, I assumed, was for her love of the water. Little did I know then that her radiant smile and childlike glee were portable features that would arrive wherever she did.

All six of the Dunne sisters are close, but I got to see firsthand how two of them, separated by eight years, transitioned from siblings to friends.

Both would earn education degrees at Chicago State University; both would begin teaching in Beverly; both would culminate their careers in District 124 in Evergreen Park.

Never far apart, they shared stories, advice, dreams, their children's clothes, family gossip and vacation destinations in Wisconsin's NorthWoods.

When Monica needed a guinea pig from whom to draw blood while training to be a phlebotomist before she became a teacher, Marianne stepped up. When our son Michael was rushed to surgery to save his life following an auto accident, Monica's was the first reassuring face Marianne saw in the waiting room.

Once while browsing at the Venture department store, with Janet seated in the shopping cart, Marianne was greeted by a stranger who asked how she was doing. After an awkward minute, Marianne realized the woman mistook her for Monica.

Their bond grew stronger after retirement, when they've been able to enjoy a few more extended periods of time together.

Monica tolerated me as her sister-pal's husband, and was often Marianne's bemused ally in our constructive disputes. She especially liked calling me out on my fanciful theories on child-rearing or the Battle of the Sexes with the equanimous logic of her scientific mind ("Sure, Dave").

Her loss changes everything and hurts in every way. It's a cliché and a truism that the good die young. But Monica would be the first to remind us that because she and Joe were high school sweethearts, they have enjoyed a mathematically greater length + intensity + volume of happiness than the rest of us.

Chicago Tribune (Southtown) & Sawyer County Record, June 26, 2020

-A Generation's Emotional Roadblock

"I love you, Dad," said Janet.

She is the younger of my two daughters, and we were exchanging goodbyes at the end of a phone conversation.

"Me too, Honey."

"Me, too" was pretty easy to say. Occasionally, I have even been able to substitute, "Love you," for good-bye, when any one of my three children is ending a visit.

But why do I find it so hard to say to them, "*I* love you"? Why does the English language's tiniest pronoun weigh 2,000 pounds when I try to insert it in that sentence?

My difficulty likely astounds readers in the year 2023 for whom intimacy and declarations thereof are commonplace, which I envy.

Yes, I can voice the three words to my wife at the end of the day. But even with Marianne, it involves heavy lifting, such as first turning off the reading light.

When speaking to the woman to whom I've been married for decades, "Love you," absent the first person subject, is way lighter and easier as I'm hanging up the phone or leaving for an overnight.

Since Marianne can cut to the core of an issue faster than I can, I asked her the difference between the two expressions while writing this column.

"'I love you' makes a direct connection with one individual," said Marianne. "'Love you' is something you just flip in the air. No real investment. Like 'love you guys,' or 'love that song,' or 'love the White Sox.'"

"So why," I added, "is it easy for me to say, 'I love you,' to Summer?" I asked. Summer is our six year old granddaughter.

"Summer won't think you're weird," said Marianne. "But

our kids would probably think you are dying."

And that's the crux of it: there's no precedent in our family because there was no precedent when I was growing up. My father never said it to me.

Certainly, we felt the love he harbored for all eight of his children, giving up so much in his own life to raise us. He performed selfless, sacrificial acts for each of us, like the day I previously wrote about when he left work to take me to Aqua Pool in Evergreen Park to help me overcome embarrassment over an unsightly scar on my side.

For men of the "Greatest Generation," stoicism was a coping mechanism for the horrors of world war. The only time I ever saw Dad drop his guard was after my brother Patrick was drafted and walked out the door for his ride to the airport and the flight that would take him to Viet Nam. My father wept quietly on our front porch.

Our succeeding generation saw our forebears' stoicism as a badge of manhood, perceiving it as an Earnest Hemingway/Humphrey Bogart ideal, not a shortcoming.

Accordingly, I am hesitant to make myself vulnerable, to tear down the wall I built to project a strong father image, but which my erudite children characterized as "aloofness."

Though my mother did not similarly withhold affection, she bestowed it sparingly. Strategically. My older brother James reminded me about how whenever we were angry over punishment or parenting we considered unfair, she never failed to tuck us in at night, saying, "I love you," melting any resentment, restoring our worlds.

Obviously, I need to change before it's too late, lest my children be saddled with the same lack I'm describing.

This past year, I went on a three day fishing trip with my oldest friend Tom Booth. Every year, since our first fishing/camping trip in Quetico, Canada when we were both 19, we have spent countless hours together in boats, talking about families, friends, dreams, discoveries, aging, and everything else under the sun, during long periods when the fish aren't biting, which is often.

When I used him as a sounding board for the "love you" vs. "I love you" question, Tom offered corroboration, since his father of the same generation as mine, never said the words, either.

At the end of our fishing day, when I handed Tom the rope to hold the boat while I got the car and trailer, he said with a slight smile: "Love you."

He is wont to wear things out for the sake of comedy, so for the rest of the drive back, including when we stopped for something to eat, then later for gas, we alternated between "love you" and "I love you," at opportune times, and inopportune times in front of strangers, up until the moment he got on the plane and headed back home.

Tom is not a psychologist. Inane, repetitious, funny, he succeeded, however, in reducing the weight of both phrases.

Mike, Jackie, and Janet: I love you!

Yes, I can write it here. We'll see what happens later today when the rubber hits the road.

Chicago Tribune, June 19, 2023

-Connections Rekindle at Sacred Piece of Northwoods

My plan in July was to visit long-ago familiar places: The cottages where we spent summers with the kids. The waterfall on the Brunet River where we used to cool off. Treeland's restaurant where we frequently dined and laughed with our Winter friends Terry and Jane.

I was curious to see how the places have changed. And I looked forward to visualizing the memories that the old places would trigger.

My wife Marianne, however, has a different view. She prefers new destinations and is loath to return where she has been. "Loved that old house," she might say, "but I'm done with it." Or "I'm glad for our time on Dauphin Island. But I'll never go there again."

She says she wants to move forward and not dwell on the

past. And I can somewhat understand her preference not to revisit a place associated with distant memories of irretrievable experiences.

But something different happened when our grown children and our grandchild Summer joined us in a visit to Trap 'N Fish Lodge on Fishtrap Lake. It was an event that underscored the importance of place in everyone's lives, which did not conform to the expectations of either me or Marianne.

Trap 'N Fish Lodge, or "the Trap," as it was affectionately called, was just down the road from our cabin on Bluegill Lake. Close enough, in fact, that you could holler, "Hey, Joe," to the owner as he was opening up the doors in the morning, and Joe Donaghue would turn with a big smile and flash a thumbs-up sign.

We first met Joe, his wife Honey, and his kids Wendy, Randy, and Wanda, when we went out to dinner at The Trap in the spring of 1986. When I told them our plan to build a cabin down the road the following summer, Joe was delighted and he found a house nearby that we could rent during the construction.

Later, in the summer of that same year, Marianne, along with Mike who was 10, Jackie, 8, and Janet, 4, would pass The Trap each day as they marched down Fishtrap Road to bring me lunch at the work site. I'd climb down the ladder for a family picnic down at the lake, trying not to show the worries I had as a school teacher trying to complete an 800 square foot cabin that my family could safely inhabit.

Without being asked, the Donahues helped assuage my concerns. Both a small business owner and handyman extraordinaire, Joe had ready answers to my questions about carpentry, plumbing, and electricity challenges, and was happy to lend me any tool I might need from his huge collection.

One night, in the middle of a rainstorm, he and son Randy left their busy bar and towed my work van out of the mud with one of their army surplus vehicles. And at summer's end, when I feared not completing the cabin before having to return to school, Joe summoned Wendy's husband Dave Shotliff to finish the roof. A local hunting guide, Dave also later helped us deal with a young bear habitually visiting our lot and rooting through our rowboat for nightcrawlers.

Once we moved in, we returned from grocery shopping one day to find that Randy had delivered a load of sand for building castles, something our children had been clamoring for. And after field mice moved in when we did, Honey shared her secret strategy to evict them.

Throughout our entire 10 year residency on Bluegill Lake, it became clear how much Joe loved his children, his grandchildren, and the remote woods and waters of the Chequamegon Forest. So much love, that he had enough to spare for a new family that had become his neighbors.

We weren't the only ones. When Joe Donahue died in 2014, all those whose lives he had touched felt a familial loss. The Trap eventually closed. The music and laughter were gone. The Lodge with its jukebox and a hundred baseball caps stapled to the ceiling, and where we always felt welcome, turned ghostly quiet.

But now, eight years later, we spied an OPEN sign on The Trap's front door. Cautiously, we entered, then met the new owner, Andy Shotliff, Joe's grandson!

Andy had taken ownership, remodeled the building, reopened it to the public, and was operating as the manager of the bar and restaurant.

Although Andy was but a toddler during our days at Bluegill, it felt like we were members of the same family. We swapped stories about Grandpa Joe from the good old days, including when a bush pilot made an emergency landing on Fishtrap Road, and Joe and Randy plowed a runway across the snow covered lake so he could take off again.

And when Andy brought out The Trap's photo album, with images of Joe, Honey (now 85), Randy, Wanda, and Wendy from bygone days, there were several moments of silence, as we suddenly felt part of a reunion much larger than we had planned.

The rest of that week, my grown children Mike, Jackie and Janet, and their respective significant others, Gen, Gene, and Kevin, along with granddaughter Summer, would tube on the Namekagon

River, canoe on the Flambeau, visit the cabin on Bluegill Lake and swim at its beach, same as we used to 35 years ago.

And as Marianne and I watched 5 year old Summer run joyously down Bluegill's familiar path to the pier, we both experienced a brand new feeling: a mix of happiness, connectedness, and family, through intimacy with this sacred place.

Duluth News Tribune & Madison Capital Times, August 5th, 2022

-Friendly Ghosts

Halloween originated with the ancient Celts of western Europe as a celebration of ghosts and spirits in acknowledgement of and hope for an afterlife, according to The History Channel.

Yet, my mother Gertrude McGrath may have had a better idea, which we learned about this past summer.

Mom died ten years ago, but it wasn't till last July, during a family get-together in Wisconsin, that my sister Nancy hauled out all Mom's old photographs for us to see.

Predictably, we did a lot of reminiscing that night, laughing, drinking, and shedding some tears while sorting through old black and whites. There was Uncle Eddie in a thin jacket and his "Untouchables" era Fedora, pushing Nancy and Kevin on a sled down "Piggy Toe Mountain." Or Grandpa Joe, a wad of TipTop Tobacco in his cheek, standing next to a fuel pump at his gas station.

Suddenly, Nancy dug into another of the shoeboxes and pulled out a thick wad of cards bound with a wide brown rubber band, and she handed the stack to me.

The card on top was a two by four inch satiny color photo of a smiling Jesus, his heart visible and aflame. I slid it out of the stack and read this inscription on the other side: In Loving Memory of Daniel J. Whitters, Born Into Life September 7, 1916; Born Into Eternity September 26, 1992.

"Oh, man, Uncle Dan!" I said. "I used to lie on the floor on Saturday afternoons, listening to him and Dad talk baseball, while they drank Drewry's beer. This holy card must be from his wake."

"There must be two or three-hundred of those in the pile," said my son in law Kevin. "Did Catholics collect those like trading cards, or what?"

Not that I knew of. Baseball cards, yes, which my brother James collected. He bought packs with six cards and a flat stick of bubble gum for five cents. In 1959, he had every major league player except for Ted Williams who refused to sign with Topps card company. James kept them all in a couple of Velveeta cheese boxes for a year or two before they got tossed during spring cleaning.

James wasn't the only one. Kids collected stamps, movie posters, hit records, coins, and comic books. But my mother was the only person I've ever known with a treasure trove of funeral cards.

If you ever attended a wake, you likely received one. They're a little smaller than playing cards, with a saint or a religious scene on one side, and the name of the deceased on the other, with their birth and death dates, and the time and place of their funeral and burial.

Below their i.d. is a prayer, perhaps authored by the saint pictured, which you could read or recite, thereby earning "indulgences" or time off from Purgatory for the dearly departed and for yourself.

Mom's hoarding them was news to me. I knew my parents attended wakes every month, but she never mentioned her impressive collection.

I read aloud another card with the same Jesus picture, same flaming heart: William Doyle, At Rest December 23rd, 1976.

"Bill was Uncle Jimmy's best friend," I said. "He had penetrating blue eyes, so when he dressed up like Santa Claus at our house one year, all the little kids knew it was Bill because of those eyes."

We took turns reading:

Katherine Z. Chrustek, 1896-1979; Section 35, Plot 198. She was the mother of my mom's friend Stella who lived in

Naples. Certainly, Mom didn't fly to Florida for the wake, so she must have gotten it in the mail after sending a sympathy card.

William McGrath at Rest, November 1, 1988. " Wild" Uncle Bill used to sing a-cappella when he visited, like the comedy actor George Burns. Old Bill would start tap dancing right there in our kitchen.

Edward J. Cichoszewski, "Kayo,"1922-2006: my mom's brother. You could see in some of the old snapshots how when he was a kid, he resembled the character Kayo from the "Moon Mullins" comic strip.

As we dredged up our memories of the departed, the neighbors, relatives, and friends whom I had not thought of in decades were reincarnated right there on our Wisconsin hotel balcony. Their faces, their individual voices, the look in their eyes: All sparked alive thanks to Mom.

We read some more:

Robert Vojtech, 1945-1990. Bob was the smack-dab middle child of the ten Vojtech kids, which included Jack, Alan, Kenny, Joyce, Mary Lou, Bob, Don, Joe, Bill and Bonnie. We loved going to their house because each of us eight McGraths had their own Vojtech kid to play with.

Frances R. Plecki, 1936-1993. I did not know her, but the funeral card featured a photo of her beautiful, smiling face, and I could see why.

Ray Russell…our late neighbor from two doors down. William J. Farrell, M.D. …the McGrath family doctor. Ted Iverson…He let our family vacation at his Saddle Lake home where I caught my first bass. Mary "Monty" McGrath, Born Into Eternity 2010. When she first started dating my brother, she passed muster with all of us kids by instigating a huge water fight in the backyard.

Thomas Dunne, 1910-1976. Shortly after meeting Tom, my father-in-law, I took him perch fishing on the lakefront. But I had to tend his pole, since he walked up and down the shoreline all afternoon socializing with the other anglers.

*

Often at gravesites, priests, rabbis and ministers routinely say the same old words about how the dead will go on living in our hearts.

But to my Mom, talk was cheap, and she took matters into her own hands, making a special place for our beloved "ghosts," so that she and her descendants would remember them always.

And we will, Mom, thanks to you.

Chicago Tribune, October 28, 2023

Romance

-The End of Summer

Summertime: Like that brief moment in the morning when you first open your eyes, arch your back and stretch. You hold it. You purr luxuriously. You try to prolong the delicious feeling. But it never lasts.

I learned the truth when I turned 12.

I grew up on the far south side of Chicago, Evergreen Park, when there were battalions of kids. Children of war, baby boomers, swarming every block. Day after day, from the time I was awakened by the milkman opening our back door at dawn, till the tingling bells of the Good Humor ice cream truck slowly moving down 96th Place at dusk, we played outside, incredulous about our uninterrupted span of time without coats, parents, or homework.

A kid's concept of summer was of a vast, endless plain, filled with sidewalks for biking, trees for climbing, and "prairies" (South Side term for vacant lots) for exploring. We played free and wild but were wary of crossing an invisible line, lest we attract the attention of adults.

But it all went south in the summer of 1961.

With no parks in Evergreen Park, if you didn't count the swing set in front of the volunteer firehouse on Washtenaw Avenue, we would ride bikes to Chicago's Beverly Park on 103rd and Maplewood each morning to play baseball. We'd pack baloney and mustard sandwiches, a can of shoestring potato chips, and a gallon of red Kool-Aid in a glass milk jug, which I'd precariously transport by hanging it from my handlebars.

Sustenance was required because we'd play ball for hours. We would have played till twilight had our parents allowed us to pack our suppers, as well.

But on a sun-soaked weekday in August, while in the second inning of a game with four boys on a side (a ball hit to right field was an automatic out), Debbie Glick showed up, settling on the bench behind the chain link fence along the third base line. She wore a peach-colored top and bright white shorts.

John O'Neill, playing shortstop, turned, cupped his mouth with his hand and said she was from St. John Fisher. Catholics, of course, lived in parishes, and Fisher was somewhere near the park. We lived in St. Bernadette's.

Mickey Michau hit a bouncer to Tommy Booth who was pitching. With only four on a team, it was "pitcher's hands out."

O'Neill was not great at baseball but was older than the rest of us, and he knew things. Between batters, he decided to leave the infield and trot over to where Debbie Glick was hugging her knees, the heels of her Keds — no socks — tucked in against the white shorts.

O'Neill rested one foot on the bench where she was sitting in order to talk. Talking to a girl.

"There's only one out, John," I called.

O'Neill did not turn around. But Debbie Glick tilted up her head and gazed toward the outfield.

She turned back to O'Neill and smiled at something he said. She rocked once from side to side on the bench. She fixed the cloth purse beside her — more like a small beach bag — then threw back her head to smooth her long brown hair with her left hand.

I moved in a few steps from left field. We would play without him.

Sure enough, my brother Kenneth hit a slow grounder through O'Neill's vacated position and stretched it to a double. I called a timeout.

The Kool-Aid jug sat in the grass in foul territory, against the fence and opposite the bench. When I got there, I could hear O'Neill gossiping about some boy on St. John Fisher's basketball team whom apparently both he and Debbie Glick knew.

Is that what you talk to girls about?

I lifted the jug with both hands and took a long drink and a longer look through the glass bottom to see what was wrecking our game: No more than one girl. With very white teeth. Sparkly earrings.

The cold drink left a sharp stitch in my gut. My eyes returned to her face, but the earrings disappeared momentarily when she leaned forward to nod and politely laugh at some other boring thing O'Neill said.

But there it was again, at the intersection of ear and slender neck. A tiny sparkle, glinting behind the waterfall of hair shining in the sun. How could such a small and fragile thing give me a dizzy, soaring sensation? I reached a steadying hand against the fence wire.

I turned to where the others were walking toward our bikes that lay in the grass. I turned back, magnetized by the earrings.

Debbie Glick's bare knees touching each other. Her eyes, omniscient fireflies, met mine.

O'Neill, yapping, oblivious.

Our game ended.

September coming fast.

Summer, slipping away, would never be the same.

Notre Dame Magazine, August 17, 2020

Savor the Last Dance

I was in my first year at Chicago State College (CSC), and I had yet to have a Valentine, better known as a serious girlfriend. I was too shy to ask anyone out or to even approach a female.

Most people at that age harbor insecurities. But I was the only one hoofing it to the lunch counter at Woolworth's on 69th and Halsted every day to avoid having to mingle in the school cafeteria.

I was assigned four classes for the first semester. Three of them were in my wheelhouse: English, world history and German. The fourth, however, a P.E. class in ballroom dancing, might very well have ended my college career as soon as it started.

Any other version of physical education would have been

acceptable: tennis, golf, wrestling, even badminton.

But CSC was jam-packed with male enrollees needing a minimum of 12 credit hours for a 2-S draft deferment during the Vietnam era, so you were stuck with whatever was printed on your schedule.

My first day at college started interestingly enough. The world history teacher had Einstein hair and a Russian accent.
My English teacher was a published poet.

But at 2 p.m., wearing the required white t-shirt and tennis shorts for P.E., I felt an ominous roiling in my gut when I entered the gymnasium for dance class.

Two dozen young women in white collared shirts, baggy shorts and bobby socks were clustered in front of the folding wooden bleachers. A male student with wavy black hair, slouching like Marlon Brando, was chatting with the only blonde in the group.

They all turned to look as the door closed behind me, so I felt relieved when the teacher, a thin, businesslike woman with short gray hair and noticeably erect posture, asked for everyone's attention.

Holding a clipboard, she took attendance, pronouncing each name on the roster before giving a brief pep talk about how the objectives for this particular class, having to do with poise, confidence and so on, related to the field of education.

"Any questions?" she said.

Brando raised his hand.

"Do we gotta dress like this?" he said. "I mean, be like dancin' in our undies."

A few of the girls laughed. The teacher looked down at her clipboard:

"Mr. Romano, was it?" she said. "Drop the class, and you can wear whatever you like."

Silence.

"Other questions?" said the teacher. "Very well. We begin with the foxtrot. Partner up."

I was close enough to the door that I probably could

have exited unnoticed. I knew I might be risking a very long flight to the Mekong Delta, but anything would've been better than this.

Until the gentle tap on my shoulder: "Would you be my dance partner?"

She had long brown hair bound in a ponytail and enormous blue eyes. Her mouth was set in a half smile that seemed ready to erupt in laughter any second. It was the same kind of electrical energy which my little sister had, so I figured she came from a big family, too.

Her name was Annie, very easy to look at, and the kind of girl who would never be with someone like me. Surprisingly, though, all of her fingernails were bitten down, the cuticles raw and red. Somehow, this gave me hope.

"Pretty please?" she said, her hands folded in prayer. She was impossible to resist.

But I grew panicky. The fire started between my shoulders and rose to my neck when Annie touched my arm, guiding me to follow the teacher's instructions for the "closed ballroom dance position hold."

The rest of the lesson's logistics escape me now, except for how "The man's right hand is placed on the lady's shoulder blade." Whereas, my hand involuntarily jerked away when it felt the strap beneath her shirt.

Annie didn't flinch. Instead, she looked around at other struggling foxtrotters, making light of the shared awkwardness, glancing up at me with a conspiratorial smile, as though the two of us must humor the teacher, whom she named Sgt. Schultz, from *Hogan's Heroes,* whose "one-step, two-step" commands we dared not disobey.

In contrast with my sweaty hands and ripe man-smell, Annie was as cool as ice, with a hint of peppermint on her breath. She did most of the talking, and by the end of class, I entertained the possibility of surviving the semester.

Still in my arms, she leaned in closer and whispered, "Thank you, Colonel Hogan," before turning and skipping away.

On the long bus ride home, I was seeing those big eyes and trying to remember the way her face looked when she repeated my name. I nearly missed my transfer at 79th street.

On Tuesday, I only had German and no dance class. When I checked the bulletin board outside the registrar's office, I saw that a spot had opened up in intramural basketball.

I hesitated: The prospect of three more months with my angel-faced partner was intriguing. But was she for real or a put-on? Would I regret not grabbing that vacancy?

All I knew for certain was that ballroom dancing was suddenly expendable. So, I forced myself not to think much more about it and went inside.

A month later, when I changed buses at 79th and Western Avenue, there was Annie on a side seat next to the blonde from class. She wore a mini skirt under a wool coat and black leather boots over white tights. Her brown hair was combed out, framing a face more beautiful than I remembered.

"My dance partner!" she said, affecting a frown. "You abandoned me!"

I shrugged and smiled and kept moving down the aisle, for how could I know I'd never see her again.

Today I am older and richly blessed with three grown children I raised with Marianne. No more hurrying down aisles of any sort.

Still, all these years later, I wonder what might have been. Or what other story I might be writing had I chosen to stay in dance class.

Notre Dame Magazine. February 14, 2023

-A Lesson for Lonely Hearts on Valentine's Day

The late musician and storyteller Harry Chapin composed one of the best Valentine's Day songs ever written, "A Better Place To Be," about a man who could not believe his good fortune when a woman way out of his league chose to be with him. "You see, she was so damned beautiful she could warm a winter's frost," Chapin wrote.

I heard the song decades ago and have never forgotten it. The speaker was a night watchman in a factory, with not a lot going for him, and I felt pretty much the same way.

Like the watchman who was, "not much of a mover or a pick-em-up easy guy," I could not get a date. Not that I was getting multiple refusals, but I was too acutely aware of my physical and social flaws to even ask for one.

I don't believe I was hideous. My brother's wife Michelle, in fact, told me I reminded her of Arnold Schwarzenegger, though I don't recall the "Terminator" having thick eyeglasses or a bad complexion.

And though I had just made the freshman dean's list at my college, I lacked either the cleverness or the confidence to even speak to a girl.

Except for Marianne. With her, I was able to look straight into her eyes when she initiated one of our conversations:

"Clean up in Aisle 3, David," or, "Can you help this nice lady with her groceries," or, "Please don't place the eggs in the bottom of the bag."

She did all the talking, of course, in her supervisory role as the head cashier at the Jewel food store in Evergreen Park Plaza, where I was a bag boy.

A secretly infatuated bag boy, that is, since just like the mystery woman in Chapin's song, my boss was beautiful. Not flamboyantly, like Scarlet Johannson, but more subtly, like Mandy Moore: dark hair and eyes that said, "Can I help you?" even when she wasn't actually saying it to customers.

Not only was she way out of my league birds-and-bees-wise, but our personalities were so diametrically opposed that I wondered if I might have been born on a different planet and shipped to earth as an infant.

For while I was a hopelessly shy, tongue-tied introvert, Marianne could very well have been the prototype for the amiable and gregarious "CBS This Morning" star Gayle King. Not only personable and chatty, but sincerely interested in every human being she met. It was no surprise that the line in her checkout aisle was always the longest. And she knew many of her customers by their first names.

My one consolation in our being worlds apart, was that I could idolize her from afar — by which I mean at the end of her counter, where I stood in my red tie and white apron, holding a double brown bag, watching each of those shoppers' happy faces when it was their turn with Marianne. And though I spent most of my life in those days feeling invisible, this was the one place where I didn't mind.

Right about now, *Sun-Times* readers — more astute than average news consumers — are already guessing that Marianne and I somehow ended up in each other's arms. And they would be right. It happened when we were both invited to the wedding of another Jewel employee and found ourselves together and alone at the after-party in the groom's parents' rec room.

The question, of course, is with so many debonair and interested men available, why on earth would she choose me?

In Chapin's love song, the incredulous midnight watchman asked the bewitching beauty the same question: Why would she consent to go home with a dud like himself? In her reply she hinted about disappointment and loneliness in her past, and said that being with him might be a "better place to be," and that "'Lovin' someone is a better way to be.'"

All of which may have gotten her to thinking, since when the watchman returned after getting breakfast for him and his new love, he found she had gone, having left this note: "It's time that I moved on."

Meanwhile, in real life, I never asked Marianne the same kind of questions. And we remained together happily ever after.

The lesson being for other lonely hearts out there on Valentine's Day: Self-pity can only be self-defeating. Unless, of course, you make your living as a songwriter.

Chicago Sun Times, 2/12/2022

-The Motel Room

When I realized that Marianne wanted to be with me, warts and all, as much as I did with her, I knew she must be the one.

Especially since the warts were not metaphorical, but actual pill-shaped growths on several knuckles of my left hand.

They disappeared after a few weeks, which I attributed to a commercial hand soap in the employees restroom at the Jewel supermarket where, after starting as a bagger, I became a stock boy and Marianne was a cashier.

It was a working-your-way-through-college job paying $2.50 an hour. But after I found myself hanging around at the store even when I wasn't scheduled, I figured I may as well volunteer for overtime.

Everybody loved Marianne. Her checkout line was always the longest, and she knew her customers' first names.

Funny how much less I dreaded mopping the tile floors or stocking the shelves with cans of Del Monte Pears in Unsweetened Juice when she was on duty, right there behind Register No. 3. And the overtime pay came in handy after we started dating, so I had cash to take her to the movies, to restaurants and to miniature golf courses on our Saturday night dates.

I felt rich enough, in fact, and bold enough, I hoped, for a very special date, come Valentine's Day, at the Miami Motel.

Cicero Avenue on the South Side was "motel row," all of the establishments being within easy driving distance of Midway Airport. But the Miami stood out for its beckoning neon sign, palm branches shading the word "Miami," and the tall stucco wall along the sidewalk shielding the one- and two-bed units from traffic along the avenue.

Up till then, Marianne and I had engaged in what Betty and Veronica in the *Archie* comic books called "necking." We would gaze at the stars through the windshield of my 1964 Oldsmobile while parked at Turtlehead Lake in Orland Park.

But a motel was an adult and serious next step, and I had just reached the legal age in Illinois to register at one. Yet it still felt forbidden, for although it was 1971, California's '60s sexual revolution with its "free love" mantra had yet to establish a beachhead on Lake Michigan and the Midwest. Not to mention that both of us were Irish Catholics living with our strict (mine) and religious (hers) parents.

Friday afternoon, payday, we found ourselves alone in the Jewel's break room, where I had brought a cheeseburger I'd purchased at Wimpy's across the way.

Sitting across the table, Marianne pulled my paper plate in front of her. She sawed the cheeseburger in two with a plastic knife, sliding the tomato slice onto her half before slathering mustard on mine.

It was a game we enjoyed, minding each other's business, as when I removed a cigarette from her lips, or she, a pen from my hand. A game ongoing, unacknowledged.

"For Valentine's Day," I said, "how about if instead of bowling, we go to the Miami Motel?"

She looked up from the plate, slitted her eyes in mock disapproval. Till she realized I was serious.

"We'll see," she said.

A good sign, I remember thinking.

That night I got little sleep, going over Saturday's date in my head, visualizing it like a movie, rehearsing the transaction with the hotel clerk.

By Saturday morning, I had convinced myself it would be best to get a room ahead of time, and I drove over in the late morning to get the worrisome business out of the way.

The room rate was more than what I normally paid for two or even three of our dates. But the nickel-colored room key for No. 219, secreted in my back pocket, was worth two or even four weeks of swabbing floors and stocking those shelves.

Did I mention that Marianne was beautiful? Not in a splashy way like Marilyn Monroe, but more subtly, like Katharine Ross: Long, dark brown hair, eyes gleaming with generosity. But she was also smart, and on Saturday she knew where we were headed as soon as I said it was a surprise.

I glanced but couldn't read her face when I turned onto Cicero Avenue. And as I pulled into the Miami's parking lot, I could feel her sit back to take it all in.

"Just say no, and we'll forget about it," I said after shutting off the engine. "Bleeker's bowling alley is just a couple of minutes from here."

She scanned the U-shaped building with the iron railing along the second story.

"We should leave by midnight," she said.

*

Room 219: Shag carpet, dark brown. Framed pictures of palm trees and seagulls on the wall. A 19-inch Panasonic television with remote control. Queen size bed with a red and gray quilted spread. And a bathroom with a stack of neatly folded white towels on the counter.

"What do you think?"

"Palatial," said Marianne.

Its best feature, I realized, were the curtains. Admittedly plain: yellow, pleated, with a white, plasticky liner. But when I closed them, we were the only two people in the world.

I poured wine for each of us into the clear plastic cups. I had splurged on Lancers Rosé, since it was Valentine's Day. And we sat in dining-room-style chairs at the little round table, kitty-corner to the bed.

We talked about school, particularly German, the only

class we had in common at Chicago Teachers College. And wouldn't *Professorin* Schreiner like to see us now?

Marianne asked which of my five brothers I was closest to (Kenneth), and I, in turn, asked for recitation of the names of all five of her sisters (Betsy, Kathy, Barbara, Stephanie, Monica).

Other questions about work and parents and my dumb parking ticket, and do you want more wine, and pretty soon we ran out of topics.

Momentary silence, as she extracted a swizzle stick from the motel coffee packet and stirred the ice cubes in my Lancers.

"I don't feel . . ." she hesitated.

"Comfortable?" I said.

". . . sure."

"Wait," I said. "You mean 'not comfortable' or 'not sure'?"

"Both, I guess."

"That's okay," I said. "Maybe it's too soon."

"I don't know. I'm sorry."

"No, I understand. To be honest, I'm relieved. The pressure's off, you know?

I stood, then genuflected before her chair and put my arms around her. To reassure. More probably, to keep hold.

And then I turned on the fancy TV, tuning to Channel 9 and the Chicago Blackhawks hockey game.

"But all the money you spent on this room," said Marianne. "And the wine."

"What do you mean? This is perfect, watching my team with the person I love. And without my brothers in my hair."

The Hawks had a one-goal lead over the Vancouver Canucks, halfway through the first period.

"Why are they all stopping?" said Marianne.

"Icing the puck," I said.

I explained the rule. She opened a package of crackers and poured more wine. We spent the next 90 minutes watching Stan

Mikita, Bobby Hull and Lou Angotti.

She thought it was funny that Bobby and his brother Dennis played on the same team but on different lines. And as she started to pick up on the goals and the strategy, she decided her favorite was Eric Nesterenko, the way he prowled the rink
with those droopy shoulders and a crown of thick, dark hair that looked like mine, at a time when helmets had yet to be mandated.

The Blackhawks would win, 3-1, and we checked out well short of midnight. It's a good thing, too, since my Oldsmobile, out in the cold, would not start.

When two other couples came out to their cars, Marianne ran to intercept them. I heard laughter, and then she waved me over. They were happy to let us squeeze in. They were headed to a Valentine's party in Beverly and would drop us off at Marianne's, after which she would drive me home in her own car.

The next day, when my brother Kenneth drove me back to the Miami with his jumper cables, I was conflicted about what to tell him. To his credit and to my relief, he never asked.

The Blackhawks won more than they lost that year, and Marianne became a knowledgeable fan.

In the fall, on a trip to Iowa to see a college football game, we checked into another motel. Same carpet as at the Miami. Same towels. Same kinds of pictures on the wall.

But we had grown closer as friends and lovers. We were in a zone, like a pair of violinists in no need of sheet music. It was a gift that nothing could surpass.

What Marianne had intuited that first time at the Miami was not that the time was wrong. More a matter of that exclusive "place" we had yet to inhabit together.

A year and a half would pass before we paid another visit to the Miami Motel — on Valentine's Day, for old time's sake. Again we watched the Blackhawks on TV. But this time we arrived in a brand new Chevy and with a pizza from Rosangela's. And we signed in as husband and wife.

-The Kiss

Marianne asked me why I am not romantic anymore.

"Not true," I said. "I was never romantic."

"Ha, ha," she said, rolling her eyes.

She got me thinking, though. Admittedly, when we were younger, I was more inclined toward romantic gestures.

A month after we started dating, I sent her flowers. But since I was making only $1.60 an hour stocking shelves at Jewel, I took the cheap route and bought a bouquet of mixed flowers at Walgreens, which I asked my brother's friend Roy Osmond to deliver in his dad's car.

She was impressed, thinking it was from a fancy florist, and she tipped him $1, which was more than ample in 1969.

A year later, the night before Marianne was going on spring break to Marco Island with two of her friends, one of whom was my sister, Rosemary, I left a poem in my sister's car as a bon voyage message. Again, Marianne was moved, even though I had plagiarized a couple of stanzas from e.e. Cummings.

After we were married, I made the classic move of carrying her across the threshold of our new house in Wisconsin and threw out my back. I was bedridden for two days.

Tell me that ain't love!

By far, the most romantic thing I had ever done was on the night of my cousin's wake. Funeral rites and romance don't exactly go together, but that is kind of the point.

That morning, we had an argument, which back then was likely about money. This led to a period of not talking, which led to my driving to the funeral parlor on my own.

While paying my respects and making the rounds to greet friends and relatives, I kept watching the doorway. When I finally saw her across the room, I felt a stab of longing somewhere between my heart and my throat.

She was standing in the mourners' line, shoulders square, with a look of compassion or reverence, hazel eyes straight ahead, her mouth closed beneath that perfect nose. She was like Audrey Hepburn with long brown hair.

I walked toward her, weaving between two rows of folding chairs, when she spotted me. No smile. No frown. But a barely perceptible arching of her brow, a widening of her eyes. Like a question. Or a signal only I could see.

When I reached her, I put my hands around her waist and kissed her. And kissed her. And she kissed me. It was a long kiss. Too long for two people out in public. Too long for a married couple. Too long with relatives and strangers watching. Too long for a crowded funeral parlor and with an open casket 10 feet away.

To this day, "the kiss" still comes up in conversation. Marianne wonders if I had been showing off or else taking advantage of the circumstances, rather like the sailor who kissed the dental assistant he did not know on V-J Day in the famous *Life* magazine photograph.

But I had never been more genuine. While it may have been caused by regret over our morning misunderstanding, it was nonetheless a spontaneous expression of the intense love I felt at that moment.

So, on Valentine's Day, decades later, I plan to surprise Marianne with "The kiss II." I'll have to catch her before she reads this. Perhaps, I'll approach while she's in the kitchen pouring her morning coffee. Or later, as we pass in the hallway, just before I leave for my morning bike ride.

I've been silently debating whether it would be fair to kiss her passionately as soon as she gets up. On the other hand, it feels right to take her in my arms at the start of the day.

One way or the other, I will get it done.

And then once Kiss II is consummated, we'll replay it every morning so that it's never again a surprise.

Chicago Tribune, February 14, 2023

-A Winning Formula for Marriage

When my wife and I got married in August of 1972, I was a substitute teacher for Chicago Public Schools earning $40 a day.

Marianne had a permanent gig as a fourth grade teacher at St. Barnabas Elementary for $5,000 a year.

So, whenever we traveled, we stayed at quaint budget motels such as the Abe Lincoln in Effingham, or Millie's Winter Motel, in Winter, Wisconsin. Marianne hated most of them, but I liked the prices, along with the fact that I could park my 1964 Oldsmobile Super Eighty-Eight several feet from the door of our room.

When I finally landed a full-time job teaching English at Chicago Vocational High School, starting at $9,570 a year, we stepped up to Motel 6, where the sheets were freshly laundered, and you could splurge on extras such as phone service or a mini fridge for an additional $5 a night.

By the time Mike was born in 1975, and I'd earned a master's degree entitling me to a raise at Vocational, we would book a couple of days during spring break at a Holiday Inn with a pool, and we'd head home with one or two monogrammed hotel towels as "amenities."

All of which I've been inspired to recall after our weekend at the Lido Beach Resort in Florida, gifted to us by our three children on the occasion of our 50th wedding anniversary.

With two pools, two hot tubs, two restaurants, valet parking, and our balcony on the fourth floor overlooking the white sand beach on the Gulf of Mexico, Lido is a far cry from the Abe Lincoln, and an extravagance I would think twice about booking myself.

But in consideration of the love it came from, and the 50 years of dual occupancy Marianne and I were commemorating, we accepted it with gratitude and humility.

While golden jubilees are the bread and butter of small-town newspapers, including Effingham's *Daily News* or Winter's *Sawyer County Gazette*, big city dailies like this have way weightier urban, national, and international issues to cover.

But in these virulent times, a commentary about how such an accord might have been achieved by two perfect strangers for half a century, would seem appropriate.

So, on our first evening at the resort, at Lido's Drift Restaurant, as Marianne waited for her baked snapper, and I, the grilled shrimp, we sorted out what enabled us to arrive at this point in our lives.

"I thought you looked like actor Michael Parks," she said."

"And you, Natalie Wood. Still do," I quickly added.

Then we both got serious and agreed our longevity could be traced to a single moment when I sat on the stairwell just inside the front door of our home, several decades earlier. Our three children were school-age, and metaphorically, so was I, as I was headed out to a cocktail lounge to meet my volleyball friends for the second night in a row.

Far removed from the romantic, poetry-writing, guitar-playing folk singer she had married, I had devolved into an aloof, hard-drinking, Al Bundy clone, who felt his youth, freedom and artistic horizons had been occluded, if not sabotaged, by a needy family and a stressful job.

The adult in our marriage, kneeling on the stairs in front of me, and sensing peril to both us and the kids, extracted from me the aforementioned truth, along with several more that the *Sawyer County Gazette* could not have published in a family newspaper, before she suggested a plan.

Like the wives of half of my like-minded friends, she could have chosen to cut loose the baggage and commence a separate life. But we had known our love as a living thing, which both of us feared to kill.

Instead, I would start pulling my weight with the kids, so she could break free of her own chains, obtain an advanced college degree and cultivate a social life beyond the children, her mother and me.

And she would indulge my frat house routine — the softball, the fishing, the beer — until it ran its course. After which I could build that cabin in the woods and write the novel with which I'd been making false starts for the previous 10 years.

Meanwhile, every Saturday night would be a mandatory assessment session, which is teacher jargon for going out on a date at a pizza joint.

Maybe it was just by making a plan, or maybe the string of 2,000 dates, or maybe it was the chance for each to pursue their dreams. But I grew to know her better than before, and she, me, it seems.

Every couple must find a key, and ours was not separate lives. Instead, it was talking and more talking and granting each other the room to be who we are. Today we are grateful and amazed at each other's blossoming, and our love is the best that it's been.

Chicago Tribune, August 20th, 2022

Fatherhood

-My Red Badge of Courage

Probably because I thought it was personal, and even a little embarrassing, I had always kept quiet about that day with my father.

It was the year I stopped going to Aqua, our swimming pool complex in Evergreen Park. Instead, I stayed home that summer, watching "General Hospital" on TV or the Cubs' day games, even as my brothers and friends from St. Bernadette School were meeting at the pool every day.

Rule No. 1 at Aqua was that before entering, you must take a nude shower in a large open area of the changing room, just like in the prison movies, an experience that took a while to get used to.

But by the second summer, I had acquired an angry red scar shaped like a boomerang just above my waistline, the result of a gash from a freak accident with a jagged piece of metal while horsing around with some friends.

I was 13 years old, a gawky, guarded age for boys, so I was petrified at the prospect of the other people staring at it when I undressed.

After patiently but futilely trying to talk some sense into me, my father offered to leave work early one day and drive me to the pool. We would change together, he said, and I could stand behind him if I preferred, so no one would even see.

It was a sunny and busy Friday afternoon at Aqua, when at least a dozen other males, including a couple of boys close to my age, were in various stages of undress.

As the two of us were getting ready, my father struck up a conversation with another man about the White Sox's chances of winning another pennant.

In his 40s, my father was portly, and I was immediately conscious of his bowling pin shape and the many red marks on his skin, like a permanent rash that I had not noticed before. But his confident smile and unrushed pride about being there with me, which he somehow signaled in his steady tones and easy conversation, reduced my scar to irrelevance, if not invisibility.

Sneaking a look around, I saw the others listening to what he was saying about when to use pitchers Hoyt Wilhelm and Gary Peters.

"Who else did you say, Dad?"

He turned to me and answered with the name of some other pitcher whose name I don't remember; I had only asked to make sure everyone knew I was his son.

The relief I felt being with him was so overwhelming that I could scarcely believe there had ever been a problem. I rode my bike or walked with my friends to Aqua nearly every day the rest of that summer, unrolling the bath towel holding my trunks, not bothering to hide my scar.

Years later, when I eventually had my own son, I reflected on the ferocity of my father's love that day, when he left work to protect me. And I was just one of his eight children.

Parents ache to give all they can to their kids, and I hoped I would be able to answer the call when any of mine had problems they couldn't handle alone, the way Charlie McGrath did for me.

Decades later, though I meant to bring it up with my father and ask him if he remembered, I got busy, or forgot, and he died at age 73 before I got around to it.

I trust he would forgive that I took so long and am instead writing about him now, so that maybe other fathers out there might learn from the best.

Naturally, I still have it today: my red badge of courage, just under my belt.

Courage bestowed my dad, who had plenty to spare.

Chicago Tribune, June 19, 2022

-Parentamorphisis

The Progressive Insurance TV commercials are hilarious but also profound. You know the ones with the Sully Sullenberger lookalike as group therapist Dr. Rick, who tries to help keep homeowners from turning into their parents: "Guess what," he informs them, "the waiter does not need to know your name."

The commercial's talented actors and familiar message got me wondering about Father's Day: are we really all just clones of our parents?

Charlie McGrath had a yeoman's task as my father. He jury-rigged a system of mild discipline and Christian principles to usher six boys and two girls through childhood, higher ed, and out the door to our separate lives, without any detours to jail or rehab.

While I hope I inherited his good qualities, I swore I'd avoid what I considered his mistakes. So as funny as those characters are, I, of course, have never needed Dr. Rick's help, unlike the homeowner in one commercial who is practically getting underneath the sink with the plumber, when Dr. Rick admonishes him: "OK, Tom, we talked about this. You hired him. You're not his assistant."

Yes, my father used to do that, too, if he hired a painter, or when he summoned me as his handyman to fix something, and he stood "watch," ostensibly to make sure the work was getting done right — but probably more out of curiosity or for entertainment, to the growing annoyance of whoever was doing the work.

Determined not to replicate Dad's behavior, I always make sure to stay out of the way of hired help, except, of course, in cases when I want to watch a technician or tradesman's every move, so I know how to fix it myself the next time.

Another undesirable tendency of my father was that he couldn't stand waiting for anyone or anything. Since my late mother did not drive, and Dad had to chauffeur her to the doctor, the church, the grocery store, she needed to develop an inner alarm clock that told her when she must stop browsing in the meat section and head for the checkout.

Otherwise, my old man would be out in the car muttering to himself, leaning on the horn, his blood pressure on the brink by the time Mom finally made it out the door.

Resolved that I would never show such impatience, I decided to avoid any venue or event where there might be a wait. So we don't go to concerts or baseball games or movies or on cruises — and never to a restaurant unless we can get there before 4:30. It all works out quite beautifully.

One other bad habit of Charlie McGrath was television. The year my parents got cable TV with a remote-control device was also the year my mother became a baseball and game-show widow.

Dad's stuffed armchair was planted no less than seven feet directly in front of the tube, where he'd surf through his favorite channels around eight hours a day, making sure to watch every inning of his team's 162-game MLB season, occasionally switching to a golf tournament when he needed a nap.

Fortunately, I am not at all like my dad in the television department, either.

Because our TV is 50 inches wide, I watch it much farther away than my dad did. At least 10 feet — or a full 15 when Marianne asks me to back up so she can vacuum.

Moreover, I'm more partial to football than to baseball. Granted, I may watch more than eight hours on a Saturday or a Sunday and, of course, on Thanksgiving and New Year's. But NFL Ticket was not available in Dad's era, which pretty much compels subscribers like me to watch every single game to make the monthly satellite bill worthwhile.

All of which means, Dr. Rick, that your commercials may be funny, but the joke's not on me, as anyone reading this can easily see

What I want to say for Father's Day is that Charlie McGrath

loved his children and grandchildren more than himself — and his wife even more. He taught us through his own example that getting ahead in the world was a good goal, as long as it never compromised being kind and honest with your fellow man or being true to your own beliefs.

Those are my dad's attributes, which I wish to emulate while forgiving him those pesky peccadillos.

Duluth News Tribune, Fort Myers News Press, Pioneer Press, Chicago Tribune: June 20, 2021

-Are Dads Even Necessary?

My son Mike recalls an episode years ago that supposedly validates the "World's Greatest Dad" slogan on my coffee cup.

We were on vacation in Winter, Wisconsin, and he was wading alone in knee-deep water, casting a topwater Rapala into the whiskey-colored Chippewa River, when he hooked a smallmouth bass. Smallmouth are among the fiercest fighters, as they jet away, aerial out of the water, and pull with such strength that it feels like you're holding a jackhammer instead of a slender graphite rod.

Mike was eventually able to land the fish, but not before the creature's last dash and sudden turn caused the top set of the lure's treble hooks to bury themselves in his knee. He decided to head home, about a mile up the hill on Fishtrap Road, carrying his trophy in one hand and the rod and some slack line in the other to minimize the pull and strain of the three nickel-plated hooks digging into his leg.

Fortunately, good Samaritan and neighbor Geno Siefeldt stopped to give Mike a ride home in his pickup. The bad news was that the barbs of two of the three hooks were embedded beneath the flesh alongside his kneecap, prompting Marianne to declare a visit to the ER and Mike to struggle to hold back tears.

There may be an alternative remedy, I told them.

I had never actually performed the "string, yank technique"

for removing a fish hook; but as an avid practitioner of the sport, I had heard and read about it.

So I cut an 18-inch length of fishing line from Mike's reel and tied each end securely to the bend in each of the two offending hooks.

While his mother spoke soothingly to distract him, I pushed down lightly on the eye of the treble with my left hand, so that the shaft lined up in the same direction in which, with my right hand firmly gripping the line, I yanked upward. Amazingly, the hooks popped out, free and clear. I looked up from his knee and realized that Mike had neither felt nor noticed he was suddenly free of the hooks and the fishing line.

And although the story is cataloged in our family history as an episode when Dad came to the rescue, it actually is evidence that Father's Day might be a hoax. In fact, I believe I speak for many fathers in admitting that our accolades are mostly undeserved, and all the gifts and cards are inspired by fake news.

Before I explain, I must first caution that none of the whistleblower information contained herein applies to Mother's Day. The first Sunday in May was legitimately designated an occasion for honoring women who endure the pain of childbirth and spend the rest of their lives in sacrifice and selfless commitment to their children.

Whereas, the institution of Father's Day was a later attempt at fairness, ending up as false equivalency.

For example, removing the hooks from Mike's knee saved me from having to make a 38-mile drive to the hospital in nearby Hayward. It also spared me the cost of our Blue Cross deductible payment for an emergency-room visit, which we supplanted with a thorough washing of Mike's knee in warm, soapy water, followed by application of Neosporin and a Band-Aid.

So does it not seem more like a case of pragmatism and self-reliance than any sort of paternal dedication?

The same goes for the memorable Saturday when I

accompanied my elder daughter Jackie when she purchased her first car. Was it really a loving manifestation of dear old Dad's support or his determination to not get bested by a slick salesman?

When I used to sing "All the Pretty Little Horses" to my younger daughter Janet at naptime and read her the poetry of James Wright at night, was it really an expression of pure affection or simply a desire for a quiet evening with my wife?

Or how about teaching all three of my children right from wrong? A matter of paternal pride and principle or a pecuniary interest in keeping them out of jail and avoiding exorbitant attorney fees?

Was my fostering their love of nature all through childhood a gift of love or a strategy to distract them from cable TV, movies, video games, malls, and other forms of expensive entertainment?

Am I onto something here, calling an end to the hypocrisy of Father's Day with these dispassionate rationales?

Get over yourself," said Marianne. "It doesn't matter to the kids if you're no Tom Hanks." She was referring, of course, to Hanks' designation as America's Dad.

She went on to say that our kids loved me "flat out" because I'm their father and I'm there for them. And that the Dave Barry book they bought for me, along with the coffee mug with the Lab's head is to show their love, fierce and unqualified, no matter what.

Which shut me up.

And I'm good with that.

I mean, really good.

Duluth News Tribune, Naperville Sun & Daily Southtown, June 20, 2021

-Pivotal Moments of Fatherhood

One of my favorite fatherly recollections was when my 6-year-old daughter Jackie came home from first grade and unloaded her backpack onto the kitchen table: a box of crayons, a stack of papers with stickers from the teacher, her Bert and Ernie lunchbox, and a miniature blue race car. When I asked where she got the car, an unfamiliar toy, she said It belonged to her classmate Jason, who was very sad it was broken.

"I told him you can fix anything, Daddy," she said with a giant smile.

It took me a second or two to find my voice before I could tell her I would try. Truth be told, there were likely many things I could not fix. But as a rookie teacher with a new family, I had to learn to do things myself since we could not afford repairmen. You can bet I spent extra time repairing the tiny toy car so Jackie wouldn't disappoint her classmate.

All of my best moments as a father are similar to the toy car story: something brief and shared by one of my three children.

In 2002, for instance, my son Mike applied to medical school. He already had two different majors and seemed to have been in college forever, so his mother and I were skeptical. We didn't discourage him, but we tried our best to prepare him for possible rejection.

What really got to me was that in the essay portion of his application, he wrote that part of his interest in wanting to diagnose medical mysteries came from watching and helping me build our cabin near Hayward, and fix things for our family and friends. Months passed, the telephone rang, and Mike gave us the news that he was accepted.

This is the same boy who was born 25 years earlier as our first child. His was a posterior birth (face down rather than up), so he ended up badly bruised from the forceps. Both mother and child had to stay an extra day or so in the hospital.

I remember during that time I stopped at my mother's house, where she and Dad were packing for a move up north for a job transfer. I walked through the door to the dining room to tell her Marianne had just given birth to a boy when I stopped mid-sentence. That I felt a sob coming on was a total shock and surprise. I was not one to lose composure, especially over good news; but my mother, of course, fully understood.

Fast forward 30 years. My younger daughter Janet was driving with her "serious" boyfriend to join us in Hayward. When they arrived about two hours later than expected, Janet explained they had made many stops so she could show Kevin all the places that were special to her as a child — from the park in Cadot on the Yellow River where we used to stop for a picnic lunch to the site of our first cabin on Bluegill Lake near Winter.

Pointing out familiar places to someone is a common practice. But for a parent to hear his kid valuing childhood experiences in that way is the best kind of love and affirmation.

Probably best to conclude this immodest parental preening before I lose all my readers, so I'll finish off with the child I started with.

When Jackie was at a turning point at the University of Missouri, confronting obstacles and losing confidence, she started carrying a little book with her that she read from time to time but mostly hung onto when she needed a morale boost. When she told me it was a copy of *Artful Dodge,* a literary magazine with my first published short story, I was humbled and surprised. The timely connection that it provided between the two of us was more important than the publication or anything else I could have done.

I've had more than my share of happy Father's Days, and most weren't even in June.

Madison Capital Times, June 20th, 2021

-The Irish Raconteur

Note: The following story was written more than ten years before the McGrath family DNA test showed no trace of Irish ancestry.

Sunburn comes to mind when I remember my father. Way before I was born and when he was in the U.S. Army stationed in Panama, he used up a day pass for an outing at the beach. So far so good, but he had underestimated the strength of the equatorial sun under an overcast sky. He suffered a burn so bad that at reveille the next day his body resembled raw meat, his arms and legs stiff and on fire.

This so angered his superior officer that he threatened Corporal Charles McGrath with court-martial. But he softened when my father apologized and expressed regret for his "unfortunately fair complexion," while promising that the first-degree burn would not interfere in the least with the execution of his official duties.

I am reminded of the incident this week because sensitive skin and keeping silent about pain are both widely considered to be characteristics of the Irish. And for me and my siblings, St. Patrick's Day, the national holiday of Ireland, is less an occasion for parades and leprechauns than for commemorating the man who represents where we come from. Charlie was never one to go on about his heritage. A splashy green tie accessorizing his salesman's suit on St. Paddy's and his loyalty to the pope and to President John F. Kennedy, comprised the limit of his ethnic flourish.

Granted, he did fit a few of the stereotypes: Catholic? Check. Large family? Check, he fathered eight children.

Crazy about corned beef and cabbage? Yes. To be fair, he was crazy about all varieties of cuisine, to unhealthful excess.

An affinity for song and dance? He thought "Mack the Knife" was written especially for him, which he sang in his perfectly pitched baritone. And there was that Jackie Gleason grace he displayed on the dance floor at all eight of our weddings.

Yet either through strength of will or the natural attrition from his being three generations removed from the motherland, he escaped the Irish male stereotype of pub-dwelling philanderer. Admittedly, we reprise a running joke at family gatherings that involves the mysterious Aunt Lynn. Mysterious not only because we never met her but also because she was not even a relative but my father's co-worker who sent gift-wrapped boxes of candy to our home at Easter, Christmas and on Valentine's Day.

My brother James mused that Aunt Lynn might have been my father's mistress and the holiday gifts a form of penance for the cheating.

All of which my 92-year-old mother, Gertrude, still finds amusing, secure in the knowledge that her late husband had never fooled around and that the kindly Aunt Lynn, whom she had met, would be the last female to inspire such an inclination.

But the legend persists because, well, he was Irish, and according to legend, Irish husbands, when they were home, beat their wives; and when they were not, cheated on them.

In the final analysis of my father's proclivities, a statistician would conclude that, absent a DNA sample, it's impossible to certify that Charles R. McGrath was a member of the tribe. Except for the one detail, going back to the sunburn.

You see, the first time I heard that story, I was 10 and in bed for the night, when my parents were hosting a party. My bedroom door was shut tight, and I dozed off and on to the murmur of a dozen indecipherable conversations downstairs. In one of them I recognized my father's tones, and slowly I made out individual words and then whole sentences, as the party noise abated and peripheral conversations faded out.

As everyone else went silent, I became spellbound, transported to the coastal tropics of Panama. But something in that baritone — a vulnerable sincerity and a sense of his own surprise as he saw himself and his characters unfold anew in the eyes of his listeners — rendered every other adult in our house mute, so that the story he wove floated upstairs, its scenes still visible in my mind's eye 40 years later.

The tradition of Shaw, Beckett, Fitzgerald and Cormac McCarthy notwithstanding, anthropologists might disagree on whether an affinity for story-telling is less nature than nurture, less Irish attribute than coincidence of brain orientation.

But we remember my father as the Irish raconteur.
And the stories he told to customers, friends and grandchildren, from the Army chronicles to miles of misadventures in the family

station wagon, we retell today, perpetuating his memory and defining who we are.

Which is why March 17th will remain Charlie McGrath Day for us, with all due respect to St. Pat.

Notre Dame Magazine, March 13, 2012

Motherhood

-Sometimes Mom Was a Piece of Work

She was one of a kind, my mom.

She once phoned to tell me about Chicago's weather of clear skies, balmy temperatures and low humidity and then wondered out loud why anyone (meaning my wife and me) would move to Florida.

The morning of a hurricane, she was the first to call to ask if we were all right and what we were going to do. And didn't we wish that we had stayed in the Midwest where there are no hurricanes, mudslides or tsunamis?

"What about the winters, Ma?"

"My children always loved the snow. And ice skating."

Since she could never resist photos of her eight kids, I figured I'd win her over by ordering one of those cute albums you can customize with humorous captions. Beneath a photo of my wife and me by the sea, I wrote: "I wanted to visit the nude beach, but Marianne vetoed the idea." And accompanying the shot of the two of us at a waterfront restaurant: "Seafood is so fresh here, Ma, that the waiters and waitresses carry landing nets."

"Interesting," she said. "Don't you miss Chicago pizza?"

Once when I flew home to visit, she fixed me a plate of chicken and potato salad from the Jewel deli and immediately got on the phone to report my arrival, arranging for me to visit Net's house, Kevin's place, Rosie's condo and James' and Charlie's homes in the burbs.

When I told her I was jet-lagged and thought I'd just spend the rest of the day relaxing at her home, she said what a nice surprise it would be for Kev if I popped over there that day. He was just asking her, "How is Dave doing?" And when you go, she said, make sure to tell Kev how nice his garden is. He works so hard.

The last day of my visit, when I stood up with the rental car keys, she sidled over to her strategic spot where she would lean against the back of the couch, blocking the front door. That was the moment she brought out the big guns, news-wise: Mary Kay's new house. Last week's visit from Nancy and Jay.

I dropped my keys on the table and sat and listened. Asked some questions. And when I got up to leave a second time, she maneuvered back to her spot in front of the door: Had she mentioned to me the problem with her clothes dryer?

Gert (Cichoszewski) McGrath was born in 1920, the oldest of six children, including two younger boys who survived and two who died at birth and another at around age 5. Childhood mortality was considerably higher in the days of polio, tuberculosis and scarlet fever.

I thought that might be one reason why she and Dad had had so many of their own children and why she treasured members of her family more than her life.

On my wedding day, when I was looking forward to a quick ceremony and epic partying at the reception, Mom managed an adjustment to our plans: Her own mother, Grandma Rose, had been ailing in the hospital. You have enough to do today, she assured us, but, you know, it pains Grandma that she cannot attend, and she would be thrilled to see both of you on your special day.

We really would like to, I was about to tell her, but it was quite impossible with the schedule.

Marianne, of course, not as familiar with my mom's M.O., totally caved and directed the limo chauffeur on a detour to Little Company of Mary Hospital. How could we not spend an extra 30 minutes, Marianne said, to bring tears of joy to someone who wanted so badly to see us? Well, sure, once she put it that way.

Today, Mom is gone.

And I look back with appreciation for her patience and persistence all those years in finally making me realize that there is nothing more important than family.

And no such thing as loving too much.

Chicago Tribune, May 6, 2922

-A Mother's Lasting Impact

    Not until I became a parent myself did I fully appreciate what my mother did for her eight children.
    In the 1960s, parent-teacher conferences at Catholic grade school were for adults only. So once a year on a weeknight in October, my father, irritated to have to head out again after working at the tile store all day, would zip up his jacket to cover up his string T-shirt and drive my mother to the school, while we kids waited in the living room watching TV.
    Charlie, the oldest and in charge, turned off the lights to cut the glare on the fuzzy picture on our black and white Admiral TV. Rosie sat on the couch with Kevin and toddler Nancy, who were not yet in school, while my brothers and I retrieved pillows from our beds to lie on the carpet to watch "The Many Loves of Dobie Gillis."
    Dobie Gillis" was a teenage sitcom in which Dobie (Dwayne Hickman) would often address the home audience with monologues about his dating woes. No doubt the show was funny, especially when the beatnik sidekick Maynard G. Krebs (Bob Denver) would pop on screen and say, "You rang?"
    But I specifically recall Charlie looking askance at Jimmy, the second oldest, whose extra-loud laughing betrayed his nervousness about what would happen when Mom and Dad got home after hearing from our teachers.
    Which they did, finally, around 9 p.m., the old man's mood slightly improved, either because of good school reports or since he was finally able to open up a can of Hamm's beer.
    One by one, starting with the oldest, we were summoned to the kitchen. Down the hallway from Dobie's TV voiceover, my parents' muffled words were indecipherable while they spoke with Charlie about his progress in school.

"None of your beeswax," said Charlie when he rejoined us and Kenneth asked him about it.

But when it was Jimmy's turn, we had no trouble hearing the old man seething from the kitchen: "I don't give a damn what Willie did. It's your permanent record, not his." Though he was there twice as long as Charlie, Jimmy was all smiles when he came out.

"What happened?" Charlie asked him.

"Nothin' bad," said Jimmy. He reported that he got nearly all E's on his report card (for excellent) but that he intended to "murdelize" Willie tomorrow. And then he asked Charlie if he could switch the channel to "Wyatt Earp."

Rosie's confab went quickly. E's in all her school subjects and zero checks on the behavior side of the report card.

When it was my turn to take a seat at the kitchen table, Mom was still wearing her blue dress and silver earrings from the conferences. Dad sat at the head of the table in his T-shirt, his pilsner glass of beer half full.

"There's a check on your report card for 'self control,'" he said. "Mrs. Kelly told us that you made that poor girl cry."

It took me by surprise, since it wasn't my fault. All I did was pass along a tightly folded note that my pal, one row over, had bounced off the side of my head. On its outside he had printed with a fountain pen in tiny letters: "To Patricia M." When Patricia had opened it, she started crying, causing a giant commotion and getting both me and my pal in trouble. Mrs. Kelly was angrier than I had ever seen her, ordering us to stand in the back of the room facing the lockers to "reflect and pray" about our actions.

I whispered to my partner in crime, asking what was in the note. And though I don't remember his exact words, he smiled sheepishly and whispered back that it was something "fresh" from his nose that morning.

My father thought I should not hang out with that particular friend anymore.

But my mother interceded, reciting the grades on my report card one by one, most of which were VG's (very good) with a couple of E's, as well. My record showed, she said, that I could be a good influence on my friend and that I ought to try to make sure neither of us got checks on the next report card.

The old man shrugged, then chugged from his beer.

I got off scot-free, or so I thought. Even as I joined the others watching Wyatt Earp (Hugh O'Brien) ride his horse out of town, while Kenneth and then Pat took their turns in the kitchen, I felt the uncomfortable weight of the new responsibility Mom had given me. The upcoming semester loomed long.

Today I have three kids. They're all grown, but readers my age know that parenting never really ends.

So, today, I marvel at how I used to assume my mother's chief focus was on me and my day-to-day travails and triumphs, even though I was just one of nine kids, if you counted the old man, to whom she dedicated the same amount of effort, the same amount of love. Never ending, her entire life.

What mothers do.

Chicago Tribune (Naperville Sun) & Sawyer County Record, May 6, 2021

-A Mother's Enduring Presence

On a recent road trip to Manatee Springs State Park while stopping for gas, I smiled to think about my mother.

The service station restroom had a dispenser for soap, which came out green and silky, but had a sharp lemon-peppery smell, just like the bar of Ivory soap in my childhood home.

My five brothers, two sisters, and I always had to wash our hands before dinner, and my mother would inspect all 16 of them, invariably flagging mine which still had dirt under the nails from playing in the prairie.

She'd take me to the sink and hold one hand under the tap and rub the slippery bar across the tops of my fingers, a ticklish but warm feeling with her own hand underneath mine.

Same with the smell of marigolds, among her favorite flowers. As pretty as any other orange colored blossom, but with an earthy, musky fragrance, and, most importantly, an affordable price tag. Once or twice a year, she would buy a flat of marigolds for planting in the yard when she had a spare half hour.

Our yard never had a lawn. Instead, it had six boys and a dog, and a rectangle of dirt scoured from running bases in our makeshift ball field, punctuated, especially in the spring, by holes dug by Cleopatra, the stout family beagle.

It made for a rough picture out her kitchen window, which Mom would try to pretty up with a patch of marigolds, and we would tiptoe around them for a full day, maybe two, in deference and obedience, but which was inevitably obliterated from someone overrunning third base, or the hard skid of a bicycle.

Indeed, the nose triggers so many mom memories: oxtail soup simmering on the stove; the iron-like smell of melting snow on the back steps when she helped me take off my boots and leggings; Jean Nate perfume; scorched cotton from her marathon ironing sessions in the basement.

Most of all, it was the scent of fresh hay. It was Mom's idea to drag the ping pong table outside at Christmas time and flip it sideways to make a stable in front of the picture window.

Dad was busy selling tile, so she paid old Joe Corbett to cut creche figures out of plywood with his jigsaw, which she covered with stencils of Joseph and Mary and the three kings.

Dad bought a bale of hay some place on Saturday, which we spread on the roof and floor of the stable, which when layered with snow overnight, offered the sweetest smelling hiding place for a six-year-old, cozied between the baby Jesus and a plywood sheep.

But it's a haunting sound, instead of a smell, that has me lately remembering her through the fog of so many decades, at a time when our twilight years are electrified by our granddaughter, a 36-pound bolt of lightning who stays with us one night every week.

Now that she's four and growing more resistant at naptime, I take a chair next to her bed and sing the lullabies I once sang to her mom. After a while, running low on both lyrics and energy, I scale it back to humming. Initially, it has melody, but eventually it devolves to a 4-count metronomic chant, the beat on the final syllable: hmm...hmm...hmm...HMM. Repeated, but now lower. Repeated, but now softer. As easy and hypnotic as breathing.

And as my granddaughter finally falls asleep, I realize it was exactly the same "song" my mother invented half a century earlier, inspired partly by exhaustion, mostly by love for me and her seven other children.

And as long as I can hear and smell and love her back, she is with us, still, on Mother's Day.

Orlando Sentinel, Fort Myers News Press. Duluth News Tribune & Naperville Sun, May 9, 2021

-Mom More of a Dive Bomber than Helicopter

For once, I felt like the "big man on campus."

I had just received a letter in the mail saying I had made the dean's list.

That same evening, I learned from my brother's girlfriend, Michelle, that her best friend — older, attractive and worldly — wanted to date me.

In less than a month, I would turn 19. And I recently switched from Lucky Strikes to Marlboros, the real man's brand of cigarette.

Not only that, but since the start of summer, I had been pumping iron three times a week with my pal Tom Booth in his basement. After each workout, with arms and shoulders aching and biceps bulging, we would promenade down the main aisle at the Evergreen Park Plaza in our muscle shirts.

I connected with Michelle's friend on the phone on a Friday afternoon while I was alone in the house with my parents at work and my siblings at school. I was feeling her out while trying to impress her with the right amount of bravado when my monologue was abruptly interrupted by a clicking sound, followed by an unfamiliar voice:

"This is the operator with an emergency breakthrough request on this line."

I was totally befuddled — until I heard my mother's voice in the earpiece.

"I've been trying to call for an hour, David, and you're tying up the phone. Make sure you're home when I get there."

The line went dead. And so did my inflated ego, as I wondered how much of my mother's scolding my potential love interest had heard.

Mom's busting into my romantic conversation was embarrassing but not that much of a surprise. For I had learned long ago that nothing would stop her from doing what she thought best for her home and family.

Like the time I saw her morph into beast mode to pry a leech out of my little sister Nancy's leg as a small crowd at a swimming lake in Michigan gathered to watch.

Or how, when I was little, she would commandeer five bench seats on a CTA bus for her and her brood for the hour-long commute to Rainbow Beach on 79th Street on broiling days in August with no air conditioning at home.

Or when she stepped outside on a frigid day in December, wearing an apron but no coat, to issue a stern warning to some older boys who were vandalizing our snow fort and posturing for a fight.

Not that our mother was one of those "helicopter parents," hovering over us in an unhealthy way. She would never dream, for example, of interfering at school, implicitly trusting the nuns to administer education and "justice." As fiercely as she loved us, she resisted the maternal urge to overprotect, intellectually aware that accountability and independence would help us in the long run.

Which is why at the height of the 96th Place scandal of 1962, when my older brother and his friends were caught in an infamous act of Halloween mischief involving a freezer, a dog, a brown paper bag and a Zippo lighter, it was good old Mom who convened a block meeting to address the matter. Not to ensure special treatment for her own, but to make certain all the perpetrators were equally punished and rehabilitated.

It all makes sense when you consider what a mother raised through war and the Depression was up against.

Shortly after Gertrude Rose Cichoszewski married Charlie McGrath in 1941, she got a crash course in self-reliance when my father was drafted into the Army for service in World War II.

After my father was assigned to an artillery command post in the Panama Canal Zone, she had her first child, Charlie Jr., in a Chicago hospital. For the next 18 months, my mother had to care for him alone. A story she often told was that when her husband came back to the States on furlough, the toddler said, "Go away, man," when my father tried to enter the bedroom.

When my mother became pregnant again, she wrote to President Harry Truman to ask if he could please speed things up so that her husband would not miss the birth of his second child. The White House replied with a polite form letter. Not long after, James was born, my father still absent.

Truman did finally speed things up, dropping bombs, accepting the Japanese surrender and sending Capt. McGrath by ship and rail to the train station on Chicago's South Side.

Mom was never happier.

Still, it didn't get much easier, as she had to raise a family that grew to 10 on the erratic commission my father earned as a tile salesperson. Not to mention, it was an era when women's employment, education and political avenues were closed off or restricted. They couldn't sign contracts for loans or even own a credit card. Nor did Mom ever drive.

Yet Gertrude McGrath succeeded as a mother in spite of gender restrictions, and as a role model and leader ahead of her time, thanks to her strength, ingenuity and tough love.

And her hijacking of my phone conversation that day? A

blessing in disguise, ultimately rerouting me to find Marianne.

Chicago Tribune, May 13, 2023

Friendship

-My Oldest Friend

The weekend before Independence Day in 1971, I was 21, single and had just bought my first car, an olive green 1962 Oldsmobile Super 88.

I gave the owner five $100 bills and he handed me the keys to freedom.

I don't remember what the odometer said, but the grill resembled a smiling Charles Bronson, and there were 330 horses under the hood.

When I pulled in front of Tom's house to show off the 88, he raised an eyebrow and uttered the magic words: "Road trip."

I had known Tom since grade school, when he was the starting guard on St. Bernadette's basketball team and I was a reserve. We shared a passion for Sherwood's hamburgers, bass fishing and Raquel Welch.

And now we had both just graduated college, with summer "shore leave" before we'd enter the adult world. Absolutely nothing was expected from either of us, and we agreed to take off on Monday morning.

Of course, we had no internet, no reservations, no money for boats or motels. But Tom proposed that if we aimed toward Iowa, we could fish all day in the countless farm ponds he had seen where he went to school, which sounded like a plan to me.

Leaving the South Side of Chicago, I soon had the Olds in the left lane of Interstate 80, heading west. Seventy-two miles per hour, elbows out the open window, Creedence Clearwater on the radio. I looked at Tom and could tell he felt the same as I: we owned that blessed road.

Until, that is, I had to abruptly pull off. Thankfully, we were on a straightaway, somewhere near Ottawa, when it felt like we hit a curb, the steering wheel shaking violently and pulling to the left. I fought the wheel to pull onto the shoulder, where we got out to see the damage — a blowout of the front left tire.

Working together, we had the 88 jacked up and the spare mounted in minutes. But a portion of the flat's tread was sliced off like an orange peel so we had to buy a used spare for $5 at the next gas station (which we would need, it turned out, on the return trip).

Once we resumed, I-80 was a long straight line with nothing but silos and farm fields. We talked some about fishing, and then I asked Tom to tell the story of how he once intercepted future football pro Ken Anderson while playing safety for the Iowa Wesleyan Tigers.

Next, we talked about after-summer plans. Tom was intent on owning his own business, and I would teach until I published the next "Great American Novel."

As the Olds roared across the Fred Schwengel Memorial Bridge, 60 feet above the mighty Mississippi, neither of us harbored a single doubt.

After exiting I-80, a few miles past Grandview, we saw a perfect farm pond, an acre of crystal clear water with a thicket of bushes and trees on one end. We pulled down a gravel drive to a two-story white farmhouse in order to ask permission.

It didn't take long before Tom caught a 3-pound bass on a Mepps spinner, and I, the largest bluegill I had ever seen. We had promised our catch to the farmer's wife, a fair trade for the adventure, the surprise, the laughter and the coat of sunburn we acquired on the banks of her pond.

Later, cruising along U.S. 218, Tom thought that another pond glinting in the sun along the side of a hill seemed familiar. It was farther from the road than it appeared and we plodded through head-high grass and patches of deep mud. The fish were starving, and we caught more than 40 juvenile bass, managing to cull eight of legal size that we kept on a stringer staked in the water.

I was thinking two more and we'd have our limit and our dinner, when I saw a lone black cow making its way down the hill, head hanging low, looking our way.

"Bull!" shouted Tom. "Grab the stringer."

We still needed two more 10-inchers. But he had already disappeared into the high grass, his fishing rod moving like a periscope above his head. I grabbed the fish and followed him back toward the road.

We finally made it to the car, panting, muddy, sweaty.

"Bull Pond," Tom said. "I just remembered what they used to call this place."

Good and tired, we drove into Mount Pleasant and parked in front of Tom's former fraternity house. It was closed up for the summer, but we found an unlocked basement window around back.

The water and electricity were still on so I unpacked our gear while Tom found dishes and salt and pepper. We cleaned and cooked what we had caught: the best fish we had ever tasted. A meal that felt like a sacrament.

Over the next half century, the two of us would slowly, methodically trade many of our freedoms, one by one, in exchange for our careers, for homes and mortgages, marriage and family responsibility, cell phones and GPS tracking, arthritis medicine and 401(k) accounts, and for insurance policies on our houses, our cars, our lives, our deaths, and even on our tires.

But today we drink a beer on the patio, and commemorate that long ago time of independence, youth and intimacy with the land.

And we raise a toast on the Fourth of July to the country where, in spite of everything, you can still choose your own direction on life's highway, and determine how far you go by your work, your wiles and your will.

Chicago Tribune & Naperville Sun, July 1, 2020

-Riding Out a Hurricane With Our Friends

Meteorologists can predict hurricanes as soon as they're

born and gauge their size, speed and time of arrival with increasing accuracy — though ascertaining their precise route remains a work in progress.

But science's limits, and the manner in which information is disseminated by television networks and other media, often place the lives of those they serve in greater jeopardy.

My conclusion is not that of a detached observer but as a survivor of Hurricane Ian, among the most violent storms in Florida's history.

Following the announcement that the storm would affect the Gulf Coast, likely near Florida's panhandle, the mood on our residential block in Port Charlotte was cautiously confident. Think of Chicago's massive blizzards, when neighbors turn friendly and helpful, joking about nature's capriciousness.

Unsurprisingly by last Wednesday, Ian's path had veered hundreds of miles farther south than predicted, and the storm surge projection for our coastal segment of South Gulf Cove increased from 3 to 6 feet to 12 to 18 feet. This potentially meant that we had roughly six hours before Charlotte Harbor's waters inundated our homes, driving us outside into salty flood water filled with downed power lines, sharp and heavy debris, and alligators.

Marianne and I have been married long enough to know each other's thinking. She watched me pace room to room, searching for batteries, life jackets and important papers, while I took note of her face and eyes as she monitored AccuWeather on TV.

"Ready?" I said.

"Let me get my Kindle," Marianne said.

We had decided ahead of time, along with our friends and neighbors Tim and Sarah, to shelter in place. Our houses are hardened for severe storms and elevated to stay dry in a substantial surge. Experience has taught us we are safer staying put than helping swell the chaos of statewide traffic — a decision Gov. Ron DeSantis recommended for those who could.

Since Tim and Sarah were already harboring two other

couples, family also originally from Maine, we joined their party.

The entire country knows what happened over the next eight hours, as Ian's winds strengthened to 155 mph and turned sooner and sharper than forecast, making landfall at Cayo Costa, a barrier island near home where I camp and fish.

Over that same span of time, we got to know Tim's cousins Bob, Lil, John and Linda, residents of North Port. We swapped stories, ate ham sandwiches and sipped beer while monitoring Ian's progress with an old-fashioned transistor radio.

At 4 p.m., we had to raise our voices over the intensifying cacophony of banging corrugated metal shutters. We took turns reporting what we could see outside through a slit between two shutters: another palm tree snapped in two and a 10-foot aluminum gutter sailing like a paper airplane. And then the power went out.

Tim turned on two lanterns, and Sarah retrieved a deck of cards. Seven stud proved an effective time filler, though no one could maintain their poker face whenever a sudden boom spelled a crash involving a building or a boat or a tree. Tim scooted more frequently to the "viewing window," measuring with the long beam of a flashlight the water line on his neighbor's dock.

"Is it time to head upstairs to the second story?" I asked.

Sarah didn't think so. All of us, in fact, were skeptical of a super surge since there had never been one where we live. But we also acknowledged the rash of unprecedented weather events in recent history, so Tim maintained his vigil.

At 10 p.m., the shutters quieted. Ian had passed. Once again, no surge in South Gulf Cove.

The next day, a celebrity TV news reporter hitched a ride in a rescue motorboat south of here. He asked the first responder at the helm to find a victim of Hurricane Ian who would talk on air, and they coaxed a mother and her 6-year-old daughter onto the porch of their flooded mobile home.

"Why didn't you leave?" were his words. While his tone was incredulous for the benefit of his audience, it translated as condescension toward anyone not wise enough to heed his network's warnings, some of which were not wrong — *this time.*

"We didn't think the storm would be this bad," she said, her daughter staring blankly at the camera.

Off-camera, she may have expressed her own astonishment at the inability of a media star with an eight-figure income to understand the calculation necessarily made by her and her neighbors: That unlike for him, the usual low odds of dying in a hurricane constitute a risk she'll take over incurring the financial and psychological costs of evacuation.

And to maintain a grip on all that she has in this world.

*

More than 100 lives in Florida have been lost to Hurricane Ian.

Weather experts, government workers, civil engineers, charitable organizations and first responders deserve gratitude for doing all that they could to minimize that tragic number.

But the hope is that from lessons learned through Hurricane Ian, self-absolving mandates and overestimates will give way to more effective, practical help before and after the next storm.

Chicago Tribune, October 5, 2022 (Reprinted in Fort Myers News Press, Buffalo News, St. Paul Pioneer Press, Grand Haven Tribune, Charlotte Sun, The Press of Atlantic City, and others.)

-My Pal Mick

"Hello, who is this?"
"It's your wife. Do you need anything from the store?"
"Are you in traffic?"
"Yes."
"I'm hanging up."
"Wait."
"We'll talk at home."

That call took place after I returned home from the Surgical-Neuro Intensive Care Unit at Christ Hospital in Oak Lawn, where I had been visiting a patient by the name of Michael Michau. My friendship with Mick began 50 years ago on Piggy Toe Mountain, a steep alley in Evergreen Park where we used to go sledding.

Mick won't be sledding soon. He won't be talking soon. On his way to work two weeks ago, he was hit head on by another driver, a 70 year old who was reaching for her cell phone.

The woman had had a sudden impulse to call home while driving 50 mph through a suburban intersection in morning rush hour traffic, and now my pal Mick won't be working soon, walking soon, even thinking soon. Doctors have induced a coma and put him on a ventilator, while trying to figure out what to do about his multiple injuries, which include two broken femurs, a shattered hip, broken ribs, a broken clavicle, bruised heart, and damaged lungs.

His vehicle's airbag burst open as it was supposed to do, breaking bones and burning skin, while saving his face and head and brain, so that doctors are optimistic that he will be restored to full consciousness.

His recovery is obviously important to his wife Carol, daughter Laurie, and sons Mike, Jr., and Steve. It's also important to the clients at his accounting firm, as well as to me and countless friends. You see, Mick is a big man, both as a physical specimen and as a human being. It's no accident we've been friends so long, since he is a man who has always been adamant about his family maintaining connections, and by family, he means two to three-hundred friends and relatives.

Hours after the crash, his wife was at his bedside, answering the emergency physician's routine questions, while Mick lay in a semi conscious state of shock and pain. As she was assuring the doctor that her husband was not allergic to anesthesia, was on no medication, was not a smoker, and had no previous serious health problems. Mick squeezed her hand and hoarsely whispered, "Better tell the doc I'm a little fat, Carol."

Though he faces many surgeries and many months, if not years, of rehabilitation, he should be able to live out his years and enjoy his future grandchildren.

The same cannot be said, unfortunately for Guadalupe Gonazalez. While he was riding on the Dan Ryan Expressway on Oct. 5th to visit his grandson, the driver of an SUV reached for his cell phone, lost control of his Pontiac Aztek, and caused the accident that killed Mr. Gonzalez.

Michau and Gonazalez are two of approximately 2,600 men and women killed, and 330,000 injured each year, by drivers distracted by cell phones.

Researchers at the University of Illinois have determined that cell phone users behind the wheel are less adept at reacting, stopping, and avoiding accidents than drivers with blood alcohol levels that exceed .08 percent.

And although outlawing cell phone use on the road seems to make sense, it is not an end-all solution. The city of Chicago has such a law, so the chatty driver who killed Gonzalez was cited for violating the ordinance, a small consolation to Mr. Gonazalez's family.

It will require public education, awareness, and empathy to reduce cell phone user carnage. A good place to start might be with a campaign to hang up if your caller is hung up in traffic.

Previous public awareness campaigns, like the one that reinforced the caveat against pregnant women consuming alcohol, have been enormously effective, even when there is no legislation to prevent the act.

So a campaign to boycott dialing while driving can be equally successful. Don't reach for the phone if you're driving. And when you receive a call from someone you learn is in a car, hang up after you tell him why. If he or she is offended, tell him you're doing it to save his life, not to mention the life of the driver on the other side of the yellow line.

We can shame each other into compliance on this.

Shame is good.

And if this catches on, who knows but that people might start to concentrate and even start re-acquiring old skills, like using turn signals.

Chicago Tribune (Southtown), November 7, 2006

-My Friend Ed

I heard the groaning as we walked off the elevator at Christ Hospital in Oak Lawn. The closer we got to Ed's room, the more certain I was that the anguished sounds came from him.

Ed lay on the bed, eyes closed, his skin tan and green. He was in the late stages of prostate cancer that had spread to other organs.

It was August of 2013, and I had just arrived in Evergreen Park for St. Bernadette's 50th grade school reunion when I learned that my boyhood pal Ed Lepore was in critical condition. My closest friend, Tom Booth, picked me up to visit Ed so we both could say good-bye.

The same age as us, Ed fully expected to live another 25 years. He was funny and creative, and had a job designing display ads for a small newspaper. He loved drawing and film and music, and playing nickel-ante poker on Friday nights.

But after being laid off from the newspaper, Ed never fully rebounded. He lived in the house he had inherited from his late parents and bought groceries and Montclair cigarettes with money drawn from unemployment compensation and sporadic part-time gigs.

His most recent job was as a maintenance worker at a nearby hospital. In his last two years, Ed's lifelong friend Mike Michau and several others helped pay his bills.

For a long time, Ed complained of pain in his hips and groin, but he never saw a doctor because he could not afford health insurance. By the time an ambulance was called, it was too late.

The Affordable Care Act, which would not take effect till January 2014, was intended to prevent tragedies like Ed's, a way for Americans to acquire insurance and safeguard their health. Though the ACA enabled 18 million more people to purchase insurance, many now fear they'll lose it if the ACA is repealed, as Republicans in Congress and President Donald Trump have threatened to do.

To resolve this national headache once and for all, Sen. Bernie Sanders of Vermont has proposed a bill to insure all Americans by extending Medicare, which seniors now receive, to cover everyone.

Sanders is convinced it will be cheaper, more effective and more humane than our current system.

Presently, citizens pay out trillions of dollars to health insurance companies, pharmacies, doctors and hospitals for deductibles and copayments. The paperwork alone adds billions of dollars to national medical costs. Yet, despite all we pay, when someone has a really serious injury or illness in this country, friends and relatives often must mount a fundraiser to get them through it.

Critics say Sanders' plan is "delusional" because it is too expensive and amounts to socialism.

But the same critics mischaracterize the cost of Sanders' plan, implying there is no money to fund it. They are disingenuous in omitting the fact that it would be paid for with the massive sums now spent for private health care insurance, which would be redirected, via income taxes, to finance universal care.

Here, in a nutshell, is how we can replace our patchwork private health care network with Medicare for all:

Currently, the United States spends $2.8 trillion on private health care. Switching to the single-payer universal system that Sanders advocates would cost $2.3 trillion, according to a study by economist Gerald Friedman of the University of Massachusetts.

Sanders' plan would thus save $500 billion a year in health

care costs. And it's easy to see why, since it would bypass countless middlemen, including health insurance corporation tycoons like Michael Neirdoff, the CEO of Centene. In 2016, Neirdoff pocketed a salary and bonuses worth more than $22 million.

Nor would Sanders' plan resemble socialism even remotely, since Medicare would make payments to doctors, hospitals, clinics, medical suppliers and pharmacies that already exist in the private sector.

Ed died several weeks after our visit. Before Tom and I said good-bye, I asked Ed if he had a message for any of his former classmates at the reunion. Ed bellowed out an expletive and a harsh suggestion that they do something that was anatomically impossible.

Pain and anger, understandably, incited his outburst. The same pain and anger which, hopefully, will incite Congress to do what's right and moral, passing Sanders' bill for universal health care.

Chicago Sun Times & Duluth News Tribune, September 23, 2017

-Farewell to a Kindred Spirit

"A popular belief is that altered cognitive processing, whether from sleep, insanity, or alcohol use, sparks creativity among artists, composers, writers, and problem-solvers." (*Psychology Today,* 4/12/2012).

I loved Jimmy Buffett's "Margaritaville."
Of course, it's because I was a drinker. And I assume that the 20 million Americans who have bought the record since it was first recorded in 1977, making it a multi-platinum mega hit, were also drinkers.

In fact, the National Institutes of Health states that 30

million Americans have AUD, or Alcohol Use Disorder; so my assumption and my numbers can't be very far off.

Singer, songwriter Jimmy "Bubba" Buffett died at 76 last Friday of Merkel cell skin cancer.

We loved the artist, and we loved his iconic song, because it made drinkers feel like heroes.

I don't mean hero in the sense of Superman or Sully Sullenberger or Babe Ruth. Instead, Buffett romanticized people with AUD as *tragic* heroes, examples of which might be Macbeth or Kurt Cobain or the character Rick Blaine portrayed by Humphrey Bogart in *Casablanca*. Yes, they failed at what they wanted to do, or experienced a tragic downfall. But they were spectacularly cool, lyrical, and admired during the process.

Likewise, "Margaritaville," the song which made Buffett a billionaire, is the story of the unfulfilled, aimless existence of a failed musician in the Florida Keys, who has nothing concrete to show for his life except a new tattoo.

But the heroic elements, which Buffett ingeniously accentuated with his voice, his melody, and his tone, mainly derive from the poignant details enumerated in the song, including lost love ("some people say there's a woman to blame"); the hero's noble acceptance of blame ("my own damn fault"); his insouciance and humor in the face of the pain ("brand new tattoo"); and his bravery in withstanding the depression, and soldiering ahead with the help of the "frozen concoction that helps him hang on."

Buffett hit upon a winning formula that combines Hemingway's *"grace* under pressure" philosophy, with the "blackout drunk" mission statement of college fraternities nationwide, turning it into a half billion dollar corporation of music, books, hotels, t-shirts, and tequila.

I don't mean to imply that Jimmy Buffett was an enabler. On the contrary, he was more like a therapist, bringing together thousands of drinkers to sing, celebrate, and relieve the loneliness, wistfulness, and sadness symptomatic of AUD. His concerts qualified as some of the largest outdoor AA meetings ever assembled, absent the abstinence.

Nor is Buffett's story of success a unique phenomenon.

Psychologists have long acknowledged the close association between creativity and alcohol use. Some of the greatest artistic works in history by the likes of Earnest Hemingway, Dorothy Parker, Vincent Van Gogh, and Tennessee Williams, among others, were conceived with the help of boozy concoctions, frozen or otherwise. Which also applies to "Margaritaville," which Buffett confirmed as being mostly autobiographical, though he severely curtailed his drinking in the latter half of his life.

Buffett was a gifted artist and a skilled musician, who tapped into the "morning after" syndrome of pain, regret, and longing, familiar to everyone who's ever been hungover, including myself. Thank you, Son of a Son of a Sailor, and farewell.

Chicago Sun Times, Duluth News Tribune, Madison Capital Times, September 12, 2023

-My Friend the Writer

This year as we celebrate the 100th birthday of Jack Kerouac, author of *On the Road*, we might also anticipate the release of *The Long Way Home* (Ice Cube Press), the latest offering by *Notre Dame Magazine* contributor Tom Fate, for its banquet of pleasing parallels to Kerouac's masterpiece.

On the Road, published September 5, 1957, and considered by some critics as America's greatest novel, chronicles the chaotic journey of Kerouac, thinly disguised as young writer Sal Paradise, as he travels back and forth across the country, in search of adventure and purpose.

Though categorized as fiction, the novel is based on time Kerouac spent in New York, Denver, New Orleans, Mexico City and San Francisco, as the contemplative narrator grows from exasperation and uncertainty about the world, to a sense of confidence and happiness about his role in life, as a result of his experiences and friendships with other young artists.

Fate, who lives in Glen Ellyn, Illinois, and is a former writing professor at College of DuPage, writes about his own travels to Nicaragua, Canada, the Philippines, South Dakota, Minnesota, Iowa and elsewhere around the globe, in a similar search for meaning, while using the real names of colorful characters he encounters in a work of nonfiction.

Full disclosure: Fate has been a teaching colleague and friend, but also a rival freelance commentary writer for the *Chicago Tribune*, other Midwest newspapers, and for this magazine. Although I am not certain about the exact tally of our competing essays over the past two decades, I admire his talent and have marveled at his four previous books. This is a commentary, therefore, and not a book review, which I write with the desire and expectation that Fate's latest will win the National Book Award, catapulting his career to such heights that he'll finally relinquish the periodical venues to me!

A fair-to-middling bass and trout angler, and a graduate of the Chicago Theological Seminary and of the University of Iowa Nonfiction Writing Program, Tom Fate is, at his core, a storyteller.

The first chapter in *The Long Way Home* is an alluring trap rendering us captive through the rest of this provocative memoir. We're hooked when Fate writes that he both loved and hated being a preacher's son, ushering us to the climactic moment when he makes up his mind that he will not get confirmed. He's 14 years old and he is about to tell his father, the minister at the Congregational Church, that he no longer believes.

So as not to spoil the ending of chapter one whose title is "Fishing For My Father," suffice to say that it is one of over a dozen stories in this slim volume that took me luxuriously long to read. The stories go fast because they're compelling and relatable, but page by page you slow down as to pause and gaze into the distance, scanning your own memory to recall how you felt and what you thought at comparable junctures in your own life.

It's time well spent, as Fate poses questions identical to those of Kerouac: Why are we here? What is love? How do we respond to loss? Share the earth? Respond to suffering?

Fate calls his process of traveling and writing a form of "fishing." He mesmerizes us with a colorful evocation of a trip, for example, to the Pine Ridge Reservation, where he's almost immediately robbed at gunpoint, but later invited to a sweat lodge. Or his trip to Nicaragua during the Sandinista revolution, armed with a press pass from *The Daily Iowan,* accompanied by Carol, the woman he fell in love with months earlier, and whom he would marry in the middle of a war zone in Managua.

His prose, better than Panavision, makes us forget Netflix, Facebook and even food while immersed in another of his tales. And throughout each story, he tells us what he thinks or is puzzling over, "fishing" to learn what he felt, what he feared, where he failed or what he did not know.

In a "A Map to Somewhere" (chapter 11), Fate relates the sometimes harrowing, sometimes hilarious adventure of a fishing and canoe camping trip in Canada with his three brothers, Robin, Paul and Kendall, when they had to resort to Plan B after most of Quetico Provincial Park was closed because of raging wildfires. Smoke, inclement weather, unreadable maps, dead cell phones and salty arguments ranging from fishing strategies to the correct return route all impede their return to civilization.

But amid all the perils and yet unsure of where exactly they are, Fate returns to a sense of *home* around the campfire each night, when they reminisce about past trips and share stories about their late father:

"It was the balm of memory that always knit our frayed egos and tired bodies back together again, so we were once more *at home* with each other. No matter what happened on those trips, or in our lives, that was where we always ended up."

For Kerouac, the search was for "it," or what he wanted out of life. For Fate, it is finding the way home.

All the experiences comprise a journey with a tangle of detours, a very long way to home, which, literally, is where he grew up in Iowa, although figuratively, it can be anywhere he feels a sense of belonging, understanding and relevance. It is where, even if he hasn't found the answers to all his questions, he's found where he fits in the universe and its scheme, and it usually entails some sort of harmony with family, the earth, time, God and society, though not necessarily in that order.

    The best thing about Fate's writing is that you don't have to read or contend with the paragraph I've just written. Just sink into the stories, and Fate's wonder and insights will sink into you.

Notre Dame Magazine, April 26, 2022

Education

-The Redemption of a Middle School Benchwarmer

At the end of every October, I grow anxious. Irritated.

The reason, I tell everybody, is that it will take a month of restless sleep before I acclimate to the time change.

But an underlying cause, I suspect, is the memory of a bit of trouble that happened around the end of daylight saving time in 1962 after I made the cut for St. Bernadette's eighth grade basketball team in Evergreen Park.

I wasn't much of a player. Surely, I was strong and dogged, from playing in the yard with my brothers, and I did all right on defense. But I could not dribble, shoot, rebound or pass, and I was neither tall nor particularly fast.

My pal Jack said I made the team only because Coach Walsh knew my father who was a "big shot" as a village trustee. Everybody else in the locker room laughed when he said it, including me. But after a couple of months of never playing and being strictly relegated to the practice team or "reserves," I thought maybe he was on to something.

Practice was every Tuesday and Thursday night at Evergreen Park's Southeast Elementary gym, when I'd work up a sweat and feel like part of the team.

The last Tuesday in October, after the clocks were moved back, we ran out of daylight by the time practice ended. The good players, including my pal Tom who was the starting guard, were picked up by their parents. But TJ, Jack and I, the core" of the reserves, packed our duffel bags and headed home in the dark.

TJ's older brother had been a 6-foot-4 eighth grade basketball legend at St. Bernadette. TJ had all that to live up to, but he was only an inch taller than me and confined to the reserves,

But he was blessed with a different kind of talent: He could talk like Maynard G. Krebs on "The Many Loves of Dobie Gillis" TV series, or Amos, the old farmer on "The Real McCoys," or just about anybody we knew. And though shorter than his brother, he had long arms that swung out when he walked, so that with his flat-top haircut and grin, he resembled the comic book character Jughead, only with muscles.

All the way home, TJ imitated the coach yelling at the players and cursing at the reserves, which gave me and Jack cramps in our sides from laughing.

"For cripes sake, the game is basketball, not air ball, McGrath," said TJ, in Coach Walsh's booming voice, and Jack held his stomach as he dropped to his knees on the parkway.

Maybe you had to be there to find it funny or else just realize that this was a raucous, rolling release after being foils for the starters and having the coach yell at us to stay frozen in our zones so the varsity could practice set plays.

Halfway home, TJ wanted to stop at the Jerazol drugstore for a bottle of 7UP. Jack and I covered our mouths to keep from laughing as TJ proceeded to talk to the old pharmacist in his Amos McCoy voice. It was disrespectful, but the old guy didn't have a clue.

After TJ got his soda, and we'd gone a block down the street, Jack opened his duffel to show off the ice cream bars he had snatched from the freezer while TJ was flummoxing the old man.

Just as proudly, I whipped out an Oh Henry! and two Payday candy bars I had slid from the rack into my coat pocket.

We howled about it all the way home, about not getting caught like the sorry criminals on "Dragnet" or "Hawaii Five-O."

The next morning, I felt sick from guilt for what we had done, and I resolved to never do it again. But the following Thursday, something about our intoxicating laughter, our unity as the shunned reserves and our escape with our loot into the cold and darkness all superseded the risks, the Ten Commandments and the rules of conduct posted for athletes. Rules left back at the gym with the coach and his hollering and parents picking up their varsity players each night.

Being outcasts, as long as you were not alone, felt powerful. A strange feeling, fiercer than love.

It was weeks before anyone caught on; the drugstore must have called school. The coach convened an unusual meeting at practice, calling for any player who knew about the shoplifting at Jerazol to step forward.

TJ raised his hand: "Coach, are they giving a reward for catching these varmints?"

Jack erupted, stifling his laugh with a coughing spell, and Coach ordered him into the hall to get a drink of water. I was able to hold my breath until TJ shut up and the Coach got back to lecturing us about good athletes being good Catholics. I avoided looking at TJ's face, but then the word "varmints" rang in my head, and I, too, had to be excused to the water fountain.

Bernadette's won two tournaments that year and lost a close one to Holy Redeemer. I rode the bench, cheering on Tom who led the scoring.

With no more practices and no three musketeers, I felt worse about our secret and went to confession. Father O'Brien administered penance but said I also had to make restitution, a word I had to look up. And for five or six days, until Jerazol was fully restituted, I bicycled over there, pretending to browse, until I could slide a quarter or two onto the counter when no one was looking.

I don't know if it restored Jerazol's bottom line. But I had to hand it to Father O'Brien for knowing how to stop a life of crime, while inspiring an attempt at another, as a writer.

Chicago Tribune, November 11, 2022

-How to Thwart Chat GPT

An administrator at the college where I was teaching

English called to say a lawsuit had been filed against the school by a student with hearing loss, alleging I violated his rights under the Americans with Disabilities Act.

It was the late 1990s, and the news was a surprise. Through three decades of teaching, the only complaints, by and large, were from students who received failing grades. Whereas, the plaintiff in the lawsuit, a man in his late 20s who paid close attention during lessons and whom I could always count on for a smile when I told a joke, dropped the class before grades were issued.

I puzzled over the basis for the legal action. Granted, my seminars included a lot of oral discussion. But the student had been assigned a sign language interpreter who conveyed everything said, whether by me while writing on the whiteboard or by other students participating in discussions.

There were no quizzes or tests, and the final grade was based primarily on five essays that students completed during the term.

But two of the essays had to be written in class and turned in by the end of the 80-minute period. Those two assignments were what the student objected to, alleging that I did not make accommodations, under the ADA, for his individual learning style and needs.

Before he withdrew, he told me that he required more time for the in-class essay. I conceded that he could finish at home, as long as he started it here and showed me the unfinished work.

This he wouldn't do, sitting at his desk, signing with his interpreter.

My suggestion that he at least get a couple of sentences down on paper, or a brief introductory paragraph that I might read before he left, was also declined.

When I related all of this to the attorney deposing me over the telephone, he asked why I did not allow the student to do the work at home. I explained that 40% of a student's grade must derive from writing that I know is authentic and not plagiarized. I told him that I hang on to the in-class essays to use as a "control," for judging the ownership of the other three.

Later, I learned the lawsuit was unsuccessful. The "W" remained on the student's transcript, no refund was issued and he retook the class with another teacher.

More importantly, a simple teaching practice for ensuring academic integrity was affirmed. And this is the same method that can be just as effectively employed today to detect and deter cheating in college with ChatGPT.

The language-processing artificial intelligence bot generates competent, focused writing, which many fear will be used by college students to produce papers for their professors.

It's a free program invented by research company OpenAI that can swiftly provide cogent-sounding sentences and paragraphs in response to a question or a prompt.

For example, a student doing a paper on climate change might feed ChatGPT four prompts that produce four 500-word blocks of text explaining climate change and elaborating on its causes, possible solutions and the potential consequences for not taking action. Voilà! A 2,000-word term paper.

It works a bit like Google. But instead of responding to a search prompt, as Google does, by offering and excerpting articles, blogs and websites, ChatGPT generates a direct answer to the prompt in nearly flawless text and at reading and vocabulary levels as basic or as advanced as you want. Rather like a robotic term-paper mill.

ChatGPT uses artificial intelligence to "write" an article by cribbing from an enormous amount of data it has been fed from millions of sources — without citing those sources.

This last fact alone makes it a lousy cheat sheet, since college professors routinely require documentation of sources used in essays and term papers. And for informal or personal essays requiring no research, an in-class written essay or timed essay test would thwart a cheater.

Of what practical use, then, is ChatGPT?

It may prove to be an effective time-saver in situations in which plagiarism is acceptable or forgiven. For example, a speech writer might use ChatGPT to produce a 15-minute stump speech for a politician, which can then be easily adapted for each town they visit. A second draft can be pumped up by directing ChatGPT to add topical humor or an inspiring anecdote.

A teacher in a hurry can use ChatGPT to craft a class lecture or discussion, with a prompt such as: What were the four major causes of the Civil War? Anyone in need of a toast, instructions for CPR, a letter of apology or a humorous set of wedding vows might also benefit.

I would use it to generate a term paper right before my students' eyes and then show them every sentence I would flag with my red pen, for its obvious undocumented appropriation from a published source.

If you're a student, beware: 9 out of 10 who cheat with ChatGPT would likely be caught, earning an F for their trouble or outright expulsion. (See the article "Cheating in class at new level" published in the Jan. 19th *Tribune*.)

And the 10th student, smart enough to evade detection, is probably smart enough that they don't need ChatGPT in the first place.

Chicago Tribune, January 27, 2023

-What Changed My Mind About School Reunions

After reading the invitation to my Evergreen Park High School reunion, I forwarded it to my wife for laughs, just before deleting it. The prospect of attending a gathering of senior citizens whose faces evoke only unpleasant flashbacks from the 1960s seemed like torture to me.

Marianne tried gentle persuasion.

"Isn't there anyone you'd like to see?" she asked.

Well, OK, there's Jerry Kamper, but we became good friends

long after high school. And maybe Joyce Russell, one of the two girls back then I was not afraid to talk to. The other, Lynn Seermon, was already a mature adult when the rest of us were still idiots.

But too many other memories from my time at E.P., I'd just as soon forget.

Like how I never set foot in the cafeteria. My excuse was the bland food; the truth was my painfully acute shyness.

Instead, I hoofed it to the diner at 95th and Kedzie every day and had a "home dog" and fries alone at the counter.

Or the Barry Goldwater fans in Coach Dykstra's civics class who derided my defense of the Democratic Party during a debate, and for the rest of the semester, jeered, "For the people … the people," whenever I was called on.

Or the mortifying response I gave my young German teacher, on whom I had a crush, when she asked why I wasn't keeping up with the vocabulary lessons. Still too cringey to reveal.

Or bullies ceaselessly tormenting freshmen, such as the one who was trashing a poor kid's locker at the end of the school day. When I tried to step in, the bully challenged me to fight in front of a swelling crowd of onlookers. I had little choice, and the entire blood-lusting horde followed us outside to the CSX railroad tracks, where after one or two wild punches, we ended up in the mud, in a clinch, till we both grunted assent to a draw.

So, given a choice between attending a school reunion and passing a kidney stone, I'd opt for the latter. At least I wouldn't have to dress up.

But a funny thing happened since the arrival of that invitation: I went to another reunion in May for a different school that I attended before transferring to E.P.

Again, I absolutely hated the idea. But Marianne somehow talked me into it (don't ask), and I bit the bullet and showed up at the Oakbrook Embassy Suites hotel.

I had equally dreaded seeing these other former classmates, since I was even more puerile at age 14 and 15. I vaguely remember having said and done cruel or ignorant things to people who I prayed would not show up at the hotel.

I was wrong; they were there. But I was also wrong about everything else: They either didn't remember or just didn't care about my defensive, smart-alecky responses back then, or my social dysfunction.

"That message you wrote on the mirror in the bathroom," Tom said, "was the funniest thing I ever saw."

"You were one of the brains," Steve said.

And that's how the evening ensued. Everyone was kind. Charming, even. I listened with fascination to their life stories. And they asked me about mine.

When Marianne called, since I'd asked her to ring my cellphone as a pretense for leaving early, I told her I was having a wonderful time.

"You're saying that because there are people nearby?" she asked.

No, I protested. The reunion was remarkable, and I would explain it all tomorrow. Don't wait up, I told her.

The next morning, I did not change my mind, wishing I had spent more of my life with the convivial, authentic and generous group of classmates from 55 years ago.

After I asked Marianne for the checkbook so that I could send for my ticket for the E.P. reunion scheduled for Sept. 24, she asked what, exactly, reversed my opinion: Had the people at the previous night's reunion changed that much from when they were high schoolers?

She made a good point. They were all pretty much the same people I knew as teenagers, only with gray hair and stringy necks, like Danny, whose nickname had been "Motormouth," or Mike, quiet and inscrutable, still reminding me of Gary Cooper.

But we were now able to appreciate each other for our differences, eccentricities, talents, passions and each person's endearing human touch.

Because there is one big difference between then and

now — the one biochemical element of elephantine significance inside everyone who goes to high school, from the bullies and brains and greasers, to the stars, the mean girls and the nerds, but which is now conspicuously and thankfully absent: fear. Unrelenting, life-dominating *fear* of adulthood, self-image, peer pressure, the opposite sex, the future and, heaven forbid, of wearing the wrong shoes.

Fear, without which we are finally free to be ourselves.

Chicago Tribune, September 10, 2022. Reprinted in Duluth News Tribune, Naperville Sun, & Daily Southtown.

-My Extremely Brief Acting Career

Count me among the nearly 10 million viewers who will watch the Academy Awards on Sunday. Not just because I look forward to the daring comedy of this year's host Amy Schumer. Or because I'm gaga over the fashion and celebrity of Hollywood's beautiful people.

I will watch because of the awe and deep admiration I have for the work that professional actors do, an appreciation gained from … humiliation.

That's because in the late 1960s, I had my own moment on stage and under the lights while working my way through college on Chicago's South Side.

Mind you, I had no aspirations for theater or the cinema. I was majoring in English at Chicago State University because I was partly interested in writing, partly interested in teaching and mainly interested in maintaining my 2-S exemption from the military draft.

One of the classes filling out my 12-credit hour schedule in the winter term was a 300-level course in drama with Dr. Klein. It was a seminar in literature, not acting, in which we studied classic works by playwrights like Henrik Ibsen, George Bernard Shaw and Eugene O'Neill, among others.

The readings were long, the class hard, and much of

what Dr. Klein would say in his lectures went right over my head.

I was 19 at the time, but had a set of fake IDs for hanging out and my first real girlfriend. My attention in class waned, and I started cutting sessions once and even twice a week.

After two absences, when I decided I'd better make an appearance, Dr. Klein took special note of my presence, smiling and eyeballing me at the start of the hour.

"Mr. McGrath," he said. "So nice to see you again." Several students turned around, and I'm sure I blushed, knowing I was on the hot seat.

Professor Klein then asked if I'd be willing to help out with the play the school was producing, since one of the minor performers in his theater production of Herman Melville's novella *Benito Cereno* had broken his arm.

Something in the tone of his voice told me I'd better say yes in order to pass drama, and I started attending after-school rehearsals that afternoon. I was assigned a single scene, non-speaking role as one of the American sailors aboard a 19th Century ship that intercepted carrying slaves who had revolted and taken over the Spanish vessel.

The play was a bold but relevant choice for Klein as theater director, since both war and civil rights protests were heating up in the city and on our campus. My sole interest, however, was getting through the play and the semester as quickly and as painlessly as possible.

With two weeks left in the term, we staged a live performance in the school theater. I was not that nervous as I put on my two-cornered hat and navy cloak backstage. Robert was the other sailor, dressed the same, in our own black pants and shoes. We were to wait about 40 minutes behind the curtain before entering stage left, where we would remain on the ship's deck, poised with our muskets, until two of the slaves rushed us at the climactic moment, just before we shot them dead.

Robert and I bided our time, talking in whispers, when

finally the make-up artist came by to dab foundation and rouge on my cheeks. That's when my heart started to pound, and a bead of sweat trickled down my back.

Trying to catch my breath, I never heard our cue, and Robert nudged me onto the stage.

Instinctively, involuntarily, I turned to look out at the audience, and 1,500 pairs of eyes stared back. Their scattered laughter gave me an odd and momentary sense of relief, until I realized it was all terribly wrong. My body went numb, my head, dizzy.

When the slave rushed at me with his dagger, I could not, at first, move, finally mimicking the recoil of my musket well after the sound of gunshot over the P.A.

I ended up earning a B in drama, though it had nothing to do with my acting debut.

After the curtain closed, I scrambled backstage, stripping off my cloak and navy hat, and dropping them into the costume bin on my rush to the exit.

On the way home, I pondered my chances, calculating that marathon cramming of iconic playwrights' lives and works each day and night until the final exam would be the only way to avoid a plane ride to South Vietnam.

The surprise was not so much that the studying was successful, but that Dr. Klein was so sanguine in our remaining class meetings. Students were congratulating him on the play, making me wonder if I only imagined that I single-handedly ruined everything for the other actors, the 1,500 people in the audience, the school's reputation and the entire world of theater.

Or maybe Professor Klein was cutting me some slack, since acting is so damned hard. Certainly, he would have known that any awards going to Javier Bardem, Denzel Washington, Penelope Cruz, Kristen Stewart or others on Oscar night are not for beauty, privilege and luck. Instead, they go only to those who have developed this nearly impossible skill for concentration and immersion in an alternate reality, even as the real world is everywhere they look. Unique aptitude and innate talent, but mostly, again, the skill they develop, hone and practice through endless days and nights, over an entire lifetime.

Decades later, I still break out in a cold sweat trying to imagine it.

Chicago Sun Times, May 25, 2022

-Teachers:First Responders

Like a lot of teachers, I began as a substitute for Chicago Public Schools, making $40 a day filling in for faculty members who called in sick. As a 22-year-old English major, however, I was seldom placed in classes for which I was qualified. Once, for example, I was completely clueless, subbing in a kindergarten at Altgeld Elementary, and I fetched my guitar from the car to strum all afternoon while the 5-year-olds danced around the room.

So after a year of subbing that was more like babysitting, I was thrilled to land a permanent job teaching English at Chicago Vocational High School, known as CVS, for a 1972 salary of $9,570. I was handed a schedule of five classes totaling 140 students; a "division," or homeroom, for overseeing the attendance, grades and academic schedules for an additional 28; and one "duty" period.

My duty assignment for one semester was to monitor the lunchroom during seventh period. CVS' cafeteria was bigger than a gymnasium with seating for hundreds. Teen chatter mixed with laughter made the hour pass tolerably, though some of my fellow faculty monitors routinely wore earplugs.

Less tolerable was when students in one section would suddenly and seemingly all at once hop onto the tables for a better view of, say, a classmate who was having a seizure or, more commonly, two students spoiling for a fight.

Standing on tables was, of course, a violation of rules, but at least it let me know through the crush of students that a brawl had broken out, while also leaving room in the aisles for me and hopefully another faculty monitor to reach the combatants as quickly as possible.

I can't say how many fights I broke up, but I got used to pulling a brawler away and sometimes pinned their arms, provided another faculty monitor on the scene was simultaneously restraining the brawler's adversary.

I was still young and quick enough to avoid a wayward left hook and restrain a high schooler for however long it took for them to calm down.

Some fights were worse than others, as when I was the lone referee between two girls who turned out to be in rival gangs. I concentrated my attention on the more aggressive of the two, whose adrenaline-fueled surge of strength caught me by surprise. I had to use a hammerlock to separate her from the other.

The rest of the day, in between classes, I patrolled the hallway outside my classroom. I took to wearing loose fitting clothes and sneakers, so that I could chase down troublemakers and deliver them to our lone police officer. Often, I failed. One time, a 16-year-old suffered a serious head injury from someone wielding a ball-peen hammer when I couldn't get through a crowd fast enough.

At the end of each day, I reported for bus loading to protect our students at the bus stop while toughs made menacing gang signs from across 87th Street.

Some of my colleagues should have gotten combat pay. CVS' athletic director at the time dislocated his knee while chasing a gangbanger through the school's icy parking lot. And a veteran gym teacher wrested a knife from an enraged student attacking another just outside the English faculty office.

Such experiences were not unique to CVS, as teachers monitoring the lunchrooms, hallways, playgrounds, study halls and bus stops at Chicago's 600-plus other schools will attest.

Yet, in addition to all my fellow teachers and I had to contend with during our tenure in secondary education, today's teachers in Chicago and elsewhere face even more obstacles than pupil behavioral problems. These include inadequate compensation, stricter time demands, lack of administrative support, book bans (in 37 states and counting), and more and more school boards restricting instruction on gender or race issues and threatening to suspend or fire teachers for perceived violations.

At least half a million educators have left the profession since the start of the pandemic. In a National Education Association survey last year, 55% of educators declared they were going to leave earlier than they had planned. Burnout in K-12 teachers is widespread.

Increasingly ominous are school shootings, which have been on the rise in the last decade. Last year, there were 51 shootings that led to injuries and deaths; this year, there have been at least 27. With most schools conducting active shooter drills and calls for arming teachers increasing with each incident, there's little question that more teachers will exit before adding "armed guard" to their job description.

Low pay and physical demands notwithstanding, I remained at CPS for 20 years because I loved the freedom and art of teaching writing and great literature. Stripped of this autonomy, today's teachers have even less incentive to stay.

"Our nation is undergoing a mass exodus of teachers leaving the classroom," U.S. Rep. Frederica Wilson, a Florida Democrat, told ABC News in December. "We can choose to take this issue head on or lose America's teachers and have the education of our students severely impacted."

What better time than Labor Day, therefore, when we pay tribute to the American worker, for us voters to commit to solving the nation's teacher shortage? We can do so by electing legislators and school board members who support salary increases, collective bargaining rights, mental health programs, academic freedom, freedom of the press and sensible gun regulations.

Chicago Tribune, September 4, 2023

-Lucky Boys

A teacher for 35 years, I learned a crucial lesson about

the profession when I was still in high school. It happened when I was 15 and addicted to Lucky Strikes.

In the 1960s, Luckies were a man's cigarette, because they were unfiltered and had a strong tobacco flavor. In *Rebel Without a Cause,* one was clenched between the lips of James Dean, the coolest male actor who ever lived.

As a sophomore with a bad complexion and a problem talking to people, I depended on Luckies. The lightweight, square package fit snugly in my shirt pocket or tucked under the sleeve at my bicep. The prominent red circle on the label felt like a shield.

Emulating the iconic actor, I practiced flicking my wrist to eject a single cigarette. Holding it gently, I would tap it into my palm until the edge of the paper beveled and "packed" the tobacco on one end. Finally, I would strike the match and touch the flame to the other end, while caressing the whole business in cupped hands.

Essential for me, as with Dean, was remaining silent during the entire ceremony: Inhaling the "toasted" tobacco flavor. Tightening my eyes for the deep draw. Blowing the smoke not randomly but in a direction that appeared calculated, so that anyone could see that I was not just thinking but deeply reflecting. Planning my next move.

Better yet, I was biding my time, possessed therefore of gravity and inevitability. Whereas without my Luckies I was just an idle, pimply faced adolescent, looking lost.

One day in early October when I had run out of cigarettes, Frank Oberle agreed to cut class with me and hike to the new Oakbrook Shopping Center to replenish our supplies. Frank was always up for anything, like the time we stole a case of ice cream sandwiches from the school cafeteria. He also had a face girls liked, and the young cashier at the mall smiled as she handed him a carton of Luckies along with our change.

Everything was going smoothly, and we lit up and did some window shopping, since Oakbrook in its early days was an outdoor mall. But things went south when we decided to take a shortcut back to school through the polo grounds of the rich and famous Butler family.

The area resembled a vast farm field with no fences and nothing else in sight until a man on horseback appeared on the horizon, cantering in our direction. He pulled up 20 feet in front of us. He could have been my grandfather and was wearing one of those riding helmets with a chin strap.

Here it comes, I thought. I knew little about the Butlers but plenty about the trouble in store. Not just trespassing on old man Butler's precious property but ditching school, and smoking on top of everything else, which would come as a shock to my parents. The worst, though, was violating the closed-campus rule, which could lead to our being expelled.

My first instinct was to run, but the guy was on a horse. Plan B: I fished the open pack of Luckies from my shirt pocket. Time to light one.

"Nice horse, Mister," said Frank.

Leave it to Frank. I tried to read the man's face, which was shadowed by the bill of his helmet.

"Good call," he said. He informed us that his horse was a polo pony, and that this particular thoroughbred was an extra large specimen.

"Are you from the high school?" he asked.

"Yes, sir," said Frank. "It's where we're going."

"I thought so." He said he figured us for a couple of varsity football players, because my shoulders suggested linebacker and Frank's "lean" and fleet profile spelled wide receiver. I did a double take, glancing at Frank, who never looked anything but skinny to me.

Frank started talking a mile a minute, explaining how we were on our lunch period, which was technically true, and had lost track of time and were rushing back, cutting across these "amazing" fields, provided we had his permission. "Sir," he added.

The man sat back in the saddle. He said to please call him Paul.

Frank went and told him our real names. The horse, its hide dark brown and silky, seemed restless as it stepped up and down with its forelegs, and the man raised the reins before lowering them again.

"It's lucky you weren't intercepted," said Butler. The groundskeeper, he explained, carried a two-way radio to call for police.

I felt a knot of warm dread in my stomach at the mention of the police. But Butler's tone was different, as if he were sharing a helpful tip with the fellow athletes we had suddenly become.

I slid the Luckies back into my shirt pocket. A smoke could wait.

"I should let you two men be on your way," said Butler. He added that it might be to our future advantage to steer clear of the groundskeeper. Which later I realized was an awfully nice way to tell us to keep the hell out.

I caught the earthy scent of the horse as he steered the animal away. Not in the direction from which he came, but resuming his original route.

We got going as well, giddy about the close call and congratulating ourselves for getting off easy, though I sensed that credit for the escape was hardly ours.

In the days following, I thought about our chance meeting with Paul Butler, and I wondered why, with all his money and land and power, he would take the time and trouble to treat us the way he did. Any other adult would have regarded us as two punks playing hooky and up to no good, and would likely not have rendered us as whole and addressed us as "men," as Butler did.

I learned that the Butler clan had amassed a fortune in the paper industry. And Paul Butler is recognized as a founder of the town of Oak Brook, Illinois, and of Butler National Golf Club.

Paul Butler did not sit on his millions but, instead, achieved individual greatness as a six-time winner of the U.S. Open Polo Championship. I came to suspect that one secret to his achievements in business and in sports was how he used his status not for what more he could take, but for what he was able to give to others, which in our case was a feeling of self-worth.

His "secret" was a lesson I never forgot, and it became the key for whatever success I've had as a teacher, having learned that young people respond earnestly, honestly and with their best effort when regarded not as trainees or numbers or tobacco-stained lost causes, but as individual human beings deserving of dignity and respect.

Notre Dame Magazine, Spring, 2022

-What I Learned About Role Models

I may owe my livelihood to Bobby Hull, one of the greatest players in NHL history who died Jan. 30 at age 84.

I was 14 when my father followed Blackhawk games on WGN's Channel 9. One evening I watched with him as Hull waited with the puck behind his net.

Players didn't wear helmets back then, and Hull struck a statuesque pose with his blonde locks, square shoulders and a body builder's physique evident in spite of the protective gear and padding.

I thought I detected a smile in his closed-mouth glare, right before he started skating up ice in rhythmic fury.

Not a fancy stick handler like Stan Mikita, Hull trained the puck ahead with one hand on the stick, the better to pump his legs and flex his core to generate more and more speed as crowd clamor intensified.

Nor was it a straight path as he careened in wide loops around opponents who couldn't catch him, the puck glued to his curved blade.

Once he passed the blue line, when I expected him to move closer to the goal, he launched a slapshot from 50 feet. A compact backswing, the low lean on one skate, the forward stroke, a blur, and all in a fraction of a second. The goalie stood paralyzed as the 118-mph puck went screaming past his ear into the net.

Announcer Lloyd Pettit's hoarse exclamations at the

unassisted, rink-long rush and far flung but lethal blast confirmed I was witnessing an immortal.

Something happened in that moment, an obsession born, and I became a Bobby Hull apostle. I read everything I could about him in the local papers, but it wasn't enough.

So I was first in my class to master the *Reader's Guide to Periodical Literature*, and I hunted down every story, photograph and reference to Hull in magazines and other cities' papers. Premature prowess in research would pave the way for a career as an educator and writer.

I once Xeroxed several pages from a news magazine at our library that featured an article on Bobby, accompanied by a photo of him shirtless. I was astounded to read that he never lifted weights but came by his build through arduous labor on his family's farm.

His record-breaking goal totals, hat tricks, MVP awards and his role in Chicago's 1961 Stanley Cup championship have nationally chronicled in the myriad obituaries written about him since his death.

What I recall best was his skating speed, once clocked at 28 mph. Opposing coaches assigned "shadows" to trail Hull around the rink. How I hated the shadows, like Eddie Shack or Bill Ferguson or the despicable Boston Bruin Derek Sanderson, who tried to goad him off the ice and into the penalty box with cheap shots and trash talk.

One year as an early Christmas gift, my father called an influential friend and got two tickets to a sold-out game at the Chicago Stadium for my brother and me.

Imagine our disappointment when we learned Hull was sitting out the game in a contract dispute. We'd have to content ourselves to watching the likes of Tony Esposito, Pat "Whitey" Stapleton and Pit Martin.

Just before the opening faceoff, while seated high in the stands, I heard what sounded like a fight in our high school cafeteria, the kind of noise that's generated as gawkers start cheering for blood. It started in the far corner, but the excitement rose and spread throughout the stadium till Net and I looked at each other and knew it had to be true: Bobby had signed at the last minute and flashed out onto the ice.

The roar would rise again later when he blasted in a goal. And I would hear it again over the TV and the radio for years to come, including when Bobby led the Hawks to the top of the standings. They should have won another Stanley Cup when they outplayed the Canadiens but couldn't get the winning goal past a different kind of superstar, goalie Ken Dryden.

Later, when ugly stories circulated about Hull, including racist comments and domestic violence against two of his wives, I didn't want to believe it. I only accepted the truth after a talk with my father, when I learned elite athletes with the speed and strength and charisma of Superman are also human beings with peccadillos and paradoxes like Achilles or Odysseus or the other flawed heroes of classic literature. And many, like Hull, are felled by pressures, expectations and alcoholism.

As I think back on this, my hope for my young grandchild is that she, too, will enjoy exulting in her favorite athletes' skills and "super powers" as much as I did with the incomparable No. 9. But when it comes to emulation, she'll stick with Momma and Papa, the heroes who are raising her.

Chicago Tribune (Naperville Sun, Daily Southtown), February 14, 2023

-What Every Teacher Needs

Chicago Vocational was not the worst school. Its football, basketball, and baseball teams were repeat championship contenders. And while it was the city's 2nd largest high school with an unwieldy enrollment of 4,000, it had a tough and charismatic principal in Reginald Brown who tried to hold things together.

Rival gangs operated in the surrounding neighborhood, and students were occasional perpetrators or victims of crimes involving drugs, guns, theft, and violence. Brown instituted a closed campus policy to mitigate such problems. A paltry security budget, however, and the school's multiple cavernous buildings, including an actual airplane hangar, all spread over 22 acres, made the policy difficult to maintain.

My first year as a teacher there was baptism by fire. An English major with a minor in education, I never received training, for example, in how to keep 98 pupils quiet in the study hall I was supposed to monitor.

In my composition and literature classes, my lack of confidence was blood in the water to any juvenile shark intent on savaging my lesson plans in a toothsome tug of war for each class's attention.

One memorable class clown, for example, was Bernard McCullough who in 1972, made my 8th period freshman English as chaotic as a Jerry Springer show. McCullough changed his name to Bernie Mac when he hit the comedy circuit, after which he became a movie star and suffered an untimely death in 2008.

Into my second year, I could finally turn my back to write on the blackboard without worrying that someone might try to sneak out. And I could smile and initiate discussions on literary themes involving love, loneliness, or death, without the class collapsing in laughter.

It remained a challenge, nonetheless, to get everyone committed to serious learning. Sophomores were the most difficult, not necessarily because of the "wise fool" stereotype of 2nd year high schoolers who think they know it all. Call it more of a legal problem, since there were plenty of 15 year olds who wanted to be somewhere else but who, by law, could not drop out and escape "incarceration" in my classroom till they turned 16.

Eugene, for example, liked to sit sideways and chat with his pal Stephen directly behind him, when I was teaching or trying to hear another student's question. They could have gotten away with it by whispering but willfully chose not to, a fact they made clear with their body language, rolling their shoulders in response to my reprimand.

Keeping them after class, I asked each separately to explain his animosity, using a man to man tone they weren't used to from me.

Of course, I had learned by then not to corner a youth, so I added the observation that they were smart and could potentially be leaders whom struggling classmates might look up to, and we ended up shaking hands and pledging a truce.

What was surprising but also telling was when Eugene graduated (Stephen would drop out), he confessed that our talk didn't mean as much as the handshake, since my calluses and sandpapery palms from the home repair I had been doing on weekends, was what had earned their respect.

Another year, I thought that teaching one of my favorite novels, *Of Mice and Men* by John Steinbeck, was bound to be transformational. Even sophomores would like central characters Lenny and George, I thought, and could hardly resist Steinbeck's gracefully accessible prose.

"Mr. McGrath, they be talkin' jive in this book," said Norman.

As much as I loved Steinbeck's masterpiece, Norman and others led me to perceive its disconnectedness with their era, culture, and age group. Nor did the book's thematic dream of settling on your very own plot of earth resonate for teenagers newly into Pong, Space Invaders, and nubile cheerleaders.

So with a sophomore class in 1985, I thought S.E.Hinton's *The Outsiders* might change attitudes about education.

Other than being white, Hinton's characters mirrored my CVS students in age, in economic levels, and in problems with gangs, peer pressure, dysfunctional families, and self image.

I assigned the book, and for a bonus before the Christmas break, I rented a video recorder and the largest screen TV available from the local Rent to Own store, which two burly men wheeled into our classroom on a chilly, sunny afternoon (CPS did not provide enough textbooks for its students, let alone AV equipment).

I slid *The Outsiders* video cassette into the machine, lowered the shades, and we all sat back to watch the first half of the 90 minute film. While most students already knew the actor Ralph Machhio from *The Karate Kid,* few were familiar with Matt Dillon, Patrick Swayze, or Diane Lane.

The next morning, many arrived early, grabbing the desks closest to the TV.

The usual suspects were late. They had to be shushed once the tape started playing, after which I leaned into the film with the rest of the class.

As the movie's action ramped up, the tension in the room was palpable. During the climatic episode, when Johnny (Machio) was on his deathbed, uttering his last words to his best friend, Pony Boy, I noticed a commotion in the far corner. I started to stand in order to quell any disruption that might ruin the moment, when I realized what was happening and sat back down.

Chris Zorich, one of the better students in class and a linebacker on the football team, was crying. The scene on the screen was highly emotional, and Zorich tried but could not stifle his sobs. Certainly, there's nothing unusual about an award winning film triggering tears. But someone exposing such vulnerability in front of streetwise classmates in an inner city school is risking harassment and ridicule.

I kept one eye on the TV from which sad music was emanating, and another eye on Zorich.

One of the latecomers sitting across Zorich's aisle, turned to locate the source of the crying, a smile of glee on his face. He was poised to scorn and laugh derisively.

This was not going to turn out well, I thought.

But his smile faded when he saw it was Zorich. He caught my eye before he turned back around.

Another of the latecomers, clearly aware that it was the linebacker who was so powerfully affected by the tender moment in the movie, fidgeted in place, careful not to look at him.

An impactful lesson in vulnerability, courage, and

authentic manhood had just been imparted in my sophomore lit class to at-risk inner city teens. And their teacher hadn't said a word.

Of course, neither had Zorich.

*

The next day, my sophs surprised me with the intensity of their reactions to *The Outsiders*. They passed judgment on the characters. "Two-Bit, he be trippin'" became a refrain (Two-Bit was mouthy and liked to drink beer for breakfast.)

Lorraine said she loved *The Outsiders* because it was just like her "stories," or soap operas.

Ordinarily, forty-eight minutes into each of my fifty minute classes, students begin closing their books and wrapping in coats so they could quickly bolt from the room.

But the day after watching *The Outsiders* film, several students were hotly debating with one another over who was to blame for the church fire in Chapter Six, even as the dismissal bell was ringing.

It was the best I felt about this class all year, thanks to S.E. Hinton. And, of course, to Chris Zorich, whose example effected a receptive climate for learning that would last for the remainder of the semester.

Not that he was the top student. Nor would I have considered him outspoken–he was too polite for that. But the sincerity and curiosity he exhibited about literature and composition, and the trust he manifested in what I was trying to do, made others in class aspire to that ideal.

Being a linebacker on the football team made him "cool" even to the passive aggressive males, who acceded to an "if you can't beat 'em, join 'em" mindset in English. Zorich had emerged as the class's alpha wolf.

*

In those days, I seldom attended football games, since most were played at 3:30pm when I had to get home to my wife and new baby. The only reason I knew Zorich was even on the team, was that he wore his No. 50 jersey to class on game days.

But I saw John Potocki, football coach, every day when we would both duck into the faculty washroom in between classes to smoke a cigarette.

"Is Chris Zorich good?" I asked.

"Definitely," said Potocki. "We moved him up to varsity."

"He's not very big," I said. I would have guessed 5'11", 180."

"He's fast as hell," said Potocki. "And strong. He fills the gap like nobody else," he said, pointing with his cigarette at the space between our chairs, as if it were the narrowest of openings between two offensive linemen.

The blonde 6'3", 270 pound varsity coach who later became the school disciplinarian bore a close resemblance to "Handsome" Jimmy Valiant, a popular pro wrestler on TV.

Nominated as one of Mount Carmel H.S.'s top athletes of all time, "Potts" was a standout defensive tackle for Northern Illinois' Huskies in 1969.

As the coach of the first and only CPS team to win the Prep Bowl, beating St. Rita in 1976, Potocki was perceived with a mix of affection and trepidation by our students. He also was often the first staff member they saw when arriving at school, as he routinely jogged on the snowy sidewalk encircling the campus before the start of the day.

He had taken a job as a history teacher and Coach Bernie O'Brien's assistant in 1972, the same year I was also a rookie teacher. It was through smoking–Kools for him, Marlboros for me–that I got to know him, forging a friendship that has outlasted our unhealthy habit.

Publicly, he was an old-school coach who yelled a lot and had zero tolerance for anything he deemed detrimental to the team dynamic, from tardiness to practice, to missed homework assignments. Privately, he had a soft heart and keen sense of humor—-more Sergeant York of the film of the same name, than Sgt. Hartman (*Full Metal Jacket*). His players couldn't get enough of his tough love, which he dished out in military fashion as an active member of the Army reserve.

One morning, he stood in the doorway while I was leading a discussion about *The Odyssey* in a freshman class. After I waved him inside, he stood at the front of my room, his eyes simmering with menace, before posing a question to my students.

"Who is the greatest writer that ever lived?"

The eyes of half a dozen students swiveled to me, as they weren't sure what to make of the big man's interruption, and whether it was a prelude to some stern lecture about their behavior.

"Homer?" said Brenda.

"Shakespeare!" said Potocki, and he slammed his fist on my oak desktop, knocking my attendance looseleaf onto the floor.

"You'd better start hitting the books for Mr. McGrath," he said through clenched teeth. "I'll be back."

Some of the freshmen were puzzled, while others barely concealed their amusement. But even those who suspected he was playing up his role, would never think of challenging him.

The CVS region had changed radically since the days when Potocki was raised nearby by his aunt and uncle, and steel mills dominated the skyline.

After the mills all closed, Potocki became a familiar figure in the now predominantly African American community for his role as championship coach and educator, and his imposing physical presence.

When he drove up and down the streets, old timers waved. So did gangbangers on the street corners.

"I tried to keep the lines open," said Potocki. "The gangs' leaders left my players alone. They wanted black athletes to succeed."

Just don't cross that line. Prior to the 2nd half of a CVS game at Gately Stadium, someone in the stands flashed a gang sign. When Potocki saw one of his players reciprocate, he made him strip off all his CVS football gear in front of the packed stands before sending him off the field in his gym shorts.

*

"So I'm driving near school," Potocki told me on the phone, "and I see Zorich on the sidewalk holding hands with some girl."

Potocki had a rule that none of the players could have girlfriends. It was a coaching anachronism widely debunked since University of Alabama and New York Jets superstar Joe Namath made no secret about violating it. But Coach Potocki retained it for his Cavaliers to ensure that their main focus would be football.

"Immediately, I pull over," continued Potocki. "I roll down the window and say, 'See me in my office tomorrow morning. Both of you.'"

The next day, Zorich and his girlfriend were waiting outside Potocki's office door when he arrived at 7 a.m.

"I look at them and start to fish for the key in my pocket, when Chris stands up and says, 'Coach, we're both virgins!'"

It took several seconds of Potocki holding his breath before he could look at his linebacker with a straight face.

"I don't want to hear about any of that shit," Potocki said.

He waved them into his office where he reiterated the reasoning behind the "no girlfriends" policy.

Over time, Zorich would interpret his Coach's rule as more of a "don't ask, don't tell" rule, managing to hang on to his sweetheart by being more circumspect.

Later, in his junior and senior years, when Zorich was no longer in my class, he frequently stopped by the office of the *Trademaster,* the high school newspaper for which I was faculty advisor, to purchase a personal advertisement for each month's edition.

"Personals" was a regular and popular feature among the students, enabling them to send messages to classmates, teachers, the school administration, and most often to their girlfriends, for twenty-five cents a line.

Like the Bard himself, Chris composed compliments, declarations of love, and once even a marriage proposal to his steady girl.

His monthly odes were not anything unusual: the "Personals" section would fill between ten and thirty column inches each issue, with scores of Chris's classmates romancing in the same fashion.

And it was certainly not out of character for the sensitive kid who had been so deeply affected by *The Outsiders.*

What was unique is Zorich's backstory, by now familiar to most readers, and which offered insight into the young man whom his teachers and coaches knew in high school.

He grew up near CVS, raised by his late mother Zora who was white and whom he credited with not just his success on the football field, but with his very survival.

His father, who was African American, abandoned them while Chris was a young child, and his mother did her best to provide for them both on a $250 welfare check each month, which sometimes led to their sifting through dumpsters for food.

"We never had this conversation, my mother and I," Zorich told me when I interviewed him at home, "but I'm…thinking back how there were white neighborhoods where we could have moved, and it wouldn't have been as hard for her.

"She raised me in an all black environment where she was a target. But she made a decision, like, 'you know, I think it's important that he knows his black culture, so I'm going to live here.'

"If I could be just 1/8th the person my mother was."

It wasn't just his mother who was a "target."

"He got his ass beat every day in elementary school," said Potocki. "They'd call him 'Honey' and 'Sugar.' They thought he was soft."

When the young Zorich wasn't being bullied or punched because of his mixed race, it was for lack of insulation within a gang. In sixth grade, he succumbed to the pressure and would have been initiated into one of the area's street gangs, were it not for his mother's tearful pleadings.

"He stuttered when I first met him," said Potocki. "That's

from childhood trauma. I knew, since I'd been there myself, that you could work all that out in the weight room. And on the football field."

By his senior year, Potocki was spotting Zorich as he bench-pressed 400 pounds, far more than anyone else on the team. He became a battering ram on the gridiron.

"He wanted to make his mother proud," said Potocki.

*

He was also an elite and teachable athlete with a relentless work ethic. Off the field, he was a role model who was personable, honest, and almost excessively polite. During our interview, decades after he was my student, he addressed me as "sir" or "Mr. McGrath." And ten minutes into our conversation in his own home, he asked if I minded if he loosened his tie.

It was the same character whom Potocki would defend years later when Zorich's charitable organization was cited for tax violations and mishandling of funds, saying, "Chris had nothing to do with all that," attributing the errors to well meaning but unwitting relatives whom he hired to run the charity.

Potocki's contention was affirmed when the judge presiding over the case sentenced Zorich to probation, observing that he led an otherwise "exemplary" life, while praising him for years of charitable work.

*

When you're an English teacher, you read hundreds of first person essays by your students, so I had gotten to know many who were raised by a single mother in a violent environment. Some, like the sophomore males I previously described, grew a sizable chip on their shoulder that played out in mistrust and resentment toward men, with challenges to authority expressed through tardiness, non-compliance with classroom rules, inattentiveness, indifference, disrespect, and outright rebellion.

Zorich was an exception. He was humble, soft-spoken, and interested in others.

"Did you play football, Sir?" said Zorich. "You look

strong."

I was fat.

"Just sandlot," I said. I told him where I played with my five brothers.

Oh, man! What's that like, Sir?"

As I tried to convey how we relied on one another, he nodded, his eyes veering into the distance.

"Chris's family was the football team," Potocki had told me.

But it seemed clear that the chief reason for Zorich's exceptionalism–his gentleness and curiosity–was his mother Zora who devoted her life to him, doing her utmost to replace whatever her child's upbringing lacked by marshaling all her strength, wisdom, and love, and imparting it to her son.

Her dedication was obvious on Open House night at CVS, when I met her and gushed over her son's character and commended her for doing a wonderful job. She reacted skeptically, worrying whether Chris was doing enough homework and being sufficiently challenged in class.

*

After starring as an All State linebacker at CVS, he was awarded a scholarship to Notre Dame.

When I congratulated him, he surprised me, shaking his head in apparent frustration. He told me of receiving advice from others at school to decline the ND scholarship and accept, instead, some other offer where he had a better chance of succeeding academically.

"Can you believe it, Sir?" he said.

He had no doubt, despite earning unimpressive test scores, that he possessed the will and work habits to succeed at ND. He was more angry than hurt that anyone would doubt him. Or lack faith in him.

Meanwhile, Potocki told him about the Notre Dame legend. Its history and reputation. How it was filled with "rich white kids" and that he must show them who he was. His pride as a south sider.

As a Cavalier.

His first year at ND, he was redshirted.

"I saw him coming out of a barbershop on 79th street and asked him what he was doing there," said Potocki. "Why wasn't he at ND? He said they were switching him to nose tackle, and he wasn't happy about it. 'I want to play linebacker, Sir,' he told me.

"I said, 'You play whatever position they tell you.'"

Potocki reminded him, in so many words, that football is not a ballroom for debutantes. It is war, and he was a foot soldier who must do whatever he was told to help win it.

The rest, of course, is sports history. Zorich visited his former CVS teachers after his freshman year at ND, and we were wowed by the physical transformation after he went from a 200 pound linebacker to a 266 pound nose tackle.

It paid dividends. He became a unanimous first team All-American and the winner of the Lombardi Trophy for best lineman in the country. And the "most vicious player in college football," according to *Sports Illustrated*.

I understood what the sportswriter wanted to convey. But the English teacher in me would have flagged "vicious" in his first draft because of its potentially misleading connotation of malice. Or sadism.

For there was never anything sinister in the kid I knew who radiated pure joy: His grin when he spotted you in the hallway. The irrepressible smile with friends and classmates. Love and longing when he spoke about his mother, his best friend, his teammates, his coach.

The athlete who once said, "Football was a physical reaction. It was like breathing for me," was hardly a vicious human being..

Yes, he wrecked opponents with brute strength and violent hits. But like another sports star who led the Chicago Bulls, Zorich loved playing the game and exhilarated in his superiority.

He was at his happiest in an arena where he knew he

could finally win.

*

In 1990, I watched him play in the Orange Bowl on TV. What I saw was not my earnest student from English II impersonating a wild man, but a hungry and ebullient lineman with a perpetual motor, living in the backfield, making ten tackles–two for losses–and a sack. He was named defensive MVP in a monumental struggle in which Colorado eked out a 10-9 victory.

What Zorich will not forget, and what broke his heart and the hearts of those closest to him, was his coming home and finding that his beloved mother had died of natural causes just hours after watching her son play his last collegiate game.

The woman he had called his "rock" was gone at age 59.

"It was the oddest wake I'd ever been to," Harry Watson told me. He was CVS's defense coach under Potocki.

"It was unbelievable," said Watson. "I was agonizing over what I was going to say to this kid who just lost his mother who was his best friend. Instead, he comes up to me, to all of us there, wearing that big smile, like we're so great to have come. He's going all out to comfort us, to make us feel good. It was backwards."

In 1991, as the type of "lunch pail," effort-player prized by Coach Mike Ditka, Chris Zorich was drafted 49th by the Chicago Bears. He complemented the team's 1985 Super Bowl defensive line over a six year career and was named as an alternate All Pro in 1993.

One Saturday evening, as my wife Marianne and I were driving down LaGrange Road on our way back from dinner out, we passed a marquee advertising, "Tonight: Chris Zorich."

He was doing a guest appearance at Champs Sports Grill and Pub in Orland Park, and I turned the car around, hoping to get a peek at the only Chicago Bear I've ever personally known.

Approaching the entrance, I saw it was not to be. A long line of fans outside snaked into the building before disappearing up a staircase.

A beefy young man with "Security" printed on his jacket

was monitoring the line outside the door. I gave him my name and I asked him to tell Chris I said hello.

By the time we returned to our car, the same staff member was running toward us. He had spoken to someone on his two-way radio and received instructions to bring us back.

He led us past a couple of hundred people and up the staircase to where Zorich was standing behind a greeting table. My worry that he wouldn't recognize me vanished when he sprang forward, his arms outstretched.

Despite the lump in my throat, I was able to tell him how proud he made me and his other teachers. And I was about to thank him for having us delivered to the head of the line, except that he was doing the thanking. For everything, he said. For helping him on his way.

Of course, I knew he would have been here without ever having met the likes of me. He would have overcome all that he did to realize a dream because of what was inside him, instilled by his remarkable mother.

But as he did with Harry Watson and so many others, Chris Zorich made me feel as if it were *my* name on the marquee.

Chris Zorich earned a JD from ND and leads the Diversity, Equality, and Inclusion Practice for Randall Partners in Chicago. John Potocki teaches adolescent development at Calumet College of St. Joseph in Hammond. This essay is adapted from one written for the Tribune for Christmas of 2023.

-Teachers Exiting Because of DeSantis

One story behind Florida's severe teacher shortages captured in a favorite photograph.

It's an image of my late father on a fishing trip, taking advantage of the time he had left with his grandchildren, one of whom appears in the snapshot: our youngest child Janet, 7. She went with Grandpa, she said, "to teach him how to take the fish off the hook."

My wife and I are teachers, as is my elder daughter Jackie. Janet, now 41, followed a similar path, earning a master's degree in English at the University of Illinois-Chicago before taking a job at Chicago's Lake View High School.

Though she had graduated with high honors, earned national board certification, and would have been prized at any of the affluent suburban schools, she insisted on teaching where she was most needed.

There, she managed a room full of teenagers by being exceptionally prepared, and by perfecting what she calls her "teacher eyes," to cast a penetrating glance to compel attentiveness or proper behavior, without a word. She also coached the swim team and pioneered a book donation program to encourage teen mothers to read to their infants.

Though sad to leave Lake View after seven years, she and husband Kevin Allen moved to Florida to live near us, before she gave birth to her own daughter, Summer.

Still needing to teach, she was awarded a position at Venice High School, where she became known for the college-level rigor of her instruction and was asked to teach Advanced Placement English Literature for college-bound seniors. Administrators routinely showcased Allen's classes when VIPs visited.

Additionally, she founded and became faculty sponsor of Venice's first Gender and Sexualities Alliance (GSA), to help LGBTQIA+ students who faced intensified bullying.

This past year, Janet Allen's AP students earned the highest scores in the district; she received the "highly effective" evaluation for superior teachers; and GSA members had finally begun to feel that they belonged.

So, it was a shock to many when she announced she must resign.

The reason? Gov. Ron DeSantis inserting himself into school classrooms with his anti-woke hatred, with bans on books, on critical race theory, and on sexual orientation and gender identity discussion and instruction.

Allen believes DeSantis's stranglehold killed the creativity, autonomy, and motivation that made her profession fulfilling, and helped give Sarasota schools its annual A rating.

She had been warned, for example, to stop using Maya Angelou's "I Know Why the Caged Bird Sings," Toni Morrison's "The Bluest Eye" and other highly acclaimed novels containing truths related to sexual orientation or racism.

"The new laws are... put into place by Florida politicians who have zero classroom teaching experience, who seek to satisfy their voting base's culture war battle cries," Allen said in a recent interview for ScaryMommy.com, a popular website for young mothers.

"Teachers will be too fearful to meet the needs of their students with their creative expertise. You may as well have teacher bots, instead."

Allen refuses to be a conduit for the harm DeSantis is inflicting on thousands of students, including GSA members, after signing the "don't say gay" bill.

"I see this as purely a move to empower bigots," she said.

"We (GSA) normalized LGBTQIA+ existence, empowered club members and allies to challenge discrimination by teachers and students ... and elected the first openly gay homecoming king our school ever had.

"Several of those kids have reached out to me after graduating to let me know how important the club was for them... and how they felt like it saved their lives. I am terrified for what the 'don't say gay' bill will do to our school communities and our kids, not to mention how it stifles basic civil rights.

A survey by the group We the Parents found teachers leaving Florida at a rate higher than in other states, with 6,000 vacancies statewide, and 61% considering leaving.

DeSantis apparently thinks Florida's loss of quality teachers is a small price to pay for his national political ambitions.

It will remain to be seen in November, when he runs for

re-election, whether voters agree.

Orlando Sentinel, September 22nd, 2022

Race

-Independence Day

America, land of the free.*

But why the asterisk? I learned the reason at the end of seventh grade.

It was a summer evening in Evergreen Park, so I could stay out till dark, which didn't fully descend till 10 p.m. A month shy of my 13th birthday in 1962, I had already tasted freedom. I could go where I wished, as far from home as I dared. I decided to walk a mile to the baseball stadium at 90th Street and California Avenue where my younger brother Net, short for Kenneth, was playing for the Indians in a game against a team named the White Sox.

I never made the cut for Little League. I was good only at hockey and caught only one of the fly balls hit to me during baseball tryouts. Wary of the hardball, I would step aside and stab at it with my Wilson mitt.

Net could really hit, though, and I stood behind the chain-link fence along the third base line, feeling like a big shot watching my little brother, his baseball pants tucked into his high stirrup socks and the bill of his dark green cap bent just so.

The ball field had lights like Comiskey Park and a concession stand selling hot tamales and frozen custard.

Grown-ups sat on the bleachers behind home plate. Kids clustered everywhere. Some stood on the benches behind their parents. Others around the food counter. Three "runners," hands over their heads against the fence, waited to chase balls fouled off into the parking lot.

Some girls from St. Bernadette's were gathered behind the Sox dugout, one with long black hair. Though I couldn't see her face well from across the field, it had to be Janice.

Net, antsy to swing, wiggled the bat over his right shoulder. The first pitch skidded in the dirt in front of home plate. The left-handed pitcher aimed a strike with the next one, and Net swiveled his hips before stepping forward and smashing a deep line drive. The center fielder angled back to fetch it, and Net slid headfirst into second. Safe.

He was all business, calling time to dust himself off, not looking over when I clapped and whistled. But he knew my whistle.

Between innings, when I went to the concession for a beef tamale and cherry cola, Janice was standing by herself looking up at the white wooden menu. I had never talked to her, though she sat just two desks over in my class.

I could do it now, with no one else around. Should I? I had even brought money I'd been saving for a guitar. Loose change in my pocket, and a thin stack of bills sorted by ones, fives, and a 10 in my wallet. Money from painting my grandparents' house and a raise in allowance for my last report card. I could buy anything she wanted.

In school, Janice wore the uniform blue jumper and white blouse like the rest, but stood out for her sly smile and shining black hair. Tonight, though, I was stunned. Red shorts and long, tan legs. Like an angel in a glowing force field I dare not approach.

Better to wait till next time. I detoured around the concession stand and headed into the night. Beyond the lights of the stadium, stars saturated the sky. A chilly breeze smelled like adventure.

Skipping, floating above the sidewalk along California, I dreamed some day of skating like the Blackhawks' Bobby Hull. Or playing the guitar like Elvis, Janice waving from the audience. Or writing stories like Mark Twain. Steaming down the Mississippi in a paddleboat. Stopping with her for a picnic lunch. And some fishing.

I jumped high to pluck a green apple from an overhanging bough but came away with just a leaf. In a few years, once I'd grown, there'd be nothing I couldn't do.

Crossing at the light, I saw another boy, as thin as a blade of grass, walking past Rosangela's Pizza and carrying a white paper bag. And then this shout fractured the night:

"Whaddya doing here, N-word?"

A man in front of Sherwood's drive-in restaurant pointed his cigarette in our direction, his other hand on his hip. The boy looked, turned and hastened his step. The man came running, and I was afraid. And then I felt guilty, knowing he was not after me.

As he got close, I recognized the white shirt and rolled up sleeves of a neighborhood tough. A troublemaker the age of my older brother.

He pulled up, panting, his engineer boots no match for the fleet-footed boy who must have been halfway to the bus stop at Western Avenue. The tough returned with purpose to the drive-in, so he and two others could renew the chase in a huffing black Ford.

I had few opinions at 13. Just the hope that the boy made it back safe to a world different from mine. A world less free in so many ways I put off thinking about, but which we all would never escape.

This July Fourth, Sherwood's is long gone, and Rosangela's has expanded. And we celebrate the fact that a similar incident is unlikely to happen today in Evergreen Park and most other places I know.

Still, we're reminded by a profusion of modern-day racial crimes, from Citrus Springs, Florida, and Minneapolis to Brunswick, Georgia, and Brookhaven, Mississippi, that the story of American freedom requires the same asterisk in 2023 that it did in 1962.

Chicago Tribune, July 4th, 2023

-Time to Rename Chicago Blackhawks

In 1986, Chicago's professional hockey team changed and simplified its name from two words to one: Black Hawks to Blackhawks. Not a big deal.

In fact, I never noticed, and I had been a rabid fan since the 1960s. After learning to skate on a frozen pond in a vacant lot behind the Martinique Restaurant in Evergreen Park, I improved my skill at Michael Kirby's Ice Rink on the city's South Side. I played pickup hockey at makeshift rinks all through my teens.

During that same period, I read the Blackhawks' box score the morning after every game, feeling good when they won and not terribly bad when they lost, as long as No. 9, superstar Bobby Hull, was in the scoring column. I knew his height, weight, girth of his biceps and the speed of his slap shot, which had been clocked at precisely 118.3 mph. His skating speed was the league's fastest at 29.2 mph.

Still, I never noticed the change in the spelling and capitalization of its name, which is very probably true for most other fans.

So if in 2021, in the middle of the season, or at the end of the playoffs, which the Blackhawks may still manage to squeeze into, would it be that big a deal if they shortened their name to simply the "Hawks"?

And if instead of the head of an Indian person with war paint and feathers, they changed the logo and mascot to that of a literal winged bird? Say, for instance, the red-tailed hawk, common in Illinois, which would then not necessitate changing the team's colors.

It's an opportune time to do so, since the U.S. Senate has just confirmed Deb Haaland as secretary of the Interior, the first Native American in history to hold a cabinet post.

And after decades of protests and complaints about the stereotyping and dehumanizing that results from sports teams' use of logos, mascots and names based on Native Americans, hundreds of high schools, colleges and pro teams have eliminated offensive monikers.

The University of Illinois banished the Chief Illiniwek mascot portrayed by a white student in a sacred tribal costume, dancing around the stadium in a halftime choreography that looked to be part Britney Spears strut, part shaman incantation.

The Cleveland Indians dumped its cartoonish Chief Wahoo and is considering new names, including an earlier name, the Cleveland Spiders, according to an ESPN report last December.

The Washington Redskins are officially the Washington Football Team until a new and non derogatory name is agreed upon.

Most importantly, local Native organizations such as the American Indian Center of Chicago and the Chi-Nations Youth Council continue to call on the Blackhawks to end the stereotyping, along with the memorializing of white exploitation of Native Americans by the Blackhawks' name and logo.

Team ownership, of course, wants to keep the colorful Indian head on its hockey sweaters.

They proffer the same old arguments that Cleveland and Washington use to trot out, pleading that the hockey team's name is meant to honor Chief Black Hawk of Illinois' Sauk and Fox nation. They remind critics that the Wirtz family and business organization, which owns the team, has interacted with Native American organizations, made donations and lent the United Center as a venue where fans can be educated about Native culture.

Yet money the Wirtzes spend in that capacity is chicken feed when weighed against the enormous profits they derive from name branding, with which they are loath to tamper.

What ultimately causes their arguments to vaporize, just as they did in Cleveland and Washington, is the unalterable historical truth, related in this case by James Lewis, an associate professor of history at Kalamazoo College, and whose detailed account I paraphrase: The American government broke its treaty promises to the Sauk and Fox nation in 1830, after which the U.S. Cavalry massacred nearly 400 men, women and children in the Battle of Bad Axe, and subsequently paraded through the streets with a captured Chief Black Hawk in tow, showing off their victory trophy much the way the team has done after it won the Stanley Cup.

For the descendants of these same white Americans to show off a facsimile of that trophy on their uniforms, helmets and pricey tickets, claiming that today, however, it is an honor for the chief, is the height of irony and an egregious insult to Indigenous Americans.

No amount of donations or Native American workshops at

the United Center can rewrite the history or bury the implications of that Indian head's continued display on the jerseys of all those young athletes.

Instead, an invitation to Secretary Haaland to drop the ceremonial puck at the first playoff game of the Chicago Hawks this spring, or at the season opener of, perhaps, the Chicago Red-Tails next fall, might provide the only salve, and the only resolution, to a city embarrassment that will otherwise never end.

Chicago Tribune, April 16, 2021 (Reprinted in Sawyer County Record, Naperville Sun, Daily Southtown)

-Ban Native Mascots to Save Children's Lives

My op-ed last month recommending that the Chicago Blackhawks retire the Indian head logo and change their name to simply Hawks, ("Blackhawks name, logo need to go. Rename NHL team the 'Hawks'" April 17) was met with incomprehension and outrage that anyone would mess with the NHL's best-looking jersey.

Hockey fans sent emails deriding the column as excessive political correctness, and one even argued that the logo enhanced his appreciation of Native American culture.

But the story ("Remains of more than 200 children found buried at Indigenous school in Canada," May 30) about the corpses of more than 200 children found at a Canadian Indigenous boarding school, may open the eyes of those same fans to the fact that the name change is not about them or their sports pleasures and preferences, but about Native American youth, victims of ethnic cleansing and atrocities on this continent for centuries — people who continue to suffer today because of dehumanizing stereotypes such as the Blackhawks logo.

At the Kamloops Residential Indian School in British Columbia, the remains of children 3 years old and up were discovered underground, and more are expected to turn up in other areas of the property.

Kamloops was one of many government-funded Christian schools in Canada built to assimilate Indian children into white society by erasing their Indian identities.

Over 150,000 native youth were conscripted and then constrained from speaking their language and practicing their religion, with beatings and abuse that led to at least 6,000 deaths, including 200 or more at Kamloops.

The schools persisted in this unthinkable mission from 1800 until the 1970s. Canada's Parliament finally apologized in 2008, while admitting to the widespread corporal and sexual abuse in its 139 such schools.

The model for Canada's inhumane indoctrination of Indians was, of course, its neighbor to the south.

The U.S. led the way in instituting the so-called Indian boarding schools to implement the policy, "Kill the Indian, save the man," as expressed by Gen. Richard Pratt, superintendent of the Carlisle Industrial Indian School in Pennsylvania.

Enrollment peaked in 1925, when 60,000 Native American youth were housed in 357 Indian boarding schools. Forced from their homes, they were beaten, starved or abused if they spoke their language, wore traditional clothes, or were caught participating in Native religious ceremonies, as recently chronicled in *The Atlantic* by Ojibwe tribal member Mary Annette Pember.

Our government's effort to stamp out Indian-ness lasted from 1860 to 1978 and is what many Indigenous leaders and experts cite as the primary cause of a higher rate of alcoholism, drug abuse, and suicide for Native Americans than for any other minority group in the country.

Psychologist Dr. Stephanie Fryberg of the University of Washington completed four scientific studies in 2008 finding that sports teams' use of native logos have a hugely negative impact on native youth.

Due to the proliferation of images such as the Chicago Blackhawks Indian head, depicting the "noble savage" stereotype with feather and war paint, native children and teens perceive the rest of the country viewing them in a way that has no relationship to them or to reality. Such images, even in cases when they drew a neutral or favorable reaction from Fryberg's studies' subjects, nonetheless exacerbate their sense of confused identity, poor self-esteem, invisibility and community isolation, while increasing the already epidemic rates of depression and suicide.

Contrary to the general tenor of the emails I received, retiring the Blackhawks name and logo is not a talk-radio sports question but a humanitarian necessity for the health, welfare and very survival of Native American children.

Once Americans become aware of the serious harm suffered by Native American youth bombarded by Indian stereotypes, I have faith that they will compassionately endorse the efforts of the American Psychological Association, American Sociological Association, National Education Association, the National Congress of American Indians, and hundreds of other tribal nations and organizations urging a total ban on native names, logos and mascots in all amateur and professional sports.

Chicago Tribune, June 4, 2021

-Growing Up Racist on the South Side

"We have fought hard and long for integration, as I believe we should have, and I know that we will win." — Dr. Martin Luther King, Jr.

Racism was as integral a part of our lives in the 1960s as baseball, Mickey Mouse, TV westerns and vacations at the lake.

I grew up in a white south suburban middle class neighborhood in Evergreen Park, which was just like the town where Dick and Jane lived in our elementary school readers: No African Americans.

The only Black people I knew about were major league baseball players whom my uncles mocked at family parties and backyard barbecues. So I grew up thinking that Larry Doby was a terrible player. When one of my brothers dropped a ball, we called him Larry Doby. The same Doby who is in baseball's Hall of Fame.

Before I ever met an African American, I repeated n-word jokes I heard from my friends who heard them from their elders. So that when I finally encountered Black people on a CTA bus or at the Evergreen Park Shopping Plaza, I viewed them with a mix of pity and caution.

At St. Bernadette's grammar school, no one disabused me of these notions. Not the Dominican nuns. Not the priests.

What we learned in our religion class or in our paperback catechism about loving thy neighbor and thy enemy constituted my first lesson in critical thinking: Comparing what was written in those texts and in the Bible to the talk and behavior of everyone I knew, told me that the books were fiction. The church, I inferred, promised you heaven if you donated on Sunday and paid lip service to its doctrines without having to abide by them.

The lone African American in my high school freshman class was Wendel Winslow. An above-average student, he was short and bespectacled, strong and fast, and won the rope climbing event in our P.E. "Olympics." He was an exception to the stereotypes I had learned, and that was the reason, I assumed, he attended our school.

At 15, reading John Steinbeck, Emily Dickinson and Mark Twain, I learned that adults were flawed and oftentimes fools. At 16, reading J.D. Salinger, Ernest Hemingway and Richard Wright, I learned we were supposed to call out hypocrisy where we found it.

College classes in philosophy, history, literature, sociology and political science did what they were supposed to do, opening my eyes to the injustice, cruelty and oppression of racism.

Not just a relic of the Deep South before the Civil War, racism was happening right in front of our faces. There were redlining practices to isolate African American neighborhoods on the South Side, segregated beaches along Lake Michigan and hiring biases in the police and fire departments.

Nonetheless, many of my white peers exposed to the

same truths retained the bigotry they were raised with. It's as if the lessons from school and the great books were like those I had learned in catechism: material to be studied but then forgotten, once you've passed the exam. They went to Mass, took communion, lit a cigarette on the way out and still told N-word jokes, while checking who was in earshot and keeping their voices down.

Had my peers not paid close enough attention in school? Did they have a different learning style? Were they born without the synapse in their brain that enabled empathy?

No to all three questions.

What was different for me was taking a job alongside African American teachers at Chicago Vocational High School. And though it was initially culture shock for an Irish Catholic Evergreen Parker, you can't help unlearning stereotypes and forming friendships with people you live and work with every day.

Because my school colleagues had endured myriad social and economic obstacles all their lives, from which I had been spared, I benefited more from them than they did from me.

Friends like Willa Carr, Rich Cook, Rev. Malcolm Walton, Delores Greyer, Gwen Abston, Chris Randolph, Jimmy Grisset and Pam Cox, among others, shared hard-earned lessons in judging character, motivating youth, overcoming tragedy and withstanding daily slings and arrows, while still maintaining optimism with humor, faith and love. And they treasured family values all the more because of the greater struggle required to preserve them.

Later, I would think about my friends from Vocational when I read about the strength and forgiveness shown by the elderly African American survivors of the horrible shooting massacre at the Emanuel African Methodist Episcopal Church in Charleston, South Carolina in 2015. They also had to survive that most debilitating obstacle imaginable, racial hatred, all their lives.

And that's why I subscribe to Dr. King's belief, then and now, in the importance of integration, as inspirational as it was for me.

Busing back in the 1970s is often said to have been a failed experiment. But the reasons behind it — enlightenment, transformation and racial harmony — remain valid.

As President Joe Biden's administration begins to carry out its racial equity agenda, it must find new ways of bringing blacks and whites together to allow the better parts of our human nature to breathe free.

Chicago Sun Times, Minneapolis Star Tribune, Sarasota Herald Tribune, Madison Capital Times., Duluth News Tribune, Sawyer County Record, January 24, 2021. Selected for inclusion in CHICAGO EXPOSED, a Chicago Sun Times photo archive produced in association with the Chicago History Museum.

-Racial Progress Through Truth, Not Denial

If only Florida's governor Ron DeSantis would watch the classic TV series "Roots," he might gain the insight his Ivy League education failed, somehow, to convey.

Based on Alex Haley's novel about an African American family tracing its history from royalty in Gambia, Africa, to enslavement in America, "Roots" was broadcast in January 1977 over eight consecutive nights.

At the time, it seemed every person I knew or talked to watched it, a fact later confirmed when Nielsen ratings showed there were 130 million viewers, a record for a TV miniseries. It was the blockbuster television event of the year, earning a Golden Globe and nine Emmy awards.

Why such an explosive impact? Before "Roots," most Americans had been raised with an intellectual notion of slavery as an unfortunate economic and political controversy leading to the Civil War, as portrayed in textbooks by white historians.

But new perspectives were achieved 46 Januaries ago, when ABC brought slavery into everyone's living room, subjecting beloved TV actors like John Amos, Cicely Tyson, Ben Vereen and Lou Gosset Jr. to graphic episodes of torture, lynching and sexual abuse. Adding to the shock value was that the sadistic perpetrators were portrayed by familiar TV favorites like Chuck Connors, Sandy Duncan and Ralph Waite, the gentle and empathic patriarch of "The Waltons."

Though "Roots" was categorized as a work of fiction, the accuracy of rape and other acts of violence being committed by slave masters had been well established by historians.

I was 28 years old at the time the miniseries aired and in my fifth year of teaching writing and literature at Chicago Vocational High School, where enrollment was 99% African American. Walking into my classroom and facing my students after the first episodes had been aired, I felt the acute discomfort from which DeSantis wants white people shielded.

It's the reason his Tallahassee legislature rubber stamped his "anti-woke" legislation banning books and teachings that expose America's history of racism. His rationale is white students should not be subjected to literature or lessons that are "divisive" or make them feel guilty or uncomfortable,

But what I felt after watching "Roots" had less to do with discomfort, shame or guilt than with horror and regret over our country's legal enslavement of indigenous Africans in order to maintain America's robust economy. Our ancestors bought and sold kidnapped people and treated millions of human beings like cattle, purely for profit.

Nor was "divisiveness" a consequence of the TV series. DeSantis maintains that teaching the truth about racism only fosters "hate" in schools. Nothing could be further from the truth. A week's exposure to slavery's horrors did not make my students hate me. A collaborative learning climate had already been established in September when I started each year teaching Richard Wright's "American Hunger," based on the true story of the dehumanization of black maintenance workers at a Chicago research hospital.

And contrary to what DeSantis seems to believe, African American students are intelligent enough to distinguish between despicable personages in history and their current teachers, classmates and friends.

What is divisive and harmful, however, is when DeSantis and others censor or deny the truth about America's past. For it's only through ongoing conversations about history and racism in books, films and in our classrooms that we can hope to make things better or, at the very least, prevent destructive reoccurrence.

The importance of history, particularly those portions that are painful and regrettable, is an absolute truth likely valued by every Harvard professor DeSantis sat before. Which is why I have a sneaking suspicion that he doesn't wholly believe in his outrageous claims and initiatives, but only espouses them to curry favor with a vital segment of Republican voters as he contemplates a run for the presidency.

His Machiavellian strategy is disturbingly reminiscent of that of another recent president whose reign was a disaster for the United States.

Let's hope that segment of history doesn't repeat itself, either.

Chicago Tribune (Naperville Sun), February 27, 2023. Reprinted in Daily Southtown, Duluth News Tribune, Fort Myers News Press, Naples Daily News.

-Implicit Bias from Those Who Think They Know Better

Three years ago, while teaching one semester at a college in Florida, I drove to school on my day off because Leonard Pitts was going to speak. I had reason to be excited, but also worried.

Pitts is a Pulitzer Prize-winning columnist at the *Miami Herald* and among the best in the field. Whether commenting on a complex legal question facing the Supreme Court or explaining why one of his favorite musical hits from the '60s is so enduring, Pitts seizes the reader's attention with a compelling personal voice, astute analogies and graceful sentences of luminescent clarity.

I spotted him seated at a table in the lobby outside the school auditorium, where teachers and students might say hello or get an autograph. He was a little heavier, a little older than his column mugshot. But then, who isn't?

I got in line to tell him how much I appreciated his work and that I use his columns to teach writing. What I feared was that in mentioning my classroom, the subject of our textbook might come up.

That's because the school's required textbook contained over a hundred essays from newspapers and periodicals, none by Pitts. I was embarrassed that it did not have a single work by the journalist invited to speak that day.

Even worse, the textbook had not a single op-ed by any of the other African American syndicated columnists in the United States. It featured work by William Safire, Paul Krugman, Nikolas Kristof and Eric Schlosser but nothing by Eugene Robinson, Charles Blow or Clarence Page.

The school is predominantly white so a typical English class of 25 might have two or three African American students. And it's not very hard to imagine how different and remote and unequal the education is for those two or three who must study from a book in which none of the texts was written by someone who looks like them.

While I did not know the faculty members who selected the textbook, I assume they did not consciously exclude premier African American journalists. Instead, they probably felt good about their selection based on criteria such as topics, teaching methodology, exercises and cost.

And therein lies the problem, part of why African American progress toward equality has been too little and too slow. By *not* adding race to their criteria, the faculty members unwittingly allowed "implicit bias" to deny equal representation to African American authors and equal education to African American students.

Many white employers or teachers or police or politicians think there is no racism as long as they ignore race. If they no longer say the n-word and don't purposely commit acts that deride or deprive African Americans, they believe everything is now equal and nothing more needs to be done.

But just trying to be color blind does not eliminate the implicit bias of white Americans. Their internalized, unconscious preferences rooted in culture, society and upbringing influence their choices and attitudes if no overt and ongoing effort is made to counteract them.

A recent example of implicit bias was uncovered by investigative reporters for the *Sarasota Herald Tribune* who wrote that trial judges throughout Florida consistently gave longer or harsher sentences to African Americans than to whites for identical crimes. Judges were incredulous and ashamed even as they acknowledged the evidence.

And an example of an action taken to counteract implicit bias is the Rooney Rule in the National Football League, which mandates that team owners interview African American candidates for coaching vacancies. The rule was deemed necessary in 2003 after investigations found white owners were ignoring qualified African American candidates in a league in which 68% of players are African American.

When I finally greeted Pitts, he was cordial and funny, and we spoke briefly about a recent column of his which I used in class. Then he addressed the audience of approximately 150 about the increasing importance of journalism in today's world.

The main point and happy ending to this recollection at the start of Black History Month is that the school eventually changed to a different textbook with many more essays on topics of race, with increased representation by African American authors.

Not just that, but these days more people are cognizant of implicit bias and its potential harm thanks to studies and articles like, "How to Think About 'Implicit Bias,'" in *Scientific American* in 2018.

It's one small step forward in a long slow process of overcoming generations of racial oppression.

Chicago Tribune (Naperville Sun), February 7, 2020.

-My Kind and Bigoted Neighbor

A relative, friend, or colleague dies, and you feel bad that you canceled a lunch date with them, or never made the phone call you had intended but kept putting off.

It was different with my neighbor. More serious than a ping of regret when he died last month. Before I met him, I would never have thought of turning in a friend to the police. But I'm getting ahead of myself.

My neighbor was an older man, a retired truck driver, who lost his wife ten years ago and lived alone. You never get over losing your spouse, but he seemed able to move on, spending hours every day tending his flowers, shrubs, lawn, and trees.

Gardening was his passion. Twice, Marianne asked if he'd accept a potted plant someone gave us as a gift, but which was struggling under our care. He nursed each one of those back to life, and you can still see them out in front today, ten times the size when we had them, thriving and flowering and adorning his place.

Once, near sundown, I stepped outside and heard conversation drifting over from an open window in his kitchen. When I asked the next day if he had company last night, he smiled and said it was his late wife.

"Oh, I talk to her all the time," he said. "I tell her everything."

I told Marianne about it, theorizing that it was a healthy thing for him to do. And that I would probably be bending her ear after she was gone. She scoffed that I'll be "pushing up daisies" long before her.

Fact is, I did worry a lot less about my neighbor after that.

And then came the weekend when my four year old granddaughter was staying with us. As I wheeled her in her wagon into his driveway, his entire countenance changed: The look people have when they spot a rainbow. I had never realized his eyes were blue until he stepped back and *beheld* her, I guess is the right word, as he cleared his throat and spoke softly: "Howdy do, Little Miss."

Thereafter, when my granddaughter visited, she would wave to him from our yard, or when we passed his house in her wagon. He'd call out the same greeting to her in the southern Indiana dialect from where he grew up, and she'd point to all his "pretty flowers."

One day in the middle of the week, he walked into my garage where I was cleaning a paint brush and handed me a stuffed animal for her. I said he could give it to her directly next weekend, but he insisted I take it.

It was after that when the trouble started.

It involved a tree encroaching on his property. Not my tree, but that of the couple whose house was on the other side of his.

I had never heard him say much about them until now, when he tried to tell me confidentially that there was going to be big trouble over the tree with those "dumb Mexicans" who couldn't even learn proper English.

The couple were our friends and two of the kindest people Marianne and I knew. I tried reasoning with my neighbor about stereotypes, informing him that the husband had actually been born in Spain and had risen to the rank of supervisor with the Ford Corporation. But my neighbor just glanced away, looking towards the offending tree, while bragging wistfully that his hometown was still all white.

Then he turned sideways, caught my eye, and said with a sly smile that he had a "persuader" under lock and key inside his house with which he could settle the dispute.

I studied him hard. He was very old. And I convinced myself it was just talk. Empty talk of a curmudgeon.

I should have told Marianne. She would have had wisdom about what to do or say. But it felt like a shameful thing. A dirty thing to report only to the police, or to keep to myself.

Meanwhile, the couple had already paid a tree service hundreds of dollars to comply with the old man's wishes. He resumed his gardening, often on his hands and knees. Things quieted down. I considered the matter resolved. And I hoped that maybe his perspective had changed after all this. Until the florist rang our doorbell: A vase with red roses: A birthday gift for the wife of the couple, sent by her daughter from Michigan. But the couple wasn't home, and the old man in the house next door with all the beautiful flowers, refused to accept the roses for them, the florist said. Would we kindly see that they got them?

Later in the year, the couple moved away. They said they wanted to be closer to their children. But things were never the same with me and my neighbor.

We spoke less. Said what neighbors say. He was getting on, and I helped when he needed it.

It was easier that way.

What was hard was to detoxify hate. To cure his blindness.

Surely, it must be possible because of his humanity: His wife, after all. My granddaughter. The miracles in his garden. Clearly, a capacity for love and empathy.

But the clock ran out. And that's what I regret.

Chicago Tribune, October 2, 2023.

Conservation

-Slaughtering Wolves for the Thrill of the Kill

In Shirley Jackson's classic short story "The Lottery," the villagers of a small town randomly choose one of their own to stone to death for no ostensible purpose other than the cathartic thrill of the kill.

A similarly macabre lottery recently was conducted by our neighbors in Wisconsin. Following the Trump administration's controversial removal of the gray wolf from the federal endangered species list, just days before Donald Trump left office, 2,380 Wisconsin hunters chosen by lottery from 27,151 applicants "won" the privilege of buying licenses to kill 119 wolves over a seven-day period.

But the hunt was cut short this week, on Wednesday, when the quota was exceeded and 182 wolves wiped out in just three days. This was likely because the wolves were more vulnerable due to heavy snow cover, said George Meyer of the Wilderness Wildlife Federation.

Why did more than 27,000 people pay for a chance to shoot a gray wolf? It certainly wasn't for food. As one might expect of this apex predator, gamey-smelling wolf meat consists mostly of muscle and is widely considered inedible.

A market may exist for wolf hides in some states, with a pelt fetching an average price of $210, according to Alaska Fish and Wildlife News. But when you add travel and hunting expenses to the cost of a tag for a single wolf, any gunman in it for the fur is more likely to end up in the red.

And when Luke Hilgemann, president of Hunter Nation, the out-of-state organization that filed a lawsuit to force Wisconsin's Department of Natural Resources to stage the hunt without delay, explained that wolves needed to be exterminated to protect livestock and pets, even hunters had to smile. Official statistics available from

2018 show that under provisions of the federal Endangered Species Act, $144,509 in compensation was paid to Wisconsin farmers and pet owners for 33 cattle and 19 hunting dogs lost to wolves. That's 33 cattle fatalities out of Wisconsin's 3.45 million head of cattle, according to the U.S. Department of Agriculture.

Important to note, in view of hyperbolic wolf legends and lore: there has been only one human fatality (in rural Alaska) in the United States from a wolf attack since 1900. And only 32 attacks at all since 1782, according to Field and Stream.

Whereas, Farley Mowatt, in his 1963 classic memoir "Never Cry Wolf," documented the beneficial role that wolf packs (complex, extended families dedicated to the care and feeding of its young) play in ecosystems, such as keeping healthy the Arctic's caribou herd, and, arguably, doing the same for Wisconsin's deer population.

Hilgemann was more candid, however, when he added that another reason for his organization's lawsuit was to protect "hunting traditions." Which, if he's honest, amounts to stalking and shooting wolves for fun.

I confess, as a fisherman, that this is a rationale to which I can relate. Anglers take to the water partly to harvest and eat fish, but mostly for sport in an escapist immersion in nature. We fish for recreation and pleasure. The difference is that we release, unharmed, any fish we don't eat. The wolves trapped or hunted down this past week, on the other hand, were shot where they stood or finished off while tangled in a trap, never to see another day.

In President Trump's last month in office, the U.S. Fish and Wildlife Service delisted the wolf as an endangered species, citing its recovery over the last few decades. But the Trump administration had a record of a wholesale loosening or elimination of worthwhile environmental restrictions, as well as ceding power over wildlife and resources to private industry and state governments. And Republican legislators in Wisconsin, still smarting from Joe Biden's electoral upset in their state, had made known their fervent desire that the DNR fast-track a wolf hunt before the new Biden administration could restore protections.

Environmental groups including Earthjustice are suing to restore federal protections for wolves, maintaining that the recovery of these animals is a fiction insofar as they remain extinct in 80% of their former habitat. Wisconsin's wolf population of approximately 1,000 was reduced by at least 15% in this week's deadly shootaround.

Years ago, on a foggy summer morning, I came face to face with a wolf on the edge of the Chequamegon National Forest in Wisconsin's northwoods. I had been walking with my dog on Barker Lake Road, where we had a lake cabin 30 miles east of Hayward.

Our black Lab, accustomed to chasing everything that moved, halted suddenly, its back hair standing up like porcupine needles: A gray wolf stood on the high bank on the right side of the road, looking down. Though it was the first I had ever seen, it was unmistakable for its considerable size (100 pounds), its legs splayed wide, head slightly declined, its amber eyes intently focused on the two of us.

A single moment of silence, of fear and reverence, of holding my breath, before its head visibly relaxed, and it turned and vanished into the pines.

There is a chance that the wolf I saw was among this past week's victims. Though wolves have inspired frustration and even hate in some, and awe and inspiration in others, it's a disgrace and a crime if this wolf was shot to death for political vindication. And fun.

Chicago Sun Times, Feb 25, 2021 (Reprinted in Madison Capital Times, Duluth News Tribune, Wisconsin State Journal)

-Seeking Relief from Climate Change

"The frequency of heat waves has been steadily increasing in the United States, from an average of two per year in the 1960s to six today."— U.S. Environmental Protection Agency

When the wolf is outside your door day and night, it wears

on you physically and mentally. Our son Mike lives in Phoenix, and that's more or less how he characterized the city's record-breaking heat wave of 31 straight days of 110 degrees or higher this summer.

A physician and a mountain hiker in his mid-40s, Mike is used to Arizona's triple-digit temperatures and doesn't worry about falling down and suffering burns on the 180-degree sidewalks or running out of Gatorade.

But the last week of June he traveled 1,800 miles with his girlfriend Gen to join me and my wife Marianne and the rest of our family in Bayfield, WI, among the few places in the country where the AC hasn't been running 24/7.

Less than two hours east of Duluth, Bayfield is a historic commercial fishing town on the steep shores of Lake Superior. No matter how hot and humid it gets in the rest of the country, you almost always need a hoodie on the banks of Gitche Gumee.

Air temperatures ranged in the 70s during the days we were there, and in the low 60s at night, and we were fortunate to find accommodations for ourselves, our children, grandchild Summer, and my sister Nancy and her husband Jay Anderson from Wausau, Wisconsin, at the Pier Plaza hotel during one of the hottest months on record.

While dining on fresh sauteed whitefish at the Manypenny Bistro after arrival, we caught up on family news, from 6-year-old Summer's promotion to the highest level in swim class to the jubilant announcement by Nancy and Jay that they are officially in remission after battling cancer for the past three years.

My elder daughter Jackie and her husband Gene commiserated with Mike and Gen's need to escape, comparing it to their own condition as Midwesterners afflicted with a maddening form of cabin fever during a prolonged January cold snap, when they check the thermometer daily, watch weather catastrophes as lead stories in national-news broadcasts, and wake up every morning with a sense of dread about the next electricity bill and the very future of our planet.

Nonetheless, we made the most of our vacation with a kayak

tour the next day, paddling in and out of Superior's rocky nooks and crannies, stopping midway for a breathtaking swim in the sparkling water of a sandstone cave.

Summer got her first paddling experience with her father Kevin, a writer and actor who captained from the stern, so that Summer's mother, an English teacher, had to pair up with Grampy in an 18-foot, yellow sea kayak and abide the same nautical commands she heard from him decades earlier in a 17-foot Grumman canoe: "Less gawking, Janet, and more paddling!"

The next day, Lost Creek Falls proved to be worth the mile-and-a-half hike through the woods, since the 10-foot waterfall had been supercharged by an early-morning squall, allowing everyone to climb behind it for a nippy shower. Mike, along with Gen, a student nurse, and Gene, a Marine, assisted the less-sure-footed among us through rivulets and over logs that we might stick our heads under the icy cascade.

A two-mile ferry ride to Madeline Island on Thursday for a dip at Big Bay State Park's beach concluded our scheduled activities, where I was surprised how simply knowing about the rest of the country's sweltering state provided sufficient motivation to plunge into 67-degree waters without hesitation. Young Summer, teeth chattering, braved the chill, even laughing as she called out Grampy's real reason for moving off into deeper water: "to meditate," in his words.

The felicitous effects of the cold-water therapy lasted several days, including until we arrived back home, where we read a text from Jackie and Gene saying they spoke with a Realtor about possible and permanent relocation to Bayfield's haven from climate change.

Haven for the time being, I thought, as millions of other Americans contemplate contingencies, alternative locations, and emergency evacuations in the face of wildfires, tornadoes, unprecedented floods, mudslides, hurricanes, and heat waves this year, next year, and for many years to come.

When my neighbor Dick indicated on a recent morning that I needn't worry, claiming (baselessly) that the latest weather events were part of the natural cycle that will likely return to normal next year, all I could think of was Summer: her freckles, her smile, her future world.

Duluth News Tribune, August 8, 2023 (Reprinted in Naperville Sun & Madison Capital Times)

-Florida Fish Farm An Environmental Monstrosity

I don't have the exact coordinates for the proposed fish farm in the Gulf of Mexico for which a Hawaii-based company, Ocean Era Corp., is seeking a permit from the U.S. Army Corps of Engineers.

But its reported location of 45 miles southwest of Sarasota, Florida, puts it smack dab in the middle of the state's fishing grounds, where tens of thousands of Midwesterners vacation every year.

Permitting this underwater monstrosity would be a tragedy.

A chain link cage, anchored to the sea floor 130 feet below, with 20,000 Almaco jack fish packed in like cattle, in a suspended swarm with waste and pharmaceuticals, would alter the ecology and pollute and deform the uncorrupted Eastern Gulf.

That the Corps would contemplate a permit is befuddling, considering what they already know. A study published in *Science Direct* in December 2019 detailed the chronic accidents imperiling Norway's offshore fish farm industry, including "mass mortality of fish during and after operations, introgression of genes from farmed salmon, the spread of disease and material damage to assets..."

The conservation group Friends of the Earth echoed the same dangers: "From the release of untreated fish waste and excess nutrients to the overuse of antibiotics and endangerment of marine life, industrial ocean fish farms are nothing but bad news for our oceans."

Ocean Era itself acknowledged that in their other existing farm off the coast of Hawaii, which they saturate with thousands of gallons of hydrogen peroxide, "leakage" is common and escape risk "high" for the penned fish invariably infected with "skin fluke parasites." They also admit to hazards for large fish and mammals (dolphins and whales) attracted to the cages that can become trapped inside and die, as happened recently with an endangered tiger shark and a monk seal.

Ocean Era argues that aquaculture would make the United States less dependent on imported seafood. But countering their argument was a report just last week that more humpback whales are being observed off the coast of New York than ever before, as they feed on massive schools of menhaden that have finally returned. Scientists say New York's bounty is due to cleaner water and stricter conservation laws, which is what the focus of the Army Corps and the federal government should be for increasing domestic fish stocks, instead of polluting the Gulf with farms to make inorganic "seafood."

As a sportsman and a human being, I also plead on behalf of the caged fish. Fishermen respect nature and appreciate the intelligence, complexity and intrinsic value of the Gulf's inhabitants. As a freshwater and saltwater fisherman, I know the freedom, speed and magnificence of the nearer dwelling native amberjack, to which the Almaco jack is a close cousin which can grow to 80 pounds. It is an offshore pelagic, a silvery torpedo high in the food chain who prowls the open ocean for prey (not pellets) in depths of 800 to 1,000 feet.

But in Ocean Era's net pens, they cannot roam. They are confined in a watery cell at a shallow and unaccustomed depth; and they lead an artificial, immured existence before being slaughtered and frozen for shipment.

Finally, the pristine character of the Gulf of Mexico must be preserved. The sea is the last frontier where sportsmen, tourists, their grandchildren and, hopefully, great grandchildren, may encounter wilderness, solitude and wonder.

Sailing over hills of sparkling blue water, accompanied by platoons of dolphin, frigate birds with 8-foot wingspans soaring overhead, flying fish gliding iridescent in your wake and curious loggerheads surfacing to investigate, even an atheist suspects that this is where God, if he or she existed, would reside.

Imagine if you were vacationing in Yellowstone National Park, exhilarating in the mountains, the rivers and the wildlife, and your path suddenly were blocked by a barbed wire corral imprisoning 20,000 cramped and sedentary bison. In many of the same ways, a 24/7 barge parked over a submerged fenced-in enclosure stabilized with floating buoys and boiling with disoriented fish and a festering stew of contaminants destroys our Gulf wilderness.

In jeopardizing our seascape and its cleanliness, the Ocean Era fish farm may pose an even more serious threat to Florida tourism, the state's No. 1 industry, than the grotesquely protruding and hugely dangerous oil rigs which the state has been successfully fending off its west coast for decades.

Denying Ocean Era a permit may seem like a no-brainer. But in view of the current federal administration's preference for private industry profits to trump environmental health, and President Donald Trump's executive order just last May to remove federal restrictions on aquaculture, I urge readers nationwide to make their views known by sending comments — before Nov. 4 — to the Army Corp of Engineers at this email address: OceanEra_VEaquaculture@usace.army.mil.

Orlando Sentinel, October 16th, 2020 (Reprinted in Sarasota Herald Tribune, Chicago Sun Times, Fort Myers News Press, Naples Daily News, Madison Capital Times, & Angling International Magazine.)

-Dragging a live shark calls into question animal-treatment laws

I was 9 when I trapped a foot-long garter snake in a shoe box. I tied a string around its head, hung it from my mother's clothesline, and stuck two straight pins into its body. Then I watched as it twisted and writhed.

Recalling the incident today, I feel shame and repulsion. But back then, I thought what I did was expected.
Snakes were evil. It was a serpent, after all, that tricked Adam and Eve into committing original sin, which started all the world's troubles. At least, that was the truth conveyed in our Bible history book, with an illustration of the fanged black serpent hanging from the apple tree, its face contorted into a conniving snake smile.

The lesson was reinforced by my mother's horrified reaction to the green and black snakes that migrated through our grass and dandelions, and her "I hate snakes" proclamation.

Still, as I watched the snake die in the sun, I did not exactly feel I deserved a medal. Something in me sensed consciousness in the animal. Something made me wonder about its pain.

I would like to ask the same questions of the four young adults in Sarasota, who are waiting to find out if criminal charges will be filed, after they posted a video on Instagram of their dragging a black-tip shark by the tail behind their speeding boat, as the helpless creature crashed and bounced in the wake.

"Look, it's already almost dead," said one of the men in the 11-second video.

Their dastardly act was nationally publicized after they sent the video to "Mark the Shark" Quartiano, a Miami shark fisherman, who re-posted the clip with the following caption:"For once I may have to agree with @PETA."

Negative fallout went viral. Florida Gov. Rick Scott called the video "disturbing."

The Florida Wildlife Commission has been investigating for months, eventually learning the identities of the culprits, including boat captain Mark Wenzel, 21.

And many animal sympathizers have been boycotting MTV's reality show "Siesta Key," all because the leading actor, Alex Kompothecras, 22, is a friend of Wenzel.

I have not hastened to join the lynch mob.

144

After all, who among us has not tortured and killed innocent creatures? Who has not stepped on an innocent ant, or swatted a fly that was not even trespassing?

And is anyone ever faulted for brutally killing a mouse, a rat, a skunk or a raccoon that is trying to find warmth and shelter in a corner of the basement or attic?

Where exactly do we draw the line? What's the difference between nuisance animals deserving automatic execution, and those deserving humane treatment?

I have been on boats with fishermen who have mistreated or destroyed carp, catfish, suckers, puffer fish and gar, acts which rarely launch Florida Fish and Wildlife Conservation Commission investigations.

Saltwater sportsmen routinely cut open perfectly healthy squirrel-fish and lady-fish, to make them more aromatically attractive as live or dead baits, for catching "desirable" species like redfish, tarpon, snook and cobia — species for which any mistreatment would draw public ire and criminal citations.

So if it turns out that the FWC does bring criminal charges against the shark draggers, their defense attorneys can point out that the questionable intelligence manifested by Wenzel and his crew only proves that they are gullibly innocent victims of confusing laws, misinformation and cultural indoctrination.

Think about it: Since the universally popular movie "Jaws" sparked worldwide fear, young men like Wenzel were led to believe that sharks were dangerous, deadly, voracious man-eaters.

And though "Jaws" was released long before Wenzel was even born, and we've become more educated about sharks, pop culture has persisted in the demonization. Consider the wildly popular scare videos online and on cable TV like "10 Unbelievable Shark Attacks" on YouTube or the 2016 sci-fi feature film "Sharknado," in which flying sharks threaten to destroy the civilized world.

My intent, however, is not to be an apologist for the shark draggers.

I wish only to pose a question: If the FWC and its legal experts need months to even figure out if laws were broken, aren't we obviously in need of more sensible, clear and well-disseminated animal-treatment laws and guidelines?

Orlando Sentinel, October 25th, 2017

-Everglades, Ever-Inspiring

Tarpon were breaking the glassy surface of the river mouth: A pod of intimidatingly large fish, just beyond casting range.

Jim Edge killed the engine. The only sounds were the whistles and quacks of shore birds. A sliver of rising sun visible over the trees. Very little wind. No other boats in sight. A fisherman's dream.

Jim turned to climb onto the poling platform. Or so I thought. Instead, he fired up the 70hp Yamaha and plowed right over those tarpon, motoring upriver.

He continued east, zigzagging from one side of the stream to the other, while I quietly seethed, having wanted to pitch a bait to those enormous fish.

When we finally pulled up again, and he shut down the Yamaha, I asked him why we left those beautiful tarpon.

"They were not happy fish," he said. "Slapping their tails. Pissed off. You could tell from their body language, they knew we were there. But the fish *here* will eat."

I hadn't even seen them till now. Agitations on the surface eighty feet away, coming closer.

Edge climbed onto the platform: "Yep," he said. "See how they're rolling? These are happy fish. Lazy ass, happy fish."

Earlier that day, Tom Booth and I had met Edge at the Outdoor Resorts boat ramp on Chokoloskee Island at six a.m.

Edge is the owner and sole proprietor of Suncoast Boat Sales who was featured in the "I Am a Florida Sportsman" segment in the Dec./Jan. issue of 2021.

Forty-four years old, he has fished the Everglades for 20 years. He can navigate its 733 square miles in his 17' Hells Bay Biscayne flats boat "blindfolded," which means he cruises the rivers, bays, islands, mud flats, sandbars, lakes, shell bars, and marshes with the GPS turned off. Its screen, he says, is a "distraction."

Tom Booth, my fishing partner since we were kids, and who has the ability to think like a fish, had flown down from Orland Park, Illinois at my request.

Neither Booth nor I had ever been down here. Nor were we accustomed to heading out on unfamiliar waters under a sky that made you dizzy with so many stars. But as Jim eased open the throttle, tweaking the Hells Bay to skim as smoothly as a figure skater across a frozen pond, we sat back to enjoy the ride deep into the heart of Everglades National Park.

The quiet monotony of the four-stroke, the gentle breeze, and the fragrant salt air nearly lulled me to sleep. But as my eyes adjusted to shadows, I could make out the shapes of islands and trees to the east, the "backcountry"; and to the west, or out in "front," the expanding luminosity of the Gulf of Mexico.

When it grew light enough to glimpse our surroundings, it felt as if we were on site to shoot a film about dinosaurs: uninhabited islands, a sound track of exotic bird calls, and a crocodile slithering along the shore.

At our second location, after having raced ahead of the "unhappy" tarpon, I was surprised at how dirty the river seemed, saturated with soil, twigs, and leaves that had all flushed downstream.

Speaking low, Jim explained that zero visibility, warmer water, an abundance of food, Gulf access, and current were exactly why the tarpon were here. He asked Tom to slip the anchor quietly into the water. A yellow float was attached to the rode in case we had to untie and chase a fish.

Tom and I took up the heavy duty Star rods with Penn 4000 Spinning reels loaded with 30 lb test Power Pro.

Poling closer, Jim said that although talking was okay, we

should minimize our movements to avoid boat noise. Most importantly, we should not rock the vessel and cause it to push water, which tarpon would definitely feel.

Standing on the deck of the bow, Tom cast a red and white swim bait ahead of the boat. From my middle position, I aimed to the left of Tom and cast a four inch gold swim bait about fifty feet.

Tom reminded me to keep my bait moving high in the water column: "We're not walleye fishing," he said. Tarpon mouths are designed for feeding upwards.

"Three o'clock, Dave," said Jim. "Cast as far as you can."

I made a hard overhand cast, though I could not see what Jim saw from his higher perch.

"Perfect," he said. "Now let it marinate for a few seconds. There you go. Raise it up and crank slowly. No such thing as too slow."

The anticipation in Jim's voice had me gripping the rod tightly and squeezing the reel handle to keep from turning it too fast.

Nothing.

I threw the swimbait back out.

"Fish," shouted Tom. I turned to see Tom whip the rod behind his left shoulder to set the hook. The rod stayed bent, as the line zinged left to right, and he reared back a second time.

I raced to reel in and reached for the camera, when Tom's tarpon shot up from the surface in front of the Hells Bay. For two seconds, it hung vertically, completely clear of the water, before crashing back down.

"Did she spit it?" said Jim.

Tom waved his rod loosely. "Yeah," he said. "I bowed to it at the jump." He showed us what he did, bending forward, pointing his rod at the place where the fish disappeared.

"Not fast enough, I guess," said Tom.

"You're fine," said Jim. "It's like a car crash. Everything happens so fast, there's nothing else you could have done."

And just as in the aftermath of a car wreck, we were quiet and subdued. Casting and retrieving, casting and retrieving, till my shoulder ached. Till Jim said it was time to go.

"How big would you say my fish was?" said Tom.

"Six feet," said Jim. "Over a hundred pounds.." At that size, Jim explained, it would have been a female. And a migrating fish. Whereas, year-round residents are under sixty pounds.

We motored downstream, passing through the river mouth, and back into the Gulf where we turned south. The sun was up, the wind still calm, the ride smooth. Tom and I ate the ham and egg sandwiches we made earlier at the cabin we rented at Chokoloskee Island Resort.

While in transit, I asked Edge about the best time of year for tarpon.

"Always," and he smiled.

But peak migration, he continued, when the odds are most in your favor to hook a 100 pound plus fish, is March through May after the water warms. Secondary migration is September through December.

Geographically, you're nearly always in protected waters in the Everglades. A strong west or south wind can make it uncomfortable out front, but you can still find sheltered fishing grounds in the backcountry.

With 1.5 million acres of wetland, the Everglades is as big as Delaware, a fact you don't comprehend till you're here. One hundred miles long and sixty miles wide, it all looks fishy to a newcomer: islands, mangrove fringes, shining rivers, brackish bays, sandbars, hidden lagoons, oyster mounds, salt marshes, and open water slicks.

Running south, wide open, Jim spotted activity a thousand yards away on our left. A school of tarpon in the middle of nowhere?

He slowed the Hells Bay, killed the motor, then poled in the direction of the rolling fish. He could feel the pole scraping limestone, the reason for their presence, he said. Limestone increases pH in water chemistry, which, along with its holes, cracks, and crevices, enhances habitat for aquatic life and prey, including marine insects and crustaceans.

Jim resumed poling, and we kept casting, surrounded by tarpon.

At the end of one of my retrieves, close to the boat, I felt a heavy fish. I wrenched the rod sideways to set the hook, but the tarpon surged in the same direction, it's broad back visible just above the surface and out in front of where Tom was fishing. And then it was gone.

I felt its weight for all of three seconds, but it would take several minutes for my heart to slow down.

Another tarpon was fooled by Tom's swimbait, breaking free after five seconds without showing itself.

"Why aren't there 50 boats here?" said Tom. "Like at Boca Grande?"

"It's too far," he said, as few anglers venture more than several miles from Chokoloskee and civilization. Besides, hunting tarpon is time consuming, often unrewarding, and a lot of work. When they eat, you might hook ten without bringing a single one to hand.

Additionally, the Everglades, unlike Boca, is not ideal for tourists. Big comfortable boats for hire cannot ply its shallow waters. Air boats are forbidden. And if a smaller, single engine craft becomes disabled, there is no cell phone service. You might not see another boater all day. Nor can you wade ashore where there are no roads, and nothing but impenetrable swamp, sharp sawgrass, and inhospitable creatures, from alligators, crocodiles, and water moccasins, bears and panthers, to rats, roaches, snakes, scorpions, spiders, worms, deer flies, tics, sand flies and bloodthirsty mosquitoes. day and night.

On the other hand, you can go when it's cool and relatively bug free, as we did in December. Stick to the channels, including the clearly marked Wilderness Waterway that runs the entire length. Bring a VHF radio to summon Everglades based Sea Tow if you crash into a hidden oyster bed. Carry an EPIRB or

PLB for emergencies.

Avoid trouble altogether with a well maintained boat with a GPS/Sonar unit.

Better yet, hire a guide.

*

As the sun rose higher, and tarpon action subsided, we headed east into the backcountry.

Edge cruised as closely as he safely could to the mangrove beaches to afford us a better look at the American crocodile, native to Florida, which coexists here with alligators , the only place in the world where they do so.

We spotted several sunning in the sand and mud on shore. They appear buff colored, lighter than the nearly black alligators, and have a longer, bulbous snout. They also seem more wary than alligators, each one scrambling back into the safety of the water as we whizzed by.

"Can you smell the water?" asked Edge.

We were speeding up one of the jungle rivers, where Edge said you could tell from a fragrance like rich black dirt, that the water was turning from brackish to fresh.

It also was crystal clear when we emerged from the river into a freshwater bay. On the bay's western shore, Edge poled us into a "drain," a mangrove tunnel barely ten feet wide, and we readied ultra lights rigged with jigs and plastic tails. It was like casting indoors in someone's hallway, and Tom's first try was straight and low, evading the overhanging branches, his jig splashing down 35 feet ahead of the Hells Bay.

Instantly, his line boomeranged back, zipping under the boat, until an eighteen inch tarpon leapt into the air behind us, nearly colliding with Jim's push pole in its successful maneuver to toss the hook.

We remained there for 45 minutes, never landing the baby tarpon, but boating young snook stacked in the drain. Despite our noise and commotion, the action never slowed. In fact, the reason we finally left the honeyhole was the hour of the day. Darkness would descend at 5:30pm, and we had a long ride home.

At the ramp, we thanked Jim for a great day.

He thanked us right back, for making the trip and learning about the Everglades.

As a witness to both its beauty and its threats for the past 20 years, he knows it's up to all of us to preserve this national treasure.

HISTORY

Everglades history is a torturous tale of trial, error, and misunderstanding which begins around the middle of the 20th century, when most people considered it a bug infested wasteland.

The original or "historic" Everglades encompassed three million acres, from Lake Okeechobee to Florida Bay. After World War II, the Army Corps of Engineers reduced it to 1.5 million acres, having executed a plan to drain half of it for agriculture, flood control, and recreation by building 2,000 miles of canals, levees, spillways, floodgates, and pumps.

By the year 2000, the project was deemed a colossal mistake. The drained portion had been turned into highways and sugar cane fields, resulting in floods, fires, and pollution affecting half the state. A majority of tropical birds disappeared.

A plan to restore the natural flow through the wetlands and save over 70 endangered wildlife species, was funded with $7.8 billion by an act of Congress.

Today, what remains of the Everglades is a rectangular wetland 100 miles long, from north to south, and sixty miles wide. It is sliced into sections by a dozen rivers flowing east to west into the Gulf of Mexico, with scores of lakes, lagoons, and sawgrass marshes in each section, along the western edge of which are hundreds of uninhabited islands.

Restoration efforts, including disassembling man made flow obstructions and building water purification reservoirs, continue today, complicated by multiple hurricanes, Lake

Okeechobee's nutrients poisoning the St. Lucie and Caloosahatchee Rivers, toxic red tides, and mounting deaths of dolphins, manatees, and oysters.

    Completion of restoration depends on continued funding by Congress, and on the will of conservation minded voters.

Florida Sportsman Magazine, Dec./Jan. 2023

Holidays

-Silent Night, Not Always Calm and Bright

Christmas at the McGraths' was not always perfect.

I was reminded of that truth by the photograph my sister Nancy posted online. It shows her when she was about 5. She is dressed for bed in her pajamas and slippers but wearing a smile since, after all, she's nestled with our mother, Gertrude, in a big easy chair next to the Christmas tree.

My mother is dressed to the nines: necklace, earrings and the fancy black dress with the lace top she first wore to Aunt Betty's wedding. She is being careful, it seems, not to muss her makeup or her hair. Although she is seated with Nancy, her "baby" and the youngest of eight, the generous warmth to which we were accustomed is missing.

Her stony facial expression, a detachment that might otherwise be considered artful by photographers, simply isn't the mom we knew. All these years later, my siblings and I, with one glance at the photo, know exactly what was going on.

We grew up in a working-class neighborhood, six boys and two girls, steeped in a brew of Catholicism and Irish and Polish heritage, for whom Christmas was not only the most important holiday, but also an obsession.

Lights and decorations went up the day after Thanksgiving and didn't come down until the Epiphany, Jan. 6. And "Santa" frequently phoned or made landings and surprise appearances all year long at the McGrath house as a discipline aid.

Our parents, Gert and Charlie, were yuletide party animals, coming close to celebrating all 12 days of Christmas. They hosted gatherings for each separate category of relatives and friends. All of us pitched in, readying for a dinner party one night, and then cleaning up the next morning to prepare for the next. Through the holidays, a hundred people might dine and drink and exchange gifts in our paneled basement, since my mother deemed it important, on the occasion of baby Jesus' birthday, to hug every person who had ever been in her life.

But before the party for the Cichoszewski side of the family, and then the McGrath side, and then the Vojtech cousins, and the Witters and Contino cousins, and then the Morgans and the Mortises from the old neighborhood on 54th and Winchester, followed by New Year's Eve with the Mittermans, Booths, Doyles, DiBennardis and the rest of the Evergreen Park neighbors — prior to them all, was the office party at the home of Dad's boss, who was also his uncle. That was the occasion in 1960 for which Mom was coiffed and simmering.

Eleven years old, I sensed her crossness but could not fathom the reason. Mom and Dad, after all, were going to our rich uncle's, the only home in Evergreen Park with a wet bar, a jukebox and an in-ground swimming pool.

Their four kids, our second cousins, had a pool table and a pinball machine, along with a fridge full of Pepsi, Coke and Good Humor ice cream bars.

But the annual office party was complicated in ways I would learn only later. For Dad sold tile for his uncle's company and hadn't had a raise in 10 years. By 1960, things were so hard that a man came knocking to take back our Pontiac.

Meanwhile, I had not realized we were poor, since didn't every boy share socks with his brothers, waiting his turn for the single pair with no holes?

Nor did I grasp that Mom resented living a real-life version of "A Christmas Carol," starring Dad as Bob Cratchit and our rich uncle as Ebenezer Scrooge, while she scrimped on other necessities to make sure we had enough food.

Exasperated with "Uncle Ebenezer," my parents turned on each other. The night of the company Christmas bash, Charlie Jr. was babysitting while we watched "Gunsmoke" on the living room TV. We heard the station wagon arrive home early, tires squealing to a stop.

Only Mom came in, as the Pontiac sped away.

Nancy was asleep, and Rosemary started to cry. The drama, however, seemed exciting to my brothers and me. Until, that is, Mom hugged each of us without a word, and I choked up, as well.

The next morning, as we ate Cheerios in the kitchen — Charlie Jr., Kenneth, and Jimmy on one side of the Formica table and Patrick, Rosie and me on the other, with Nancy and Kevin on the piano bench at the foot of the table — Dad emerged from the bedroom. He brushed past Mom at the sink, neither of them looking at the other, and our world, I feared, was coming to an end.

Iciness persisted through the next day, and the day after, even as we hosted the Witters and the Continos.

At breakfast on Christmas Eve, Rosie and I were charged with buttering 18 pieces of toast made with day-old Holsum, while my mother stirred oatmeal at the stove. When my father entered the kitchen, he stood at the head of the table, and I held my breath.

"Did you hear that noise on the roof last night?" he finally said, and Nancy gasped.

On his way to get his favorite cup, he stopped behind Mom and put his arms around her waist. She seemed startled — we were watching closely — then she turned and smiled over her shoulder.

And the words from the carol would never mean more: "All is calm. All is bright."

Chicago Tribune, December 25, 2021 (Reprinted in Naperville Sun & Daily Southtown)

-How My Brother Saved the Season

We rely on Christmas for happy endings to life's critical moments, like the December when I turned 5.

The week before Christmas was rainy, and my sister Rosemary, 6, and brother James, 8, and I were playing in the basement. As with other city bungalows, our basement housed the boiler and a storage area for coal delivered through a window-like chute. But when everyone converted to oil heat, my father walled off the "coal shed" so we could safely play in the basement.

James sat cross-legged on the floor, winding up the tin tractor he had gotten the previous Christmas. Rosemary knelt next to him, waiting for the tractor to roll past the barn they built with Lincoln Logs.

Curious, I slid Rosemary's Thumbelina doll into its path, and the tractor crashed, its spring-activated wheel snarling and tangling in the doll's dress.

Rosemary screamed, and James scooted around to free Thumbelina and right the overturned tractor. I told Rosie not to cry, and she clenched her lips tightly together as she tried to smooth Thumbelina's yellow dress.

Later, as I looked around for other toys, there was a knock on the basement door leading to the backyard. James answered, then stepped back as Santa Claus came inside. He shook James' hand and asked him a question in a muffled voice.

Rosie stood close to me, hugging Thumbelina. The manner of Santa's walk and how he bent to give Rosemary a hug were oddly familiar. And when he turned to me, his blue eyes flickered the way my mother did whenever the others tattled to her that, "David's making trouble."

Santa's beard brushed my head as he took my hand and led me to the coal shed. He opened the panel door, moved me inside, then closed and hooked it.

Engulfed in darkness, I lost my breath. The shed had been used as punishment for James, but wasn't I too little? When I could finally breathe, it came out in wet and hysterical cries, my only defense against the spirits and goblins hiding in the darkness.

After a minute — or an hour — I quieted. I cowered against the paneling, which smelled like our toy box. Slowly, things became visible: My hand. My sleeve. A blade of light across the floor in the rear corner. The tall stickman to my left: a shovel? A ghost?

I listened but could not hear the tin tractor, which my brain knew was steps away on the other side of the door. But the toys and the two good children might just as well have been in another galaxy.

Suddenly, a slow crackling sound.

Monsters? Rats?

"Mommy," I whispered.

The ray of light in the rear corner suddenly burst into a solid, yellow beam. I shut my eyes.

"It's OK," someone said. I opened one eye.

"I found the secret compartment," said the voice.

That's when I recognized James' grin. He had broken in through a seam in the paneling. He said I'd be punished even worse if I escaped through the same crack, so he would stay with me until Santa let me out.

Meanwhile, James inventoried the room's contents, now that his break-in let in light. I watched him take down tools and old pictures from a metal shelf unit.

Another larger box on the floor contained clothing, and he searched the pockets for money. He said there were probably hundreds and millions of dollars from olden days and that we could buy our own toy TV and hide it in the shed so that next time we were punished, we could watch "I Love Lucy."

Not Santa, but my mother came to unhook the door, as James retreated to the corner. My heart no longer racing, my voice calm, I told Mom about Santa and promised I'd never tease Rosemary again.

It was the last time I was confined in the shed, since we would move to a new home when I was six.

It was not, however, the last of my punishments, as my parents did their best to manage eight children in an age when experts believed coal sheds and spankings were the bravest proof of love.

But what would experts know of love, having never met my brother James? He made Christmas 1955 the best I remember.

Chicago Sun Times. December 23, 2020.

-A Christmas Confession

I could have been arrested. Or else fired.

I can talk about it now since enough time has passed. I'm no lawyer, but the seven-year statute of limitations for theft has long expired. And I no longer work for the Chicago Public Schools.

In 1980, when I was teaching at Chicago Vocational High School and struggling to pay the bills for a house and family of four, the Chicago Board of Education went broke and stopped issuing paychecks in the weeks before Christmas.

With zero savings, we would not be able to pay the mortgage or our car loan. I could disregard the auto insurance bill, since Illinois did not yet have mandatory insurance. And we could still eat, since Dominick's was the first of the chains to allow purchasing groceries with a charge card.

Gasoline was a worry. I had a 1974 Impala that got 11 miles to the gallon, which was the approximate distance I had to drive to school at 87th Street and Jeffery Boulevard from Evergreen Park. I could travel to school with Tom Doyle, another English teacher, and maybe hitch a ride back with fishing buddy and basketball coach Rich Cook.

But luxuries were out of the question, and that included Christmas gifts. We were just going to have to tell Mike and Jackie that Santa's sleigh couldn't make the trip this year. That things were lean even up at the North Pole, so that the elves could only put a comic book and maybe a candy bar in their stockings.

Vocational back then was a sprawling campus with multiple wings built before World War II. Room 102, my classroom, was at the end of the Chappel Wing, which also housed the carpentry, woodworking, cabinetry and print shops. Room 102 was at the very end, separated from the carpentry shop by a large empty room used to store old school furniture, and in the middle of which was a commercial-grade wood planer the shop teachers occasionally used.

One morning during my preparation period, I heard the planer click on next door, a sound like a low-pitched buzz saw. I strolled over and chatted with Mr. Ritter, the woodworking teacher, who was using a stick to push a slab of distressed wood through the machine. I watched it come out on the other side looking like a brand new sheet from the lumber yard.

I watched Ritter set the planer and run another piece through, careful to keep his hands and fingers from the blades.

And then I looked around the room at all the 50-year-old school desks, tables, windows and doors, many broken and stacked head high, all made out of oak hardwood. Varnished, stained, scratched, chipped oak, with cast iron legs and hardware. And I had an idea.

During my lunch and preparation periods the rest of that week, I disassembled student desks, tables and chairs, and fed them into the planer. Out came pristine looking planks of oak, with gracefully flowing wood grain in gorgeous, chocolaty hues.

I smuggled my treasure out the side door at the end of the day, and into the trunk of my Impala.

Then every night, and during the first week of Christmas vacation, I used my drill and Black & Decker saw to make a rocker for my godson, a Barbie house for my daughter and an oaken desk for my son. With the cut-offs, I made an end table for Marianne, and fishing plugs for my brothers and brothers-in-law.

I rationalized the theft, theorizing that the furniture was likely destined for a landfill. Or even if the school board planned to recycle or sell it to help replenish their coffers, that they were already getting plenty back from me in labor which lately was not being compensated.

Yeah, I had a ready defense. But deep inside, I knew it was wrong.

All these years later, Christmas remains a magical time, especially for children. And for adults, it's a banquet of nostalgia, when the smell of snow and pine needles stir childhood memories, stirring feelings of love and longing for parents and relatives no longer with us, but who live on in images of the closeness once shared during holidays.

For me, it's a little different. The scents recalled: old varnish and wood shavings. The feelings evoked: flashes of guilt from when I hustled to my car in the enveloping darkness.

But then my heart swells when I remember my daughter's firefly eyes as she tore the wrapping off her doll house.

For the glow of a child's countenance on Christmas Day reminds us that despite myriad hardships, both then and especially in the past year, our lives are still a gift and a miracle.

Joy and love, tinged with regret, is the honest meaning of Christmas. I'm grateful to embrace it in this tumultuous year — and every year thereafter.

Chicago Tribune, December 23, 2020

-The Homecoming

Marianne and I had been married 25 years when I had a brainstorm: As a family Christmas gift to ourselves, why not a tropical vacation in Gulf Shores, Alabama?

In 1997, finally, we had some disposable income for airfare for us and for Jackie and her younger sister, Janet, still teenagers, and for Mike, away at the university. Or he could meet us directly from Champaign.

Our entire lives, we never dreamed of leaving Chicago for the holidays. But the thought of palm trees, warm sand and the smell of the sea in December had suddenly become an obsession. I imagined our opening gifts on a hotel balcony, watching the sun melt into the Gulf of Mexico.

Lest the grandparents pitch a fit, we visited both their houses on Christmas Eve. And on Christmas Day, we boarded a morning flight to paradise.

The Boeing 737 was half-empty. Both girls found window seats, and Marianne and I had our own aisle. She smiled and held my hand during takeoff, and I silently congratulated myself as she closed her eyes.

Two and a half hours later, the pilot's voice came over the intercom: "Ladies and gentlemen, welcome to Pensacola. Local time is 11:47 p.m., and the temperature is 39 degrees."

It was still early, and I assured everyone it would warm up by the time we drove the rental car 40 miles west to Gulf Shores. Anything was better than the snow and ice back home.

An hour later, after we checked into our third floor condominium rental on West Beach Boulevard, Marianne made a reservation at a waterfront restaurant for five people since Mike was scheduled to arrive at 5 p.m.

Though we had urged him to fly with us, he opted for a road trip in his new pre-owned Hyundai. Like many college men, including me at that age, he liked driving fast, in syncopation with the rhythms of Dire Straits or Metallica. But so glad we were at his eagerness to reunite with us and his doting sisters, we didn't argue.

Unpacked, we headed down to the ocean and had the beach to ourselves. Waves surged head-high before tumbling and dissolving at our feet, inspiring Janet to do cartwheels, her fingers and toes grazing the foam.

Because we had left our coats at the condo, we were forced to turn back. But we made sure to grab them before leaving for dinner. Mike had yet to arrive, so we left him a message at the rental office. Cell Phone use wasn't widespread in 1997, but he might call from an oasis payphone.

Sea-n-Suds sat on stilts facing the Gulf. It wasn't serving outside because of the weather, but we got a table by the window.

The girls wanted to try Gator Bites, and I had blackened redfish. Marianne ate half her baked flounder and saved the rest for Mike.

Still no word when we checked back at the office, and the manager described how upstate was experiencing record cold and icy roads, some of which were closed.

"I hope he has the sense to stop at a motel," said Marianne, though we both knew that was unlikely once he set his mind.

Back at the condo, the girls declined to try out the hot tub downstairs. We watched a Christmas parade on TV instead, while Marianne read, occasionally peering out the window at the parking lot.

By 10 p.m., Marianne insisted on waiting outside. I went with, and we walked a mile along Beach Boulevard, watching for Mike's car.

We headed back along the beach, braving the wind. But the sky was black and the ocean invisible, the sound of the surf the only proof it was there.

Out of all the nothingness, a squall erupted, and we ducked into the shell of a beach house that was either being built or torn down. We huddled close against a cinder block wall, silently wondering where Mike might be in all the rain and cold and dark, when Marianne tilted her head and whispered:

"What are we doing here? What were you even thinking?"

"Somebody will notify us if something happens," I said.

I meant it as a comfort, but it filled her with urgency to return to our room.

When we opened the door, they were all on the couch: Jackie at left, her feet tucked under. Janet on the right. Mike in the middle, shirtless and in cargo shorts, staring at the two of us in our wet clothes.

"John-Boy is home," Jackie said.

We stayed awake past midnight, prying information from

our son, watching him eat reheated rice and flounder. He had been delayed near Greenville, Alabama, after the Hyundai skidded on a bridge and "tapped" a guardrail on the other side.

"It was not a big deal," he said, and Janet punched him in the arm.

A wrecker winched the Hyundai back onto the road, and a state trooper sent him on his way.

"How much damage to the car?" I asked.

"Can we save it for tomorrow?" Marianne said. "We've all been up since four."

I took a deep breath. Everyone got quiet. Then this from Janet: "Mike, we have the beach volleyball court to ourselves."

"Awesome," said her brother.

The next day was sunny, though still too cold. We watched the three kids play volleyball, later watching them splash in the Gulf despite the weather.

Mike told the girls about a restaurant where the waitstaff tosses you bread rolls. That's where we dropped them off, while Marianne and I went down the street to a bistro where we could get a drink.

"Merry Christmas?" I said, raising my glass.

She smiled, shaking her head.

"Just promise, whatever your brainstorm, that our family will always be together on Christmas."

Chicago Tribune, December 22, 2022 (Reprinted in St. Paul Pioneer Press, Daily Southtown, Naperville Sun)

-Valentine's Day

Valentine's Day is less about finding your one true love than finding yourself.

I was 8 when I had my first crush. It was a Saturday morning, and I walked three houses down to my pal Joseph's house on 96th Place in Evergreen Park.

"Yo, Joe," I called, since it was considered impolite in 1957 for children to ring doorbells.

While waiting, I sat on one of the swings in Joseph's backyard when I saw a girl on the other side of the wire fence. Black hair, large dark eyes, she waved and smiled brightly from the other yard, and I fell in love.

She accepted my invitation to come through the gate, told me her name was Diane, and she swung next to me while I sang the words to the song playing on my mother's radio all week long, "Peggy Sue," in which I substituted Diane for Peggy.

Alas, however, Diane was apparently only visiting for the day, since I never saw her again. Being sad enough that I had a belly ache, I sang "Diane Sue" to myself for hours, in hopes that the melody might magically produce her second evanescence.

At 14, like thousands of other teens, I learned four chords on the guitar, G, Em, C, and D, so that I could play Beatle songs. A bonus was that pretty Lynn DiBennardi, just three houses down, was captivated by what she heard, and I spent the next several weeks sitting at her backyard picnic table singing "Mr. Moonlight," "And I Love Her," and "It's Only Love."

This precipitated a magnetic attachment to Lynn's smile, her voice, her gossipy observations about people on our block, followed by her contagious laughter. All of which, of course, added up to what I assumed was love, though once again, it was infatuation with her reaction to me.

In high school, I moved on to the next block where lived Michelle, a beauty with long dark hair, who made me think of Edgar Allan Poe's Annabel Lee, Shakespeare's Ophelia, or any number of tragic loves to which I was introduced in junior English.

Lacking both money and wheels, we spent most evenings sitting on her front stoop while I explained my newly adopted philosophy of transcendentalism, from reading Ralph Waldo Emerson, and about living a life communing with nature, the way

Steinbeck's character Junius Maltby did.

Luckily for Michelle, she found somebody else who could actually take her to the Evergreen Plaza movie theater on Saturday night, while I resumed figuring out a way to turn my newest love, literature, into a career.

In college, my brother set me up with his girlfriend's friend, Jessica. I knew very little about her except that she was older, wore sharp clothes and jewelry; and together we discovered how we had more room in the back seat of the car where there was no steering wheel.

Love happened so fast, like slipping off the end of a diving board, that I needed to be with Jessica every night, and on the phone with her for hours in the daytime, even when my mother formally requested that the operator break into one of our conversations after she had been trying to call home from her job at Montgomery Wards.

After Jessica had a falling out with my brother's girlfriend when they wore the same dress on one of our double dates, my romance with Jessica ended, since after all, it was dependent on my brother's car.

Marianne was a cashier at the Jewel where I started as a bag boy. She was pretty and popular and influential at work, so I was embarrassed that she saw me up close and at my worst, fumbling with grocery items, while doing little to overcome my social phobia with customers.

She had to re-pack my bags when I made them top heavy or explain to me what kind of help was needed by a customer who had trouble communicating.

Such a miserable frump with nothing to offer, I was shocked and confused that she spent time talking to me at Jewel's Christmas party. She had known and seen the real me, absent a guitar or camouflage, jarring my brain to want to learn all about the likes, the thoughts, and feelings of this extraordinary person.

Ours became an unlikely pairing, and it took many years before I realized it was because we met on level ground of truth and mutual interest, instead of my flights of egotistical fancy.

Duluth News Tribune, Naperville Sun, Chicago Sun Times, February 10, 2021

-Bring Back the Old for the New Year

Unlike many of my boomer brethren, I do not yearn for the good old days.

Instead, I embrace change and shed no tears for the disappearance of manual typewriters, four-barrel carburetors or Meister Brau beer. But there have been some extinctions for which there was no rhyme or reason, and whose losses, I believe, have diminished us in some way.

So, in the spirit of optimism and hope for the new year, I advocate a comeback of the following worthy staples of American life for 2023.

Maps: How I loved poring over a road map spread out on the hood of a car! Not just for the adventure and satisfaction of plotting my own route — instead of outsourcing it to Google or Bing — but also for the deeper knowledge I might absorb about a region's geography and culture that I cannot get from a digital screen.

Maps in newspapers, I miss even more. A story about a bridge collapse in Moldova or a bumper crop of grapes in Azerbaijan has more meaning and relevance for the reader with an accompanying map, which used to be supplied in a box or in a side panel of the story, showing a country's position on the globe and who its neighbors are.

Such maps have been eliminated to save space and cut costs. But what more valuable filler is there for a newspaper's column inches than graphic orientation and enhancement of its content?

Gumball machines: There was never a more magical introduction to the grown-up world of pleasure and commerce than those colorful gumball machines. Grouches removed them from most drugstores, gas stations, supermarkets and diners for reasons of health, security and profit. But also because they did not appreciate how this miraculous dispenser gives a kid his first feeling of control, independence and immediate gratification: Put in a penny and turn the knob, and a reward plops into your hand.

Granted, 1950s-era gumballs rotted your teeth. But bring them back with dentists' recommended Orbit gum and restore an important fabric of American childhood.

Wing vent windows in cars: When it was not hot enough for the air conditioning but the air in the car was stale, those small triangular vent windows were the answer. The driver and front passenger could adjust them at just the right angle for cooling and for fresh air, even if it was raining.

Today's "automatic climate control" function in modern vehicles never gets those features quite right. And the claim that it can accommodate differing preferences for the driver and passenger is a technological myth.

Gas station attendants: Speaking again of cars, while we do not have to leave their comfort and safety while completing a transaction at our bank, paying a toll, getting a COVID-19 shot or visiting a McDonald's or Starbucks, we still have to get out, regardless of how we are dressed, at a gas station.

Again, I evoke my childhood, when my six brothers and sisters and I were mesmerized, watching from the inside of our station wagon, as the attendant sprayed the windshield and wiped back and forth, back and forth, until we could clearly see his smile.

The difference today, if their jobs were resurrected, would likely be the presence of a tip jar next to the pump. But at least gas station attendants, unlike a lot of store clerks or baristas, would deserve them.

Pay phones: Am I the only one who dreads talking on the phone? I'd rather converse with someone in person or send them an email, or even a letter. Which is why I held off on getting a cellphone for the longest time, compelled finally to purchase one when the last of the pay phones disappeared, and I had no other choice for emergencies.

So, yes, I'd like to see pay phones and their accompanying Superman booths returned. But they should include a digital screen and the capability to text, in which case I would gleefully fling my cellphone into the Chicago River. Just kidding: I'll recycle it at Best Buy.

Term papers: Students hate them. And teachers hate reading and grading them. Therefore, many schools have eliminated them, substituting blogs, oral reports, website creation, PowerPoint presentations and even podcasts.

But teaching students how to distinguish among logical arguments and fallacies, flimsy documents and reputable sources, facts versus "alternative facts," or truth and lies, all by applying Aristotelian principles of logic and Modern Language Association rules for research and documentation — all these skills are needed more today than ever before.

Your turn: What do you think should make a comeback: Milk trucks? Door-to-door Christmas carolers? "Seinfeld" (redux)? Float your proposal at the dinner table, or send me an email.

Chicago Tribune, New Year's Eve, 2022 (Reprinted in Daily Southtown, Orlando Sentinel, Sarasota Herald Tribune, San Diego Union Tribune, Wyoming Tribune Eagle, Arizona Daily Star, Duluth News Tribune, and others)

-Celebrating the Godliness in my Fellow Human Beings

Not till our first child was born did I start thinking seriously about Easter.

Michael's was a posterior birth, meaning that he emerged face up, resulting in a lot of unfortunate bruising. Staff at Little Company of Mary Hospital in Evergreen Park assured us he was OK, and they apologized for not taking his picture for a newborn's customary first photo.

When Marianne and I drove home with him on a snowy day in February, I was ecstatic but also dizzy with the new and weighty responsibility of a tiny life. We were suddenly alone in our one-bedroom apartment with none of the nurses, doctors, machines or medicines instantly available at the hospital.

The next day, as the baby cried, and the contusions on his head and face seemed more discolored, I carried Michael Steven to the kitchen sink and poured a half-cup of tap water onto his head, while saying out loud: "I baptize you in the name of the Father, and of the Son, and of the Holy Spirit."

I was not religious. I had, in fact, lost my faith in Catholicism before Mike came along. Higher education turned me into an empiricist, compelled to reject the magic, the contradictions and the corruption in the church.

Yet I still remembered the intriguing provisions for baptism: that a priest wasn't required and that any Tom, Dick or non believing Harry could pour the water and say the 18 magic words to administer the sacrament and ensure a baby's entry into paradise.

Granted, I wasn't sure there even was a heaven. Hell, at 25, I wasn't sure about a lot of things. But when it came to the warm, squirming 8 pounds of amazing life in my arms, I wanted to cover all the bases.

After a week, the bruises disappeared. Today, Mike is perfect and living out West as a doctor.

And all these decades later, while I'm still unsure about many of life's mysteries, I have regained my faith in a certain kind of godliness that I celebrate at Easter. I do not mean the godliness people seek inside a church. Nor is it what the Romantic poets sought in clouds, flowers, snowflakes, hillsides and other natural wonders.

What inspired my faith, instead, were the many other amazing lives I've encountered during my lifetime.

Early encounters were brief but obviously significant,

since I can recall them from childhood. Like the tears I saw in my first grade teacher's eyes when she was compelled to punish me by denying me recess for the rest of the week, after I carved my initials in my desk.

Or a year later, when Peggy Mitterman, a nurse in the house across the street from ours, tended to my injured hand, not caring one bit about my muddy tennis shoes on her beautiful carpet.

Or something more recent, when my new neighbors Dick Nolan and Michael Champagne showed up in the morning, uninvited, then spent their next two days repairing storm damage to our home.

Or a few weeks ago, when Stan Gassmann insisted on driving hours out of his way to pick me up at the airport. Something that my sister-in-law Kathy Dickinson would do as well, as long as it wouldn't conflict with her after-school volunteer tutoring program or her work at the homeless shelter, or the food pantry, none of which she would quit even after spinal fusion, two knee surgeries and her latest hip replacement.

These are just some examples of innate human goodness from my very long list, near the top of which are people making extreme sacrifices, as when my Evergreen Park hometown neighbor Kenneth Dowdell received the gift of life in the form of a kidney donation from Lenora Salazar of Plainfield, one of some 25,000 donors every year in the U.S. who undergo major surgery often for a perfect stranger.

Every reader can create a similar list, adding up to hundreds of millions of manifestations of generosity and goodwill, as if we were all starting our day by drinking the same altruism power shakes.

Of course, there is no denying the enormity of suffering in the world from war, disease, poverty, crime and injustice with which we're confronted on a daily basis in the news and in our own lives. But decades of experience have shown that no matter how bad things have gotten, the majority's predisposition for human compassion, for good, for fairness and for right over wrong, creates a powerful global momentum toward resolution and triumph over the afflictions.

Which is why at Easter, the season of spring and of new life, I celebrate hope. Hope particularly justified this past year, for example, by our excruciating survival of the pandemic; by the long awaited arrival of new cancer treatments currently saving and prolonging the lives of my sister and her husband; by global unity in support of Ukraine's defense against a war criminal; and our own country's prevailing over attacks against democracy by holding the perpetrators, at long last, accountable.

Embracing hope can be costly, and I'm sure there are readers who would rather hedge their bets with skepticism. But the godliness in our collective human heart abounds and historically triumphs, with good reason for a happy Easter.

Chicago Tribune, April 7, 2023 (Reprinted in Daily Southtown, Naperville Sun, Elgin Courier)

-Freedom Was a Dog Named Biff

Americans celebrate Independence Day because freedom is more important than food and water for making us feel alive.

And the physical, sensual, and emotional meaning of freedom was never more poignantly dramatized than in the award-winning feature film *Born Free*.

The movie is based on a true story of Joy Adamson (played by Virginia McKenna), wife of African game warden George Adamson (Bill Travers), who adopts an orphaned lion cub she names Elsa. As Elsa matures into a 300-pound adult, and the perils of keeping her become obvious, Adamson can't bear the idea of her being caged in a zoo and resolves to return her to the wild.

The rest of the film chronicles the risks, difficulties and seeming impossibility of teaching the lioness to survive on her own in the jungle. But perfect, selfless love enables Adamson, in a heartbreaking scene, to drive away her beloved Elsa so that she might live out her days in pure freedom.

Craving freedom for ourselves and those we love is a basic human need, something I felt in my gut after relocating to the north woods.

Our "Africa" was a million and a half acres of woods and waters in Wisconsin's Chequamegon-Nicolet National Forest, and my family's base camp, an 800 square foot cabin we built on the shore of little Bluegill Lake.

No lions or elephants, but a paradise of forested ridges, valleys, and streams, dense with red and white pine, aspen and balsam, free of asphalt, fences, and other human constraints, and teeming with wildlife including wolves, elk, and deer.

A former Chicagoan, I was an alien in this environment. But the black Lab we adopted at 8 weeks was essentially a native, who on his first morning walk to the water's edge, his black puppy hair stood up like porcupine needles upon sniffing fresh tracks of black bear that had passed in the night. "Biff" had yet to see a mouse or even a rabbit in his young life, but ancient knowledge of the woods was carried in his DNA.

Thus, he became our guide in the wilds. Never knowing a leash, he was our Geiger Counter for nature, alerting us to nearby wildlife or predators on the prowl. He saw, scented, or heard what we were incapable of perceiving, by whining, pointing, or leading us to the source, which even included the approach of distant thunderstorms whose static electricity he sensed in the atmosphere and telegraphed with his trembling.

Every daybreak, I went outside and unlocked the door where my daughter Jackie slept in the little guest "bunkhouse," and Biff would spring out to lope alongside on my morning jog. Invariably, new smells sent him on side trips of exploration, giving short-lived chase to a deer, and once treeing a bobcat, another time, a yearling bear. He almost always rejoined my circuitous route back home, except for the morning he was lured by a pack of coyotes, when I feared he'd never return. But he was back in the afternoon, thirsty and muddy and chastised, wearily wagging his tail.

He so cherished his freedom that he required a bribe (Liva Snaps) to ride in the pick-up. Nor did he appreciate the confines of a boat from which he'd leap while I was fishing, to visit the family of loons, or pursue his own piscatorial quarry in Bluegill's crystal-clear depths.

For 10 years, my family reveled in his freedom as if it were our own.

On his last side trip, not of his choosing, I held him in my arms, while recalling for his vet a memorable walk with Janet and me the previous April through melting snow along the Chippewa River. How he had plunged into the rushing water and swam to the other side, keeping us in his sights as we explored opposite banks. When I whistled time to go, he raised his head, paused, and galloped 80 yards upstream before leaping back into the icy Chippewa, paddling and riding the current to emerge precisely where we stood.

Many years later, a feeling of longing and love for our "Elsa," and for the gift of freedom, is what we savor and remember on the Fourth of July.

Chicago Sun Times, Fort Myers News Press, Madison Capital Times, & Duluth News Tribune, July 4, 2021

Journeys
-Quetico

Based on the original handwritten trip log from 1967.

Our food was gone, and we had three more days of paddling before reaching civilization. So when thirty knot winds forced us to shelter in camp, and with no means of calling for help, John suggested we set fire to the island next to ours to attract the attention of a park ranger in a bush plane.

It was the summer I turned 18, and it was supposed to be a trip of a lifetime: two weeks of canoe camping in Quetico Provincial Park in Ontario, Canada.

Earlier, I could hardly believe my luck in receiving a last minute invitation from Tom Booth and his brother John. Their uncle was springing for the trip as a gift to his nephews, and they needed a fourth traveler in order to have two men in each canoe.

Tom, who lived on the next block and whom I'd known since first grade, was a star athlete in high school who would attend college in September on a basketball/football scholarship. John, a year younger than Tom, worked with me at Jewel Foods where we were stock boys, and he was the lead guitarist in a garage band.

Their uncle, Pat Walsh, was a 40 year old tool and die maker, self educated bachelor, and a fan of American history, whiskey, fine wine, and travel.

Having just graduated from Evergreen Park High School, I had an interest in literature and aspirations to write. But I hadn't any plans for my immediate future and jumped at the chance for what sounded like an exotic expedition.

I had never camped, nor had I ever paddled a canoe. So the first thing I did was visit the library and check out a 1941 volume entitled *The Voyageur's Highway* by Grace Nute, about the French fur traders who were the first to portage their canoes between hundreds of lakes and rivers in the same Ontario wilderness where we were going.

The latter proved enlightening, and also frightening, as it

chronicled the depravations of men contending with hardships, often in harsh weather, in a pristine land where they subsisted on fish caught in abundance simply by trailing a colored strip cut from one of their flannel shirts behind their canoe on a hook and line.

    Two weeks before the start date, I met Tom and John at their parents' house where Uncle Pat shook my hand. Tom's mother and father sat on the couch, while Pat stood, holding a glass of wine, talking about Quetico where he had vacationed before with a community group. He described a vast, virgin forestland of balsam, spruce, and pine inhabited by wolves, bear, moose, beaver, and deer; and hundreds of rivers, waterfalls, and lakes, into which you could dip your cup from the canoe to drink sparkling, pure water.

    "What about the fishing?" said Tom.

    "Our group wasn't into fishing," said Pat. "But the water is so clear beneath the rapids and falls, you could see thousands of them."

    "Nobody brought a rod?" said John.

    "You fellows are young. You'll learn that camping is about rejuvenating your spirit. It's the primeval forest. The roots of humanity. The core, the origins, the, uh, transcendental soul."

    Tom's father smiled and took a swig of beer from his can of Schlitz.

    The next day, Tom and I walked to the shopping plaza to buy fishing line at Morrie Mages Sports. On the way, he related that after Uncle Pat left last night, his father warned him and John about how his wife's brother was a "wild card." That he had a history of switching jobs, switching girlfriends. Of not showing up. Tom's father wouldn't deny that Pat was generous to take the boys to Canada, but said they should be careful while traveling with him and take everything he says with a grain of salt.

    "My dad and my other Uncle Joe are the older generation," said Tom. "They're bitter that Pat is free, not stuck in the same old routine like them. Uncle Pat tries new things and likes adventure. More like us."

2.

The morning of August 19th, we left early for our wilderness trip. I thought it curious that Uncle Pat did not own a car and had rented a station wagon for the drive from Chicago to Ely, MN, the point of embarkation for all travelers into the "bush." Ely was a ten hour drive, and after finally arriving, Pat dropped us off at a motel and turned right back around to return the rental to the town of Virginia, 55 miles south. From there he took a Greyhound back to Ely, when we finally all went out for dinner and had a look at the town.

Main Street in Ely was a row of taverns, canoe camping outfitters, gift shops, and tackle stores with window signs advertising "leeches" and "suckers."

It was the era before climate change, when summer temperatures in the northland dropped into the forties at night, and everyone walking the street had knit stocking caps, hiking boots, and long sleeve lumberjack shirts. Crawling with fishing guides, outfitter employees, and tourists, Ely was Dodge City with canoe paddles instead of six guns. The atmosphere felt festive, as strangers smiled and said "hey" on the sidewalk, something we were not accustomed to in Illinois.

We entered a supper club on the main drag. It felt good to warm up, and we were led down a narrow stairway to a quiet, dark dining room. The waitress seated the four of us at a middle table and asked what we'd like to drink. Pat ordered a whiskey and a bottle of Grain Belt beer.

"I'll also have a Grain Belt," said Tom. John and I followed suit, the first time I'd ever done so in a restaurant, because, unlike back home, 18 year olds in Minnesota could be served alcohol as long as it was "on premises."

That first bottle was icy cold and delicious, with a slightly sweet, slightly metallic taste. We drank it fast, washing down every breadstick from the bowl on the table. Pat ordered a ribeye, and we three, cheeseburgers and fries, along with a second Grain Belt. I remember thinking how this last indoor meal we would have for the next two weeks was likely the best one in my life.

We were done eating, and while Pat was finishing his drink, he asked John about his band, and whether they did any original songs. John said not yet, and Pat described his disappointment in popular music, how the Beatles and Bob Dylan had upended the "communal nature" of song, making it all about themselves. He segued into a music history lecture, going back to Homer and the Greek chorus, some of which sounded plausible, some of it fishy.

I exchanged looks with the brothers, all of us a little buzzed. We were just happy as hell to be there.

On the chilly walk back to the motel, and likely emboldened by Grain Belt, the three of us lit cigarettes which we agreed would be our last.

I tossed my half pack of Marlboros into a trash can, and we made a pact to be "smoke free in God's country."

The next morning, the four of us sat at a round wooden table with a travel guide at Canadian Waters Outfitters. He spread out a large green and blue waterproof map, and with a red marker, traced a line our canoes might follow in a northeasterly direction across a dozen lakes and rivers, before looping back along a different route "home."

When I asked if the portages were marked, he stared at me for a brief moment.

"There are no road signs," he said. "Follow the map to where the lakes intersect, and look for a clearing: that's your portage. Most are easy: rocky, but fairly short. The longest I think you have is a mile. Do you know how to rest the bow of a canoe against a tree?"

I nodded, thinking it self explanatory.

The guide made notations on the map where we could catch lake trout, walleye and northern pike, and bass.

Meanwhile, the Canadian Waters staff had filled our Duluth packs with toilet paper, cookware, and two weeks' food rations: canned beans and vegetables, and vacuum packed dried fruit; a dozen loaves of bread; two dozen eggs which should all be eaten the first two days; the same with two pounds of ground beef.

There was also tang, oatmeal, and a family size box of Bisquick for pancakes and biscuits; bacon, salami, summer sausage, ham, cheese, jelly, peanut butter, coffee, cocoa, and powdered milk. They routinely offered a choice of an ultra-light menu of dehydrated foods, but Pat opted for the more filling conventional fare. This meant we'd have to portage a total of eight fifty-pound Duluth packs of food and cookware, along with our tent, camping gear, and personal belongings. This was in addition to the canoes, paddles, cushions, and fishing rods and tackle.

Yet, even though we had never portaged anything, we were cocky about our strength and hiking ability, certain that we could portage anvils from lake to lake, if that's what was required .

3.

The next morning, we were ferried by pontoon boat, along with our canoes and supplies, across the vast breadth of Basswood Lake for a headstart on our trip. Midway, we crossed the U.S./Canadian border, stopping at a wooden tower serving as a Canadian customs office, where we underwent inspection, signed some papers, and purchased fishing licenses.

Shortly thereafter, the pontoon dropped us off with our gear and our canoes while still in the middle of Basswood. Stepping into a heavily laden canoe in water seventy feet deep was more nerve wracking than stepping into a roller coaster at Riverview.

Yet, the anxiety was short lived, since canoes were the perfect vehicle, I found. The Swiss army knife of water craft, they track faster, sleeker, and quieter than rowboats and are able to navigate in the deepest or the skinniest of waters. Nor do they sink if capsized.

Weighing under eighty pounds so that one man can transport it over his head between lakes, a 17' Grumman can carry close to nine-hundred pounds, which means two or three people and hundreds of pounds of supplies.

You can also turn it over on land and use it as a shelter from a storm, or from a curious black bear.

Best of all is that they move soundlessly, which greatly contributed to the cathedral-like feel of the raw beauty of our surroundings: one-hundred foot rock cliffs, acres of spruce and pine forests, and an endless expanse of clear blue water whose freshness you can smell and taste.

After landing our canoes on the threshold of our first portage in the northeast corner of Basswood, we found that carrying the canoes was trickier. Tom and Pat helped set the first canoe on John's shoulders, and he slowly headed up a gravelly path towards the next lake.

I declined their help since I wanted to try doing it myself, muscling up the 2nd canoe over my head. The cushioned bracket allowed me to balance it on my shoulders, but it limited my vision to about twelve feet of the path ahead. After only a minute or two, I stopped and managed to lean the prow of the canoe against a crook in a tree, to have a look around.

The path was lined and surrounded by spruce trees and absolute quiet. The lake breeze did not penetrate here, nor could I hear John's footfalls ahead, or conversation from Tom and Pat behind. (A bird sang somewhere near, but I would not have been able to identify it even if I saw it.)

I thought of the Voyageurs I read about, and how they must have had to clear this path two-hundred years ago, in order to portage their 25 foot canoes made of birch-bark and weighing over 300 pounds. Stepping again under my canoe, I tipped it back onto my shoulders.

I had never participated in anything "historic," before, so that I was not only edified but also sublimely happy upon reaching the end of the portage, laying eyes on a vista unchanged from what some French speaking, 18 year old Voyageur must have beheld from this same spot centuries ago. I was replicating the feat of the pioneering fur traders, experiencing their same aesthetic reward as I emerged from the dark woods into the splash of light reflecting off the miraculously bright blue lake on the other side.

Something also sparkled from the shallows a foot from shore, and I waded in my tennis shoes to see if a previous canoe camper had dropped a coin. Instead, buried except for a tiny tangential edge mirroring the sun was a small compass, an inch and a half in diameter, fully intact. Its face and font looked old, and I surmised its circular case was made of nickel, given the absence of rust.

The needle reliably pointed north, and I fantasized it belonged to a Voyageur who accidentally dropped it two centuries earlier after getting his bearings. Now in his footsteps, I pocketed the treasure, undecided whether to keep it a secret in order to preserve the fantasy.

The rest of the day passed similarly as we paddled across Eden, hopscotching a series of lakes which the waterproof map labeled West, Summer, Sundry, Silence, and Shade. Between portages, we switched bow and stern positions, and often our partners.

On the water, we perfected the J stroke from the stern seat, to keep the canoe pointed straight while paddling on one side. We tried but could not master scooping and funneling water along our paddles into our mouths, the way the Voyeugers did.

And we raced each others' canoes, though that got old quickly because of the effort it took for one craft to move but a single glacial stride ahead of the other.

Everyone was in a buoyant mood, inspired by the beauty, the solitude, and the vastness of the geography. The four of us tried paddling in concert. And when I mentioned how the Voyeugers sang folk songs to help syncopate their strokes, Pat broke into a chorus of "Jamaica Farewell," and the rest of us joined in, as hard as it might be to imagine a 40 year old and three male teenagers naturally doing: "Fare thee well, I'm on my way/Won't be back for many a day./My heart is down, my head is spinning around/Because I left a little girl in Kingston Town." It was exuberant, harmonious glee, as we bellowed unselfconsciously to an audience we knew was limited to deer and bear and moose.

By the time we portaged into West Lake, I was

confident enough to wear a Duluth pack while also balancing the canoe. Still, Tom and I had to make two trips to transport all that we had. And while briefly resting on the other side, we decided to rig our fishing rods. I tied a Countdown Rapala, a minnow imitation that sinks, onto braided line on a rod with a conventional cranking reel, while Tom used a shallow diving jointed Rapala with his spinning gear.

Paddling up the southeast channel of West Lake, we set our rods to troll on opposite sides of the canoe, and it didn't take long for Tom to haul in a 17 inch walleye. Shortly after, I caught a two pound smallmouth bass which we added to a stringer hanging in the water and tied to the canoe's crossbar.

4.

The sun was just above the treeline, and after portaging from West Lake into Shade Lake, we paddled ashore to pitch camp on a pavilion size flat of granite on the lake's eastern side. Our canoe came to a crunching halt on the granite shelf spearing into the water, and I felt relief that it could finally stay in place and not have to be hauled up another portage.

Novice campers, Tom and John and I were overwhelmed by the amount of work that had to be done before dark, which looked to be but an hour away: Unloading the canoes, pitching the tent, finding and selecting food and cookware for the dinner meal, gathering deadwood for the fire, cleaning the fish, and then cleaning everything else up before retiring.

Still, we settled easily into an ethic of cooperation, appreciating the newness and necessity of it all. First order of business was for John and I to pitch the tent, a large army style canvas A-frame. Since cutting trees was prohibited in the National Park, we had to scour the vicinity for two of the straightest, two inch diameter dead limbs we could find for tent poles. John and I wrestled with the heavy canvas, working up a sweat to finally get the tent up and staked in the ground.

I then volunteered to clean the fish on a rock ledge by the

lakeshore, while John gathered more deadwood for the fire. He filled a kettle with lakewater to boil on our folding iron grate balanced over the fire pit which he built with two rows of boulders.

Tom, who often cooked meals at home, started our dinner. Since it was the first night, he had to essentially empty every food pack to find all that was needed: a frying pan for four quarter pound hamburgers; a sauce pan for a 16 oz can of peas; another for instant potatoes; a box of Shake 'N Bake for the fish; and a loaf of white bread and one of the jars of peanut butter to hold us till dinner was ready.

Pat sat near the cook fire perusing the waterproof map, and at one point, he stood and bent over the large pot to spoon and taste the simmering green peas. Afterwards, we saw him rummaging through three different Duluth packs, until finally holding up for us to see, an army shovel that had been folded in a separate pocket of the pack with the tent and sleeping bags.

"Don't know what we would have done without this," he said. He reached into another pack for a roll of toilet paper and disappeared into the woods.

5.

The fish was ready first, and Tom used the spatula to slide a portion onto each of our metal plates. It was very hot, burnt on the edges, and the tastiest I'd ever eaten.

While waiting for the rest of the meal, we tore into a loaf of bread, each of us eating two slices with a thick layer of peanut butter.

The burgers were finally ready, and though they were likely the lowest grade of ground chuck, they had a chewy, wild game texture and salty, mouth watering flavor. Likewise with the peas that had a sweet fullness I had never noticed in other canned vegetables.

Further, when we also thought that the instant potatoes into which Tom had melted a tablespoon of butter before sprinkling with heavy doses of salt and pepper tasted better than genuine spuds, John said that we were getting carried away. And that the outdoor setting for the meal, and the unusually high number of calories we burned that day paddling and portaging over ten miles, were likely the real reasons for the *imagined* gourmet quality of our very basic vittles.

And in case all the calories we burned had not been fully replaced, we concluded the meal with cups of hot cocoa and chocolate chip cookies.

Tom and Pat sat on boulders near the fire, and John and I below them on canoe cushions on the ground, and I finally realized how exhausted I was. It was as if every muscle in my body took this first respite of the day as an opportunity for rebellion and refusal to rise again.

Tom scraped half-heartedly at Shake 'N Bake Crust in the pan, as Pat sat slurping the dregs from the can of peas as if it were some fine after dinner liqueur.

In the spirit of teamwork, and in appreciation for Tom's creation of such a sumptuous repast, John and I hauled the pots and pans and dishes down to the water to scrub them with sand.

Minnows attacked the tiny food particles in the water, as mosquitoes started to nip at my neck and arms. John and I had gotten several cans of Off and bottles of Coppertone from Jewel on our last day; but rather than make another trip to retrieve it from the Duluth pack, I decided to tough it out until the dishes were done.

Any previous notions we had about stargazing, or stories and songs around the campfire, were vetoed by the mosquitoes, the rapidly cooling air, the enveloping darkness, and the general wave of fatigue which had apparently overcome us all.

We found our sleeping bags and placed them in the tent. But just as we were about to zip up the tent screen, Pat reminded us about securing our food provisions. So we all crawled back out and worked as quickly as we could to throw a rope over a nearby aspen bough and then tie and haul up two food packs to a height that a bear ought not be able to reach.

"Look it," said Tom. "Isn't that the northern lights, Pat?" Tom was not looking straight up but toward the horizon where the sun had set.

"Uh, yes," said Pat. "The aurora borealis, the polar lights.

Some call them the dancing lights."

It was disappointing that I couldn't see them. I had broken my everyday glasses shortly before the trip, and all I had were very dark prescription sunglasses. They worked great all day. At night, just inky blackness.

"The closer you get to the north pole, you're supposed to see it better," said John. "I was expecting more."

"I've seen it up here brighter, brilliant, sharper, where it looks like it's moving," said Pat.

"What's it like?" I asked. "I can't see it with these glasses."

"Take them off," said Tom.

"I tried. Just blurry black. I can't even see any stars. So what are you seeing?

"Like green streaks in the sky," said John.

"Imagine a band of green fog stretching horizontally across the horizon," said Tom. "And you can see black silhouettes of the tops of trees in front of the fog. Pretty cool."

6.

Waking up in Quetico must be why most people come: Morning light filtering through the canvas. Birdsong. Pine scent mixed with woodsmoke from the charred remnants of the campfire.

But leaving the warmth of the sleeping bag for the icy air on our faces seemed impossible.

"I'll take the plunge this morning," said Tom, two prone bodies over. He meant rising first to start the fire and fetch lakewater for coffee and breakfast.

"But we have to take turns after this," he said, while wrapping up in his sweatshirt and lacing his shoes before unzipping the flap and exiting the tent.

I looked at John awake next to me, and we shared a smile of triumph for extra bunk time. Pat rolled over on his side on the far end. I listened as Tom snapped kindling, then set and slid pots and pans onto the grill. I waited but didn't hear him strike a match to start the fire. He seemed to have walked off, leaving only the sound of intermittent breezes pushing through treetops.

And then I must have dozed, since the next sound was the roar of the cooking fire and a pot of water in full boil, rattling the grill like a snare drum. John was already sitting up, buttoning his shirt. Time to get moving.

Tom had three pots of water on the fire: one for coffee, one for poached eggs, and a frying pan for the pound of Canadian bacon we were told to use the first morning. John offered to make coffee since the water had already been boiling. But Tom said he had to do the eggs first so that the shells could be dropped into the other pot to keep the coffee grounds down. They weren't whispering, which I figured would wake Pat; but nothing stirring at the tent.

John suggested there probably was a percolator in one of the packs, and Tom said he had already looked. John went from pack to pack, searching anyway, as Tom shook his head, poured half a cup of Tim Hortons ground coffee into a quart size pot of boiling water.

Then he opened the box of eggs, extracting and cracking one at a time into a larger pot, before dropping the shells into the boiling coffee. Eight eggs swifty congealed, floating on the surface, when Pat called from inside the tent.

"I smell coffee," he said.

Now he was outside the tent, appearing to have slept in his clothes consisting of dark green corduroy pants, the same long sleeve tan suede shirt, and a ten gallon hat hanging behind his back by a string around his neck. He ambled over, leaned over the pan of bacon cooling on a side rock, and picked up several pieces before heading back behind the tent to relieve himself.

Breakfast was hot and good, though it took only ten minutes to eat what took Tom 30 minutes to cook, and another 20 for John and I to clean up. This imbalance was a revelation, though I guess I never paid much attention to the time my mother put in doing all this by herself at home.

Tom and I took down the tent, and he suggested we keep the

tent poles in the bottom of the canoe to save time at tonight's camp site.

While we loaded the canoes, Pat studied the map spread out on the top of a boulder, subsequently announcing we needed to traverse 5 or even 6 lakes today. Tom reminded him that we wanted extra time in one of the lakes where the trail guides said we would find lake trout.

"We'll see," said Pat. "Our first portage is 300 rods, so we have some hiking ahead of us."

Another revelation, another imbalance: being an adult meant having to work to have fun. Not sure I was ready to buy into it.

7.

A brilliant day: Pale blue sky. Cold, dark lake squeezed between lush forests. Unpeopled horizons in every direction. I was in the bow and Pat in the stern. I could feel yesterday's paddling in my biceps and shoulders but was able to settle into a comfortable rhythm, switching every ten minutes for balance.
Pat was chatty, his questions distracting my focus at a level sufficient enough to render the paddling mindless. Automatic.

"Teachers college is the right idea, David," he said. I turned to see him just holding the stern paddle in the water.

"Teaching is almost as good a racket as mine," he said. "Three months of vacation, which is about how much I take, though not all at once."

He explained how tool and die makers are in such demand, that he just quits when he wants to take a trip, and then is re-hired, no questions asked, when he returns.

I had told him I wanted to be a writer but had enrolled at the city teachers college for the time being.

"What are you working on now?"

He meant writing, not my work at Jewel, and the question was sobering, since I wasn't working on anything. The last writing I had done was a book review for the school newspaper almost a year ago.

"Our trip," I said.

"Excellent," said Pat. "I can't wait to read it. You keeping a log…a diary…a journal?"

"Yes. But I haven't started it yet. We've been, you know, too busy."

The portage out of Shade Lake was the one Pat warned us about. The map showed it was 280 "rods," or about ¾ of a mile. A rod, we were told by the outfitters, is the length of a canoe, and what I assumed was an attempt at authenticity by the map makers, echoing the unit of measurement used by the Voyageurs. Etymologically speaking, *rod* was an Old English unit of measurement equal to ¼ of the chain which ancient surveyors used, or about 16.5 feet, which, coincidentally, is the approximate length of a modern aluminum Grumman.

We emptied the canoes for the long trek, and then Pat found the Duluth pack with the toilet paper and headed into the woods.

"I'll be back," he said.

John watched Pat vanish, then shot me a wide grin before heading up the path laden with a pack and the tent poles. Lest Pat and I fall behind, I lifted one pack onto my back, and another across my torso. We could get the other two packs along with the canoe on my second trip, provided Pat was finished with his business.

The two Duluth "counterweights" provided surprising balance on the portage. After I deposited them at the lake shore on the other side, I started jogging back for the canoe. Two thirds of the way back, I met Pat hailing me as he emerged from the woods.

"I either came across moose tracks, David, or a very large deer."

"Their tracks are similar?"

"Both have two toes, but this one was like this," he said, holding right hand six or seven inches from the toilet paper roll in his other hand.

8.

Moose was on our minds later that evening, as increasing rainfall forced us to beach the canoes on the mainland where there is always a greater chance for encounters with predators.

We pitched the tent hastily, then gathered inside with a food pack and made sandwiches with white bread, thick slices of smoked summer sausage, and yellow mustard.

The rain continued, and we lit a candle inside and broke open the twelve-pack of Grain Belt we'd purchased before leaving Ely. It wasn't cold, but it wasn't warm, and it went well with the salty meat.

After each of us opened a can, Pat held out his hand toward me, offering a ball point pen he fished out of his own Duluth pack.

"For your log…diary…journal?" he said.

"Do you have any paper?" I asked.

He shook his head.

I pulled out my wallet and unfolded it. Inside were the pay vouchers I was in the habit of keeping from Jewel. They were the same size as dollar bills in shades of pink and green and yellow, and the back of each was blank.

I slid one out and read out loud: "Jewel Companies, Inc.; Store No. 95, Department 11; Hourly rate, 1.45; Regular Hours, 18.6; Gross pay, $26.97; Pay Period 06/17/67."

I turned it over, and using an unopened box of cream of wheat as a writing surface, backdated the first entry of my journal: *Monday, August 21st, Day 1: After being ferried several miles in a pontoon boat, along with all our provisions, we were cast adrift in twin canoes in the middle of Basswood Lake. Utterly alone.*

9.

It must have been the sixth or seventh morning, after another rainy night, when John got up first, abandoning the warmth of his sleeping bag to get breakfast started.

I wriggled onto my side and was hovering in a brain haze just before falling back asleep, when John gave a shout from outside the tent.

"A little help out here. A canoe is loose."

I sat up, unzipped, and pulled on my pants and sweatshirt. The prospect of one canoe for four men: I didn't even want to think about it.

Tom sat up as I was exiting the tent. It was a lot colder outside the tent than in. I walked down the steep granite incline to the lakeshore to see the empty canoe riding high in the calm, cold water 80 feet away.

"You think there's a tide, or what?" said John. He was breaking pieces of kindling over his knee, feeding the new fire.

The canoe was loaded with gear when we pulled it up on shore, and we should have pulled it further after we emptied it. A shift in wind direction was probably all it took.

Tom had yet to emerge. The canoe was drifting farther away. It was the coldest part of the day, but I knew what had to be done, and I bent over and untied both shoes.

"Wait a minute," said Tom.

I turned to see him on one knee, zipping up the tent door, before making his way down the hill.

"Why don't you cast for it?" he said. "Reel it in. You got that 20 pound braid."

"I think it's too far," I said.

"Bullshit," said Tom. "You just loosen the tension." He picked up my rod and stood it on his shoe before turning one of the silver knobs on the reel's left side. Then he cut the light balsa wood Rapala off my line and tied on a heavy Dardevle metal spoon.

Positioning himself on the water's edge, he made a high

arcing overhand cast that sailed over the the canoe and into the water.

After waiting a bit, he started a slow retrieve until I could hear the metal hit the aluminum hull and slide its way up the side before tumbling into the canoe. He continued cranking slowly, slowly, till the treble hooks caught the inside of the gunnel. He raised the rod, dragging the canoe in carefully, inching it shoreward, reeling in slack, till it scraped against the shore at his feet, and he grabbed the front, lifting and pulling it the rest of the way in.

"Beginner's luck," I said, though he knew my grin was one of gratitude.

10.

After breakfast, we sat a while, drinking coffee dregs, and giving our tennis shoes a chance to dry close to the fire. As soon as I smelled burning rubber, I pulled mine out and put them on over dry socks.

Pat had told us to pack two pairs of shoes so that one could dry out while we wore the other. Easier said than done, since soaked 60's era tennies never totally dried by the fire, or by propping them up on top of the Duluth packs in the canoes to soak up rays of sunlight that most days were intermittent, if not scarce.

After scrubbing pots and dishes and loading our supplies, we switched partners. Tom and Pat set out in the lead, with Pat in the stern. John and I paddled several canoe lengths behind and to their left.

We faced a slight headwind but overtook their canoe anyway about a third of the way across Sunday Lake. Tom watched our canoe slither past, and he turned to Pat in the stern.

"Aren't you paddling?" he said.

"I'm holding our course in this wind," said Pat.

"Can't you do both?"

"I do when I'm able," said Pat.

I hadn't said anything about Pat's "coasting" with me. This is his trip, I thought. He's the adult, and I could only hope he was cognizant of my diligence and hard work.

Tom didn't defer in the same way. Of course, he was on more familiar terms with his uncle. But Tom didn't defer to teachers or coaches, either. Not disrespectful. He just seemed to be ahead of the rest of us in establishing equal footing with adults.

They were still going back and forth as John and I got farther ahead. When we landed at the first portage of the day, their canoe was a mere speck and, perhaps, ten minutes behind us.

It took us less time than that to get the canoe and all our gear over the next portage, which was barely 5 rods or 30 yards long.

"You want to wait for them?" said John.

"Sure. I'll make some casts."

"Wait. Do you hear that?"

"What?" I stood still. "Bees?"

He shook his head and held up his hand. He knew what it was. And then I did.

We looked toward the treetops along the lakeshore on our left. A low rumbling vibration. Louder. And louder.
Higher pitched. A snarling whine.

And then it broke into view, clearing the trees: an apple red seaplane. Right over our heads. Engine now deafening. I could see the pilot through the windshield, and I waved as he passed overhead.

The sound immediately started to fade.

But a quarter mile past us and above the trees to our right, the starboard wing tilted upwards, and the plane banked into a wide left hand turn.

Had I waved too frantically?

"What the hell, McGrath?" said John.

We watched him loop around, complete his turn. To my consternation, he was coming back. Heading, unmistakably, right toward us.

How do I tell him we're okay? Undo what he saw as a signal for help?

The plane was now roaring just 80 feet above us, and I froze. It's all I knew to do. You could see the pilot's eyes. His sunglasses. He was going to land in the water.

But he did not. The engine groaned, the seaplane rose. It cleared the trees.

I held my breath, and it kept going. The engine faded to a hum. A tapering hum. And I had never been so thankful for silence.

We waited on the shore of Agnes Lake until Tom came through the woods carrying their canoe. He had seen the plane on the other side, and we told him about the close call.

"You arseholes had better stay close for now on," he said.

After dropping the canoe at his feet, he asked John to do him a favor and partner up with Pat for the rest of the day.

"Long story," he said, "but David and I want to fish lake trout in Agnes and that won't work with Uncle Slug."

"Don't you mean Uncle Take-a-Dump-On-the Portage?" said John.

John agreed to Tom's request but warned that all three of us would have to take turns with Pat, so that each of us could get quality fishing time.

11.

Agnes Lake: Intimidating. 21 miles long.

Depths to 200 feet.

In our canoe, surrounded by magnificent granite bluffs, Tom and I were quiet.

Agnes's heavy current is fueled by feeder creeks and rivers. And if the wind is up, there is nothing to slow it down. In a storm, it would be dark and brutal.

On this pleasant day, however, her vastness and beauty were uplifting. It's what prompted Canada's first prime minister in the 19th century to name it "Agnes" after his wife, according to John who said he read it on a wall chart at the outfitters. John has always been a compulsive reader, scouring the back of a cereal box, the classifieds in a newspaper, or the actual articles in *Playboy*.

We were paddling down the center of the main channel. And though we had no instruments for gauging depth, the cobalt color of the water and precipitous granite on both shores signaled a canyon anywhere from 100 to 200 feet beneath the thin skin of our canoe.

One at a time, we set up our rods, so that the other could keep a steadying paddle in the water.

I tied on my largest gold Rapala that would run about ten feet deep.

"Do you have any weights?" I asked Tom.

Neither of us had experience with lake trout, though Tom was pretty sure from his fishing magazines that they inhabited the deepest layers in late summer. He said he had only a half empty tube of split shot, which were BB size lead balls, partially cut, so you could pinch them directly onto monofilament to carry a plug a few feet deeper. He applied all he had in a daisy chain twelve inches above his sinking spoon.

I had nothing. Not even a cotter pin or a machine bolt or a belt buckle that I might tie to my line.

Oddly, however, pinned inside my wallet was a round metal badge two inches in diameter. It was bright yellow with a blue quotation printed on front: "I was a Pig at Sherman's Dairy." I was "awarded" the badge the previous year for consuming a huge ice cream sundae called Pig's Dinner at Sherman's Dairy in South Haven, Michigan, where our family was vacationing.

With nothing to lose, I knotted my black 20lb braid around the sharp pin that was meant for affixing the badge to your shirt or jacket, some 20 inches or so above the Rapala.

While Tom paddled at the stern, I dropped my lure and "weight" over the side and fed out line from the reel.

Surprisingly, the spherical badge caught the water rushing beneath the canoe like a scoop, plunging it more deeply, but with an erratic, spiraling, thumping action, with the Rapala wiggling after it.

By the time we were both paddling again, trolling our lures

behind the canoe, I could not be sure how deep my bait was swimming or whether or not the Pig's Dinner badge helped in that regard.

But the terminal set-up did the trick, since after barely five minutes of paddling, the top portion of my rod which I had wedged under one knee on the starboard side of the canoe started bending and jerking. I dropped the paddle and grasped the rod to feel the vibrations of a live creature.

"Set the hook," said Tom.

I must have had at least 40 yards of line out behind the canoe, and I snapped the rod sideways in the direction of the bow and felt the weight of a heavy fish.

It fought to stay down, and its short, spasmodic runs made the rod feel like holding a jackhammer.

I kept reeling steadily, the fish rising, the thrusts subsiding. Just under the surface, it turned sideways, a thick, cold lake trout.

We had no net, and I used the rod to lift it over the gunnel and into the canoe: Roughly twenty inches long, bronze with pale white speckles. Tom guessed between 5 and 6 pounds, the main entree for tonight's dinner.

I extracted the hooks, slid the stringer spear through its lip, and hung it in the water off the side of the canoe. Tom would catch another smaller lake trout, adding two more pounds to the stringer. He surmised they were feeding in the upper layer of the water column and the likely limit of our reach with the split shot and my ice cream badge. We caught up broadside to John and Pat, and Tom held up the stringer of fish.

After we told Pat what kind they were, he informed us that a lake trout was not really a trout.

John rolled his eyes: "Pat, have you ever even seen one?"

"A lake trout is actually a char," said Pat. "Not a true trout."

"Same difference when they're in the frying pan," said Tom.

"I've eaten it at restaurants," said Pat. "It's good, but not what you think."

"You never had it this fresh," said Tom. "In fact, I have a suggestion."

Tom proposed that we end our paddling and pick out a suitable island now so that we don't have to rush everything the way we've been doing, pitching camp with less than an hour left of sunlight. If we quit now, we could get the camp work done, clean the fish, finally have enough time to swim and bathe, and then feast on the trout and two other complementary courses he had in mind, along with whatever Grain Belt was left.

Everyone liked the idea, especially John, who canoed ahead with a quickened pace. We followed in their wake, matching their speed. I looked back to see the trout spinning and skidding near the surface at the end of the stringer.

After a while, John raised his short bow paddle, using it to point toward what appeared to be several islands half a mile away at about ten o'clock, if twelve was dead ahead.

"Go for it," said Tom, and both canoes made the turn as we raced onward.

We approached the outermost island which resembled an iceberg with no place to land, and we paddled further. The second island was larger, half of it also like an iceberg with steep, vertical banks. But on its back side, it flattened out with a broad rock shelf sloping into the water. There was no firepit or any sign of previous campers.

"How's over there?" said John.

"Perfect," I said.

"No worries about moose," said Pat.

12.

After the unloading, I cleaned the trout. I was getting more efficient once I realized that the macho hunting knives each of the three of us liked wearing on our belts, weren't very suitable for fileting fish with their thick handles and wide blades. Instead, I used a sharp skinny knife supplied by the outfitter to carve off each side of the fish, and then I slid the slim blade underneath the meat to separate the skin. Like peeling a potato.

Tom took out bread, Shake-n-Bake, Rice-a-Roni, a whole red onion from the sack, and a large can of Heinz baked beans, after which he gathered softball sized stones for a firepit.

John and Pat put up the tent on a carpet of pine needles at a site higher up on the island nearer where the trees started. Everything was ready in a little over half an hour, and we picked up our towels and walked in the direction of the "iceberg," stopping at a table size rock overhanging the steep bank. Several feet below the edge of the table rock, the water looked inviting in the sunlight, clear enough to see ten feet down to the hard bottom, mottled with patches of seagrass. Though it was August, and the air temperature, we estimated, at least 75 degrees, the water, cold enough for drinking, was well below that.

Tom went first, stripping his clothes and diving from the table rock. He said nothing when he surfaced, breathless, treading water.

"How is it?" Pat called.

"My legs are numb," said Tom. He rose slightly and twisted in the water, like a fish trying to shake a hook. The rest of us took off our clothes, dropping them in the sun. Not having seen another human being since we left customs, we were able to swim naked. It felt illicit but freeing. Rather than dive, I jumped off the ledge into the water, the shock of cold taking away my breath, giving me an instant headache.

I was treading water next to John, while Tom was doing the butterfly further out. Pat still stood up on the rock, naked except for his wide brimmed cowboy hat.

"This soap may not float," he said, "so you have to catch it?"

John and I both held up our hands, and Pat's underhand toss fell short of John who plunged forward, sounded, and came back up with the white, hand size cake.

He confirmed that it didn't float and said he'd hand it to me after he finished. My headache was gone as quickly as it came, but I was getting winded treading water; so I slid onto my back to float until John was finished. Suddenly I was swamped by a wave from Pat's running jump and collision with the water.

    One by one we soaped up, silent, panting, saving our breath for staying afloat.

    Sinking beneath the surface, I spun like a seal to rinse, then swam away from the cliff toward the sloping shelf till my fingers touched granite and I was able to stand. The frigid bath left me winded, while the warmer air felt luxurious on my skin. Fatigue was inviting surrender, but I was aching with hunger, too.

    The feeling must have been mutual, since after we dried ourselves and got dressed, we crowded around the firepit to help with dinner. Tom asked me to fill two pots of water. One, I knew, had to be for the Rice a Roni. John tinkered with the fire, feeding it with kindling, using one piece to push a wood chunk closer to the flames.

    Pat, still naked except for his sombrero, stood back from the fire on the windward side, presumably to get warm. Or dry.

    Uncle Pat was taller even than Tom, and on the very generous side of 240 pounds. Five days in the bush, and he already had a Hemingway-esque beard going, curly and even redder than his hair. He was, in fact, red all over, and I, along with Tom and John, it seemed, were making an effort not to look at him. He had gone on about the stress relief and rejuvenation from total absorption in nature, so I assumed nudity must have been part of it.

    Adjacent the island was a protected, weedy cut-in, or, perhaps a creek drain, which Tom was keen to fish after dinner. The rest of us were done in, so he took a rod and one of the canoes himself, its bow rising 10 inches above the water as he paddled away.

    John and I cleaned the dishes–Pat still naked on a rock next to the fire. We were nearly finished when we heard a loud clatter through the trees, which could only be Tom's canoe running hard aground. Instead, as we later learned, it was a northern pike the size of a small alligator which he had caught and lifted over the gunwale, flapping and beating the floor of the canoe, echoing back to camp.

13.

I thought we might never leave our sleeping bags on the next morning. I was awakened by the wind, a freight train steaming across Lake Agnes, relentless, colder than even the first morning, penetrating the tent walls, reddening John's nose, cheeks and ears, his head exposed and resting on his rolled up windbreaker next to me.

I unzipped and tried to dress quickly, icy air on bare skin, a new sensation. My hands fumbled with buttons, laces, like those of an elderly arthritic, a result of stiffness from the cold and of the burning need to relieve myself.

Outside, our site was strewn with dead limbs, some with live branches and leaves. I was going to walk down to the water's edge to urinate, which Pat claimed is sanitized in minutes by the current and the cold temperature of the water.

But waves lapping up onto our granite shelf from the hurricane of whitecaps out on the main lake, sent me behind the tent and into the woods where all was quiet.

From behind a large spruce, I could still see army green walls of the tent where Tom and John and their uncle had yet to stir. It was a new and bracing morning, with adventures still ahead, but I had a nagging worry about the remaining days. That's because last night's dinner, the generous, scrumptious helpings of fried lake trout piled with sweet Rice a Roni, notwithstanding, left a bitter taste this morning because of what happened later.

The evening had begun serendipitously enough. After the dishes were cleaned and more deadwood gathered for the campfire, we had settled around it to recap the day, keep a watch for the northern lights, and finish off what was left of the Grain Belt that we had submerged in the lake between the beached canoes.

We had opened three cans of beer, and Pat filled half a cup from a bottle of Chivas Regal he had been keeping in his personal Duluth pack.

"I'd like to hear what's in your journal…ship's log," said Pat.

I fished out my Jewel vouchers, took a sip of fizzy warm beer, and read what I had written of our first 4 days. Hearing myself, I was reminded of the dry prose we read in our colonial literature book in sophomore year. But my audience seemed pleased to hear a story in which they were the principals.

Not a lot of content, 900 words, maybe, and after I finished, John said I ought to include something about the dried fruit we were having each morning; so I made a notation about how the outfitters had supplied us with a dozen vacuum packages of dried apricots, dates, pears, and mangoes, which Tom had taken to soaking in water overnight, and then boiling atop the morning campfire to produce a warm, syrupy smoothie.

Tom then suggested that if I appended the details of the various lures and fishing techniques we tried today, the notes might prove valuable for future fishing situations.

Pat cautioned that I should not leave out our mistakes: "Don't censor…prettify…you know, whitewash what happens," he said. "Did you tell them, John?"

"What are you talking about?" said John.

Apparently, while in the canoe with Pat, John made an errant cast that sent his Lazy Ike lure soaring into an overhanging limb of a tall aspen where it was hopelessly snagged.

"John is more of a threat to the birds than to the fish," said Pat.

"Not as big a fright as you walking around nude," said John.

"You have some kind of hang-up with the human body?"

"Who wouldn't have a problem when you're eating dinner and some old bastard's saggy balls are five feet away from your plate?"

The exchange went downhill from there. Though it was partly fueled by the Chivas and the beer, it had the feel of inevitability after the last several days.

Antagonism had been building: Pat's didacticism; his bathroom breaks on portages; his lazy paddling.

The brothers, I felt, previously took pride in their uncle's iconoclasm decried by their parents. And you can forgive or ignore the bad habits for a relative for whom you have affection. Certainly, at least, for the short periods of time when you see them. But lengthy cohabitation strains tolerance.

14.

As the only non-relative, I felt myself viewed as the neutral party, and I wondered if I could keep trouble at bay this morning as I took my turn fixing morning camp and breakfast.

I was no cook, but I could start a fire, put the kettle of fruit juice on the grate, and start the water boiling for coffee and oatmeal.

The tent started to rustle. Fragments of voices. It had to be Tom and John.

When I walked to the edge of the table rock to fill the two pots, I could see that the frothy whitecaps, indicative of three foot seas, were going to keep us trapped on the island. Taking on my new responsibility might prove difficult.

After joining me outside, Tom Immediately began pulling packages and food utensils from the food sacks for what he called a hybrid version of eggs benedict. We had no ham and no eggs. But we did have smoked summer sausage, cheese, butter, Bisquick, and a folding reflector oven with which Tom, I trusted, would work some magic.

He was actually waiting for bad weather, he said, since his recipe required time.

The smoked salami, summer sausage, and the bread he was using had been the go-to fillers for our outsize, outdoor appetites; but I was in favor of anything he wanted to create for us to eat.

"Jesus, look at it out there," said John who had just emerged and was gazing out on Agnes's fury. He turned, squatted close to the fire, looking approvingly at Tom's preparations before standing up again.

"I'm gonna see a man about a dog," he said. "And I'll get more wood."

By the time John returned, I had set the table, placing our

steel plates, utensils, and cups for coffee and juice on a tarp, upwind of our firepit We didn't need to be on top of the flames this morning, since the wind was doing the work of keeping the flies and mosquitoes away.

A snarl from the zipper of the tent flap, and all heads turned as Pat stepped out, dressed, minus his hat. Unruly nest of red curly hair.

I said "hey" as he approached our "kitchen." Tom and John said nothing, attending to the grate where the fruit stew was bubbling, the coffee boiling, clouds of steam engulfing the oven housing our eggless biscuits. Loud absence of conversation.

"Pat," I finally said. "That nameless fishing lake that the guide said was so good: did he mark it on our map?"

"I believe on the back side of this island," he said, glancing around. "The leeward, er, east, rear half of the promontory."

"That's probably a good idea," Tom said. He kept his eyes on the pan. "It doesn't look like we can go anywhere else today. Supposed to be some gigantic northern pike in the secret lake."

Morning uncoiled civilly. Everyone complimented Tom's recipe. John and I sat on the tarp on the ground, sipping coffee. Tom on a rock nearer the fire.

Pat had gone behind the trees. When he returned, he extracted the map. The first option, he said, was to paddle the canoes, in the very rough water, around and to the back of the island, and then make the short trek to a portage on the mainland that led to the secret lake.

The second option was carrying one canoe along the shore and to the same spot, where we could paddle across the "sheltered bay, isthmus, strait," as per Pat, to the portage leading to the unnamed lake, which appeared to be only 20 or 30 acres.

"Don't we need both canoes?" I said.

"Actually, no," said Pat. He said we three "fishing fiends" could canoe to the other lake by ourselves, and he would stay on the island and explore on his own. He also hadn't yet cracked open a copy of *Walden* which he brought for summer reading.

"Let's clean this mess up," said Tom, clearly excited to spend a few hours strictly fishing. John hopped up as well, gathering the pots and plates to take down to the water. We were like school kids granted recess.

I couldn't be certain whether it was a case of Pat wanting some "space" after last night's head butting, or if it were simply the fact that he wasn't into fishing and wanted time for reading and relaxing, since it was, after all, a vacation for him. His choice of *Walden* showed, I guessed, that he was serious about living the unmaterialistic life. But Henry David Thoreau, according to what I learned in school, was all talk.

Whatever Pat's motivation, I welcomed a field trip for just us three, not to mention a chance to strategize the remaining days.

15.

After agreeing to the second option, we consolidated the fishing tackle in one box and gathered rods and paddles that Tom and John would carry, while I braced myself under the canoe.

We started our trek along the shore, leaving Pat reclining on the tarp next to the still smoldering fire pit, his head propped up on a Duluth pack, his book propped up on his lap.

The two others led the way, and the wind from the lake made marching with the canoe feel like hanging on to the mainsail of a ship. Twice I stopped till the weight of the canoe settled back down securely on my shoulders.

When we couldn't get past a cluster of elephant sized boulders half in the water, half up on shore, John led the way to the left and into the woods, presumably to cut across to the leeward side.

There seemed to be a trail, perhaps made by previous fishermen, or, perhaps originally cleared by the Voyageurs. But there wasn't a lot of headroom, as my canoe scraped and clattered through branches crowding both sides.

The trail rose for a minute or two before it started to decline, when John called back that he could see water.

"Looks like Pat knew what he was talking about," I said.

"I think you're sadly mistaken, McGrath," said John.

I had just stepped out from under the canoe and eased it onto the ground. John had been looking across the protected water behind the island, scanning the shoreline less than half a mile away.

"Don't you remember he told us to 'cleave' to the shoreline?" said John.

"Well, he was basically correct," I said. "There's always going to be a little improvising."

"'Cleave!'" said John. "Who the Christ says 'cleave'? What a dipshit."

But he was smiling. This excursion was a good idea. Tom stood to our right, looking down at the map, and then across the water, and back at the map. Finally, he pointed to an area approximately 45 degrees to the left.

"There's your portage " he said, indicating what looked like a sliver of pebbly beach punctuating the dark green bank dense with balsam. "That's gotta be it."

After we loaded the rods, cushions, and paddles, Tom pushed the canoe into the calm water and hopped into the stern. John commenced padding in the bow, and I sat in the middle, stretching out my legs, my reward for carrying the canoe.

John was pulling strong, the canoe arrowing fast across the smooth water. The wind was 80% baffled by our island, and by another island to the left, but we could hear waves from the main lake splattering on the rocks to our far right.

"Bear!" said Tom.

I strained to see where he was looking and saw nothing.

"At least, I think it's a bear," said Tom. "Nine o'clock, about three football fields out. Or maybe two hundred yards."

And then I saw it. A black head above the surface, big like a black Lab's, but with ears at attention. This was no dog. Its nose was half submerged, the hunch of its back visible above the water, head and back gyrating in syncopation with each stroke, swimming from the mainland to…our island. Taking no notice of our canoe.

"Should we warn Pat?" I said.

"Fuck 'em," said John who kept paddling.

"I don't think he has to worry," said Tom. "It's a big island. He gets a whiff of Pat, he'll steer clear."

"We should warn the bear," said John.

"Could have been on our island last night," said Tom, and I could feel him push the paddle, as we tracked more to the left. "They're supposed to be all over, judging by all the caution posters at the outfitters. But we have food up in the tree, everything is cleaned up, and Pat's by the fire. Bear is more afraid of us than vice versa, is what they always say. These are not grizzlies."

I was sure Tom was right. 99% sure.

"If Pat gets naked," said John, "maybe the bear…never mind."

As our canoe slid, scraped and stopped on the edge of the pebble beach, I could see a path hooking left into the forest. John stepped out of the canoe. I handed him the rods and tackle which he carried to the portage, quickly disappearing in the trees.

Tom was still in the stern seat, using his hand to shade his eyes, staring out at the water.

"Bear probably scented our camp," said Tom. "He disappeared past the south end and might have been headed to the other island."

"Don't tell John," I said. "He'll send Pat berry picking over there."

I stepped out onto shore and could see the seas had not let up on Agnes proper. But I felt more eager to explore the no name lake, wondering if every canoeist felt the same surge of enthusiastic strength that I did, as soon as my feet felt solid ground.

Tom said he would haul the canoe, and I grabbed a handful of gunwale to boost it onto his shoulders.

"Hold it." It was John, coming back toward us from the pathway. "Leave the canoe down. This thing is impassable." But John was not referring to tangled vegetation or granite obstructions, but to black, oozing mud overspreading the portage.

"Every step, you sink to the ankles," said John. "Like quicksand. From all the rain. No way around it."

"Maybe it's not a portage after all?" said Tom.

"Oh, yeah, it is," said John. "You could see it tunnel through the trees. If you absolutely had to, you might be able to get through. Drag the canoe. But who knows how long it is and how long it would take."

We took John's word for it. That, and a look at his gym shoes layered with mud up to his socks.

16.

"How was the fishing?" said Pat.

We must have awakened him when we got back to camp, since he was in the exact same spot and did not seem to realize we were gone less than an hour. I explained about the mud. And the three of us decided that with no other place to go, we would circle our island and cast the shoreline. The wind seemed to be easing.

We started on the lee side casting comfortably in protected water, which was calm and clear, and I could see small bass chasing my Mepps spinner right up to my feet, though not pouncing. More curious than hungry, and the larger fish were likely in deeper water, past the first break point because of the front.

We worked around to the windward side of our island, hurtling casts into the breeze, and I caught a 14 inch bass, and John got a savage strike on a Heddon Torpedo, a noisy surface plug with a propeller that was known for missed hits because of the placement of the treble hooks.

"You can't yank it as soon as you get a strike," said Tom. Tom had more fishing experience than either of us. But schooling patience when a fish attacks is like asking someone not to curse after a kick in the shins.

"The wind is blowing all the forage toward shore, which the predators are feeding on," said Tom. "That might have been a really big northern."

Farther down, Tom caught a 28" northern off a weed bed, not a monster by any means. But I took a picture, and he released it in the shallows since they were hard to clean. Later we would learn that they were great table fare once you learned to cut out the Y bone cage.

17.

When we finally sighted our camp, Pat was not alone. Four other people in a semi circle talking with Pat hardly qualifies as an extraordinary event, except here, in Quetico, where we hadn't seen another human being in days, and on our out-of-the-way island, where we may have been the first party to camp in decades.

I was excited. I swallowed, wondering what to ask. What to say.

Jerry Greenwald was older than Pat, likely in his fifties. He wore a pith helmet and white cargo shorts. He was accompanied by another man, his friend or brother, name of Art, and an attractive, blonde, sturdily built woman who might have been Jerry's wife, and mother of two boys maybe just into high school.

They had been camped about a mile north of us, they said, on the return loop of their trip, and had been waiting out the wind before shoving off. And then Pat saw them and waved them over, and they landed their canoes–one red, one green– at our campsite.

"Are those wooden?" I asked.

"Cedar and canvas," said Jerry. "Handmade in Art's garage."

"Aren't you afraid of…can they leak?" said John.

"No more than yours," said Art. "But if one is damaged, it's easy to fix on the trail."

He prefers wood, he explained, since they're quieter and warmer. And they actually flex in the water, making them easier to steer and handle in rough water like today.

"We have extra cups somewhere," said Pat.

He had brought out the bottle of Chivas Regal for our guests, and John rummaged through the food pack for the cups.

Jerry and his wife declined, and Art held out his thumb and forefinger to indicate he'd have just an inch of the Chivas. Pat filled Art's cup and then passed the bottle around our circle.

I knew whiskey since my mother made "hot toddies" when we were sick, and I never countenanced drinking it for pleasure. But our beer was gone, and meeting fellow travelers in the wilderness felt momentous, somehow validating a feeling of kinship with the ancient fur traders. I poured what I judged to be half a shot and passed the bottle to John.

"We hope to get in 10 miles before pitching camp," said Jerry.

The two men, we learned, were, in fact, brothers, and Fiona was Jerry's wife. The younger boy was Art's son and the older one belonged to Jerry and Fiona. Why Art's wife wasn't along, or whether he even had a wife did not come up.

This was the 7th canoe Quetico trip that Art and Jerry had taken since they were kids, and they told us they were passing along the tradition and know-how to their boys.

"You feel that's important," said Pat.

We were standing around a boulder with a ledge like a Pleistocene easy chair on which sat the Chivas and two extra cups and a bag of Oreos that Art asked the boys to bring over from the red canoe.

Jerry changed his mind about abstinence and filled a coffee cup a third of the way with the Chivas and turned to Pat.

"Our first trip up here, I was 14 and Art was 12," he said. "That was thirty years ago, and a lot has happened since then. In the country."

"And our lives," said Art.

"And our lives," affirmed Jerry. "But that first trip is still my clearest memory. I've taken a million trips since then, but when I smell wood smoke or hear the wind at night, I'm 14 again."

"Exactly what I was trying to tell my nephews here," said Pat. "Not just a fishing trip. Or a vacation. More like therapy. Rejuvenation. Restoration."

John caught my eye before draining his cup of Chivas. He reached for the bottle.

Speaking of fish, can you all use some walleye fillets?" said Art.

"We'll take 'em," said Tom. "Why don't you want them?"

"We're on our way back," said Art. "Cook them up and enjoy. You'll be doing us a favor."

Tom went with him to where their canoes were beached, and Art gave him a cellophane bread bag with half a dozen white wet walleye filets. He also gave him a large foil bag with what must have been 5 pounds of dehydrated onions when it was full.

"But we've got nothing to give you," said Pat.

"Your kindness," said Jerry. "'Ships passing through the night.' That's more than enough."

Pat asked, and Art described the seaworthiness of his canoes, how they can handle Agnes's rough waters, though they often have to quarter the seas, which made their routes longer.

What I was hearing about the difference between wood and canvas, versus our Grummans, wasn't convincing. In fact, it stands to reason that our metal canoes were better able to handle rocks and take a beating.

But the skill and experience and greater confidence of the canoeists was why they were on the move and we were stuck on the island. Jerry assured us we could make it, and Pat said we would probably be getting started in an hour or so.

But after our new friends paddled away, we knew we'd be postponing travel till tomorrow, when the conditions should be better. The early afternoon whiskey may have also had something to do with it. In fact, it felt like a holiday since it was our first day in Quetico that we didn't have to pack and reload the canoes with all that we had unpacked hours earlier.

18.

Tom asked if I wanted to fish off the rocks with jigs and the pork rinds he had bought in a baby food jar. I said it sounded like a good idea for bass or whatever else was lurking under those boulders, but that first I needed a nap.

He asked John, who smiled, refilled his cup, and said, "I'll watch."

"There are two ways to hook the pork tail," Tom said. He kept talking to John as he cut off the terminal end of his fishing line with his knife.

Pat went back to his book, and I unzipped the flap of the tent and lay on top of my sleeping bag. I must have not gotten enough sleep the night before and felt myself falling as soon as I closed my eyes.

Fiona sat ahead of me in the bow of the canoe. She was wearing perfume that smelled like coconuts. Or it might have been her shampoo.

I had her to myself, the others back on the island. My eyes were trained on the fine golden hairs on the bare skin of her back showing just above her white shorts.

She turned around, holding her paddle above the water, and smiled.

"Asshole!"

I opened my eyes. A black fly was crawling across the tent ceiling.

"Who's the asshole who can't hold his liquor?"

I longed to continue dreaming but was awakened by shouting. Voices of John and Pat.

I supposed I could record the dream in my journal and read it to everyone after dinner. They'd get a charge out of that. Except that the sounds outside the tent did not exactly presage a quiet evening around the fire. I went outside.

"I can't believe how two-faced you are!"

"Ha!" said Pat. "What about you? Your

sanctimonious…innocent…pious face back home, and the petulant…surly…sophomoric one I'm looking at now?

"Dry up," said John.

"Grow up," said Pat. He had not moved from his reading position, the book open on his lap.

"How about it, David?" said John. "All his talk about 'restoration' in the wilderness. Getting back to nature. Who the hell carried your canoe and all your shit last year with your community group? I'll bet they threw your lazy ass out after that trip."

Pat looked unfazed.

"Enough is enough," said Tom. He was squatting at the water's edge, balancing a rod between his knees while sharpening the treble hooks on a Mepps spinner.

"Didn't you hear, Tommy? This is why he invited…never mind." John shook his head.

We watched him pivot angrily before walking down the rocky, algae covered slope to the water. He got down to one knee and splashed water onto his face and neck. He got up and disappeared into the trees.

Pat oblivious, eyeing a page in his book.

*

The next morning, we broke camp in record time. There wasn't as much to clean or pack, since all we ate the night before were the walleye fillets our visitors had given us. The wind was down, though steady, and I could sense everyone's compulsion to be traveling again.

I was paired with John as we paddled away from the rocky island, Tom and Pat still loading their canoe.

"Talk about getting hammered," said John. "Was I an asshole yesterday? I know he was?"

"Call it a draw."

"Yeah, well, that's the last time I'll ever drink hard liquor," he said.

It occurred to me that we probably wouldn't be having the

same frank conversation if we were facing one another: Single file, both facing the same direction was like talking on the telephone.

I ventured a hypothesis out loud that his uncle was simply not up to the task of being our friend and parent at the same time, especially since he had zero experience with the latter, and likely little with the former.

"But doesn't he annoy the shit out of you?" said John?

"Yeah, but I'm in a different boat. I'm here by his good graces. I have to cut him more slack."

We paddled about two miles to the next portage, a sandy hilly trail through the woods to Beaver Lake. John insisted on carrying the canoe. Penance.

It was getting warm, and I took off my sweatshirt and paddled in the sun across Beaver Lake's two mile expanse. "We should probably wait for them," said John. "I think there's a double portage or something after this, and A-hole has the map."

"Old 'Red,'" I said. "Wait, what's his last name again? O'Day? I know it's something Irish."

"Walsh," said John. "A-hole Walsh. I like O'Day. Hard to believe he's related to my mother."

"Red O'Day, then."

On its north end, the lake terminated in a fast flowing creek, next to which was a wide clearing which had to be our portage. We pulled the canoe up onto the sand and got out to see the river.

"Hear that?" said John.

"Rapids?"

"Yeah, and I'm betting on a waterfall."

John headed along the bank and into the woods. I waited with the canoe for Tom. And for Red O'Day.

19.

Though it was not large, it was definitely a waterfall,

about a ten foot drop. The pool beneath it looked deep, with the breadth of an acre or two.

The water was clear and sparkling and bluegreen in the sunlight, making this canopied area in the forest the sweetest spot on our trip. The shade, the falls, the wet, cool air near the cascade, and the natural intrigue of a deep pool all combined to invite a longer stay, in spite of the fact that we were at least a day behind schedule and all but out of food.

Canadian Waters supposedly supplied us with two weeks worth. And we should have had more than enough since we supplemented their food supply with plenty of fish. But no one eats more than an 18 year old male, and there were three of those on this trip. Canadian Waters simply miscalculated.

"Looks like walleye heaven," said Tom.

He had to raise his voice, with the falls just to our right and behind some trees. Without discussing it, John, Tom and I started digging in the shared tackle box for walleye lures. Most of what we had were Rapalas, spoons, and spinners.

"Tom, would you set up one of those for me?" said Pat.

"You want to fish?" said Tom.

"When in Rome," said Pat. "And this is the most excited I've seen the three of you."

Tom and I were already tying Countdown Rapalas to our line, and John, a Mepps Spinner. The place was ideal for predatory fish to migrate from the lake and stage in the pool to feed on any prey that are temporarily stunned after spilling over the falls.

"Here's your bait, Pat," said Tom. He held up a diving Creek Chub, a large and clownish looking plug we could afford to lose from our supply of tackle. A beginner like Pat is apt to get a lure hopelessly snagged on the bottom or up in a tree, and our Rapalas were too precious. The Creek Chub's weight would also make it easier for a greenhorn to cast.

The water was clear enough that we could see fish following our lures back to the bank. We spread out and made long casts, targeting the farther reaches of the pool.

John caught the first fish, a plump, short smallmouth bass. I asked him where the fish hit.

"I threw towards the waterfall and let it sink," said John. "The current started pushing it downstream, and when I cranked the reel, it was already on."

Tom and I copied John's method. I felt a bump but didn't hook up, and then Tom had a good fish that took out line and jumped in the middle of the pool. He brought in a fat, sixteen inch smallmouth bass and let it go.

"We could have eaten that," I said.

"Let's target walleye," said Tom. "Not drag a bass all day."

I looked to our left where Pat seemed to be snagged. His rod was bowed like a capital C, and he was drawing it back toward his shoulder in a half hearted attempt to free it.

"Wait, Pat," said Tom. "You don't want to break it off." Tom turned toward us, rolling his eyes, which is when I saw Pat's rod quivering, his line veering off to the right.

"Fucker's got a fish," said John.

Pat was holding the rod at a 45 degree angle but doing little else. The fish, however, was racing across the width of the pool like a rainbow trout. Or a muskie. Or more likely, in these waters, a big northern pike, peeling off line like a roped bull.

"His drag is too loose," said John.

"What has he got?" I said.

"A seriously big fish," said Tom.

Tom stepped his way on top of rocks towards Pat. We hadn't brought a net–our biggest "forget" of the trip—so there was nothing for me to do but watch.

From where John and I stood, we could see Tom signaling to Pat to use the rod's stiffness to tire the fish and reel it in.

After another minute, Tom bent over, corralling the fish with his tennis shoes in the shallows, his hands held apart. And then he lifted it–a two foot long walleye—grasping it behind the head with both hands, before underhanding it onto shore.

John and I made our way over to where the fish was lying

on its side, splashing, flapping its tail.

"Is it a pike?" said Pat.

"*Walleye* pike," said Tom. "On a damned Creek Chub!"

"It's the biggest of the trip," I said. "How much, you think?"

"Seven pounds, give or take," said Tom.

"I'll get the pliers," said John.

"Congratulations, Pat," I said. "Is that the biggest you ever caught?"

"It's the only fish I ever caught."

John returned and handed Tom a pair of pliers for extracting the two treble hooks.

"Should get him back in the water," said John.

"No! What?" said Pat.

"I'll take your picture, Uncle Pat," said John, "but then you gotta release it."

"Since when?" said Pat. "And just when we could use the food."

"You don't keep a big fish like that," said John. "It's a female. It's a breeder. You kill her, you kill a million walleye fry."

"How do you know its sex?"

"The bigger fish are generally the females," I said.

"Tom?" said Pat.

"It is probably a female," said Tom. "She's already spawned out this late in the season."

"There's your million fry, then," said Pat. "She already planted them."

"But there's the other thing," said Tom. "You're not supposed to eat the bigger fish."

"You're kidding," said Pat.

"No, John's right about killing a female. But they also have, whatchamacallits, parasites. In their fat. I've seen it when cleaning them."

"Cut out the fat," said Pat.

"We can't drag that fucking thing behind the canoe all day," said John.

"We'll eat it right now," said Pat. "For lunch."

"We're behind, though," I said. "We really should get moving. We have to make it back by Sunday. I mean, what day is today?"

"I'll cook it," said Pat. "I'll cook it if you clean it, Tom."

"I can get you started," said Tom. "But I won't eat any if there are worms. Somebody make a fire, and then we'll get it ready for the grill."

"Good luck, " said John.

Tom took the heavy fish and his fillet knife to the flattest rock along the shore, and I went to the side of the falls to gather dead branches. John picked up his rod and went back to casting the waterfall.

It was midday. Routinely, for lunch, we hadn't done any cooking the entire trip, eating salami and summer sausage sandwiches the first several days, and then peanut butter and jelly till that ran out, too.

We were hungry, but Tom and John were standing by their breeder and worm theories, and I felt I had to go along. Though deep down, or not that deep down, we just didn't want to give Pat the satisfaction.

He had made the biggest catch with something that could feed all of us. And we probably could have scaled it and traveled with it in cold water, the way our visitors kept the fish they gave us. It's as though we were willing to punish ourselves in order to punish Pat.

I got a fire going in a clearing away from the waterfall and pulled the cooking grate out of the Duluth pack. Tom had finished cleaning Pat's walleye. He didn't spot any worms, but that didn't mean there weren't any, he said. He left the skin on both filets so they would stay whole and not fall through the grate into the fire.

"Where's Pat?" he said.

"Red O'Day, you mean? He's in the woods."

"Figures," said Tom. "What's Red O'Day?"

I explained the renaming as he placed the filets, skin side down, on the grate, perched on top of but safely distant from the flames (we had used all the flour). We both walked back to the waterfall to resume fishing.

We cast for another hour, but the few fish we spotted were gun shy, following our lures at a safe distance, too far to even threaten a strike. It's as if they were all on alert after the commotion of landing the walleye.

We returned to the fire, but Pat was nowhere in sight. A good portion of the walleye had been eaten. The rest was cooked and browned, the skin edge black, crispy, and curling.

"Goddam, that smells good," said Tom. He separated a sizable chunk with his hunting knife and blew on it before eating.

"It *is* good."

I unsheathed my knife and separated a chunk of the fillet.

"That's better than the lake trout," I said. "It doesn't even need salt."

We both cut off another piece. There were small bones which I picked out and tossed in the fire.

"Better take some, John," said Tom. "You don't know when you'll eat next."

Help yourselves, gentlemen." It was Pat who had just come out of the woods with the army shovel.

"It turned out pretty good, Pat," I said.

"Save whatever is left," said Pat.

"If we all want to get sick," said Tom. "Nothing worse than unrefrigerated fish. You get bacterial poisoning. One of my customers when I used to deliver newspapers at the hospital nearly died from coho that had been left out."

"What if you cook it again?" said Pat. "Seering, sterilizing, grilling it?"

"Knock yourself out," said John.

Tom and I ate our fill. Pat scooped up the rest and folded it into an empty bread bag.

We doused the fire and cleaned the site before portaging around the falls to the next lake for the sprint back to Ely.

Before getting into the canoes, Pat got out the map to review our course back. He said we had 40 miles yet to go. We had averaged between 7 and 10 miles a day, so far, and would have to nearly double that to make it back before sundown Sunday and catch our shuttle back to town.

A lot of nonstop paddling, and all we had left to eat was one can of Del Monte peas and half a bag of dehydrated onions.

20.

By this time in our journey, paddling was automatic, like breathing or walking, and we kept at it till nearly sundown: partly in an effort to make it back at the appointed time, but mainly because we knew there was no food left for supper, though none of us mentioned it.

We set up camp in the waning light on the southern end of Lake Kashapiwi. A pebbly but flat clearing right on the lakeshore, our site was also the threshold of one of our longest portages back into Agnes, which we intended to tackle first thing in the morning.

With no food and, therefore, nothing to do about dinner, we decided to take another bath in Canadian waters. Once again, Tom and John and I went first, jumping off a ledge where we knew the water was deep, while Pat watched from the clearing, wearing his sombrero, his substantial paunch sagging over the elastic waist of his briefs.

The lake was shockingly cold, and we soaped and rinsed and quickly climbed back out. We dried ourselves in the remnants of sun, and Pat stood on the ledge, reconnoitering about whether he should take the plunge.

When I went inside the tent and started putting my clothes back on, I heard John holler:

"Asshole! Jackoff! Shitbomb!"

I rushed back outside, prepared for the worst. What I saw were Tom and John standing together in the clearing, looking out on the water. Pat floating in the lake on his back, a smile on his face.

"What happened?" I said.

"What do you mean?" said John.

Tom turned around and waved me over. He kept his voice low.

"John was venting while Red O'Day was underwater."

*

A cool wind made the cook fire feel good. But our achy empty stomachs, along with having to watch Pat finish off the remaining portion of his walleye he had smuggled along, did not help the general mood.

In fifteen minutes, it would be dark. Pat stood up, pulled the folding shovel out of a Duluth pack, and headed up the portage trail.

"Does this mean he'll be available for the killer portage tomorrow?" said Tom.

"Fat chance," I said. "He's more than capable of working another one up by then"

"We don't have to haul his shit," said John.

"We already tried that," said Tom.

"We leave his shit, and we leave *him*, is what I mean," said John.

"You going to tie him up?" I said.

"That's Plan B," said John. "Plan A is kill 'em."

It was funny. Tom, I saw, thought so, too.

"I don't know," said Tom. " He outweighs you by, what, fifty or sixty pounds."

"I'd stick him like a pig ten times before he could raise his fist," said John, patting his scabbard. "But don't lie; you guys want him dead, too."

I thought I heard Pat up the hill. But there was a lot of wind.

"You could never do it," I said. "He's your uncle."

"Mom would cry," said Tom. "Her brother."

"Dad and Uncle Joe wouldn't mind," said John.

"Actually, you can probably commit the perfect crime up here in the wilderness," I said. "No witnesses."

"That's what I'm talkin' about," said John. "We tie him to a tree and leave him for the wolves. The bears. And whatever's left after that, for the racoons and crows. There wouldn't be a scrap of evidence."

"I like the part about letting the animals do our dirty work," said Tom. "But there'd be plenty of evidence: bones, pieces of rope. Hell, before any of that, some girl scouts could come paddling by, hear the fatass's screams, and untie him."

"But you know the girl scouts would have to kill him after a day," said John. "So we'd be off the hook."

"Tom's right," I said. "A smart killer doesn't leave anything to chance."

I offered that the three of us could hold Red O'Day under water, which would, at least, be bloodless. And then we weigh him down with boulders and sink him in a hundred feet of water in Basswood.

"And then?" said Tom.

"What?"

"What's our story when we get back to civilization?"

"Well, okay, that he drowned," I said. "Fell out of the canoe or something and never came back up. Or he woke up in the middle of the night to take a dump and never returned. We didn't know he was missing till morning."

"Or he went fishing by himself in the canoe," said John, "and something happened, and we retrieved the overturned canoe. But we say it happened on a different lake, not here.

That way, the search won't turn anything up."

"That's the beauty of being out in the bush with no one around," I said. "You can make up anything you want."

When Pat returned, we glanced at each other, keeping smiles out of our eyes.

He paused before putting the shovel back into the Duluth pack.

"You guys been drinking?" said Pat. "You look 'mellow'? Or maybe 'insouciant?' 'Bemused?'"

"Just musing," said Tom.

"About what?" said Pat.

"The best thing about the trip," said Tom.

"And what did everybody say?" said Pat, getting comfortable near the fire.

"Lots of things," said Tom. "Seeing the northern lights would have to be at the top of my list."

"For me, it was a bunch of firsts," I said. "First lake trout. First time camping. First bear sighting."

"And I'd have to say catching my first fish," said Pat. "The biggest of the trip. I hope those photos turn out."

Pat looked at John.

"Me? We still have a couple or three days," said John. "I'll wait to see what else happens before naming my highlight."

21.

A cold rain fell during the night, and my sleeping bag was wet. Water may have seeped through the canvas. The shoes we propped up for drying against the firepit were waterlogged.

We were out of coffee, but Tom had sifted and saved the grounds from the morning before. With no other food for breakfast, I climbed a four foot boulder to fish for smallmouth that we might grill to fill our bellies. But a cold north wind was blowing, and I couldn't get any distance.

John came over with his spinning reel and was able to sidearm a beetle spin about ten yards or so and quickly caught a rock bass that was feeding on forage blown up against the bank.

I took it off his lure and dropped down to clean it, and he soon caught another. We had a little assembly line going until they stopped biting after John caught the fifth. They're small and thin and not a lot of meat, but enough for some sustenance, and it was probably the first time anyone ever had rock bass and dehydrated onions for breakfast.

We had a lot of miles ahead of us and packed quickly, but we may just as well have taken our time, since Tom and John were nearly swamped as soon as they paddled out into the open, as a gust of wind turned the canoe broadside to the whitecaps. They returned immediately, pulling the canoe up on shore.

We regretted not going an extra two miles to cross the formidable expanse of Agnes last night, since now it seemed unlikely that the wind would diminish any time before sundown.

"This calls for drastic measures," said John.

"We'll just have to hunker down and wait till it passes," said Pat.

A discussion followed in which John suggested we set fire to one of the small islands out front to attract a ranger plane. Pat, the only one of us with a previous Quetico trip under his belt, insisted we should wait. If we were late by more than a day, he pointed out, they'll send someone looking for us. No need to start a forest fire, he said.

John scoffed, shaking his head, razzing Pat for his lack of imagination. He pointed to the second closest island which would be no threat to the national forest if set on fire.

"There may be another way," I said.

I described a passage in Nute's book about how the Voyageurs would lash their canoes together for travel in rough conditions, essentially fashioning an uncapsizable catamaran.

"We could use the tent poles to lash ours together," John offered.

Pat and Tom were skeptical as we lined up the canoes in

parallel positions. We laid one of the tent poles across the top and slightly ahead of the stern seat, tethering it with rope to each canoe's rear thwart. Then we laid the second pole over the bow thwarts, tying it securely.

I gripped the poles, shaking them to make certain they were tightly fastened.

"Should be ready," I said.

We took up positions on the seat cushions–John and I in the bow of each canoe, and Pat and Tom in each stern.

Shoving off, I thought it felt pretty good. Balanced. But then the first wave hit the bow, water rushing and sloshing up between the canoes, soaking John and me, and filling the floor.

"Back, go back!" said Tom. "Go left. Everyone left." We barely managed to get the twin vessel back around, a wave hitting us broadside and inundating us with yet more water before we straightened out and nosed up onto shore. "That was fucked," said Tom.

"I don't get it," I said. "The fur traders didn't ship water like that. Maybe since their canoes were longer with higher sidewalls? And they lashed them together several times throughout the book."

"The water gushed up between the two canoes and came inside," said John. "Maybe if you tied them farther apart, the water would have someplace to go besides into the boats."

That made sense. The two canoes together were like two hands clapping the water between them, the spillage pouring into each vessel.

I was willing to try again. And Tom and Pat seemed more amenable after our first run.

After tipping and emptying the canoes of water, we lined them up parallel again, but this time a good three feet apart. Though the tent poles didn't quite reach all the way across each canoe, there was sufficient length to tie each pole end securely enough.

We took our same positions. John shot me a grimace from his bow seat, bracing for what might prove to be another cold bath. The canoes wouldn't budge until Tom stepped out to push us off the rocks before hopping back into the stern.

I thrust my paddle in, pulling hard, as we drove straight into the oncoming waves. The first one hit, then rumbled beneath us, bouncing our catamaran up and down. But there was no sideways roll. Stable.

John and I trained our eyes on the three feet of water between us, which rose and crested, rose and crested, but stayed out of the canoes.

"Did the wind lay down, or am I imagining?" said Pat. I looked ahead onto the main lake, whitecaps like cake frosting. Looking to the left, I was able to gauge a wave height between two and three feet, sometimes more. But we were moving steadily into it, picking up speed but keeping dry.

"It's still blowing a gale," I shouted. "But John's adjustment did the trick."

"Well, Ja-heesus," said Tom. "Let's get the gear and save our strength for the crossing."

After turning around, the canoes remaining level, we scraped up onto shore. We loaded quickly, eager to see how our more heavily weighted rig would respond. Tom pushed us off again, and I paddled hard, feeling the resistance of both vessels in the water. Our "catamaran" kept a straight course in spite of the headseas, and we paddled together with pace, making good progress, plowing ahead like a rectangular barge with a paddler at each of the four corners.

I worried that the four of us paddling in such close proximity would breed more contempt. But everyone was civil on the long ride across angry Agnes.

We were canoe hardened at this stage of the journey. I paddled aggressive and steady for what seemed a couple of hours and was able to rest for several minutes while the other three continued. Each of the others could rest or coast when needed without our veering off course or losing momentum with the canoes lashed together.

The paddle across Agnes was of greater distance on the return leg of our journey, since we had to make it to Agnes's southeastern end where there was a portage that led directly to

Basswood Lake.

"We would have lost another full day waiting for the wind to let up," said Tom.

"There would have been an advantage to that," said Pat.

"How?" said John.

"I'll be asking Canadian Waters for a refund for every day we were without food. They were supposed to outfit us for fourteen days."

"That's true," said Tom. "And if we didn't have half a dozen meals of fish, we would have run out even sooner. Speaking of which, we should probably troll the rest of the way."

And we did. From his stern position, Tom let out a gold and black, four inch sinking Rapala. Our catamaran stayed on course without his paddle in the water, and it wasn't long before there was a bend in his rod–a severe bend– suggesting a good northern. It turned out, however, to be a lake trout, well over three pounds, which elevated our mood already buoyed by our improvisational success with the canoes.

Likely just one more night camped in Quetico, and we might, indeed, end on a high note.

Tom hooked another smaller laker, so we tore through fresh lake trout smothered in dehydrated onions that night. After eating, we disassembled our catamaran since we needed the limbs to build the tent. We went to bed, spent, at dark.

22.

I woke up and something was wrong.

I saw light through the tent, but it could not already be morning. You can tell when you've only been asleep for an hour or two. A noise, or, quite possibly, the light was what roused me.

My heavy bones didn't want to move from inside the sleeping bag, and I closed my eyes. But then I found the zipper, opened the bag halfway, and sat up.

Nobody else was in the tent.

I called out, but, strangely, only air rushed from my throat. No sound.

It was cold, and I pulled on my pants and socks inside the sleeping bag. The rest of my clothes. I tied my shoes. And then I stood up.

What I first saw when I exited was moonlight shimmering on the lake, flickering through the black branches of the trees.

But it was still night, and the second thing I saw was to my left: a mound of embers in our campfire, glowing orange. And there was Tom holding a stick in the embers and staring back at me.

"Gonna need your help," said Tom.

"What's wrong?" I struggled to say. "Where's John?"

"He's down by the lake." Sparks from stirring the embers lit up his teeth. A smile?

"What?"

"He's by the water, washing up."

I turned and walked toward the lake, shuffling in the semi dark, trying not to slip on the lichen covered rocks. John squatted on shore, splashing his hands in the water. He kept his back to me but knew I was behind him.

"It's true what they say about dead weight, McGrath."

I froze. He turned around.

"Come with me," he said.

John looked somehow bigger. A foot taller.

I did not want to follow, but he led me up the slope and behind the tent and into the woods. Was I sleepwalking? And there on the ground was what appeared to be a large man lying motionless against the base of a tree. Or possibly just a pile of wet clothes, the familiar tan suede shirt.

"He weighs a ton," said John. "I read this article in National Geographic. The theory about the weight of inert matter."

I did not see a face. All I could think of was that we had to get *rid of it. Drag it and carry it into the canoe to dump into the lake. But the moonlight was gone and we would have to wait till morning. So we returned to the tent to go back to sleep.*

Tom and John fell asleep almost immediately, whereas, I lay thinking how we must disappear all the evidence in the morning. We must wake early and lash the canoes together again, for how else could we three reverse our course and transport Red O'Day's remains from Basswood back to Agnes. I did not know why but was somehow certain that he would float here, and would sink only in Agnes's darkest depths.

But I must have finally dozed, since I was awakened when Tom got up and I heard him get the shovel. The dread filling my chest felt like a jagged, rusty piece of iron. It was all my idea.

I waited for Tom, my heart beating as though I had just carried the canoe up a steep portage. We had to tell the same story. Or maybe we could leave the body, not touch it, not waste another day going back to Agnes, as long as we all agreed it was some sort of accident. A tragic drowning.

I heard Tom's feet on the gravel; the beam of his flashlight penetrated the wall of the tent.

I sat up when he came in.

"Where's John?" I asked.

He trained the flashlight on the bundled figure against the far wall.

"Right there," Tom said quietly. "Next to Pat."

23.

Our last day of the trip was sunny and long-sleeve cool, but sufficiently calm so that Basswood on the other end of the portage ought not be a problem to navigate.

We found half a package of dried apricots in an outside packet of a Duluth pack which Tom boiled in water, and we each had a mug of hot and sweetened "breakfast" before getting to work.

The portage was long, but we were quiet and emotional and relieved–at least, I was–and got the canoes and remaining gear into

Basswood Lake in record time, especially since Pat skipped his morning "constitutional" and lent a hand.

Though measurably as vast as Agnes, and just as deep in the main channel, Basswood had a radically different character, polka dotted with many low lying islands and rimmed with weedy bays.

Studying the map earlier, Pat had calculated that we would arrive at the Fall Lake takeout well before the appointed pickup time. Since there was no sense in having to wait a couple of hours on the other end, still without food or drink, we paddled close to shore, on the lookout for fishy points and weedy bars for a last chance at a trophy.

"Did you have a nightmare or something last night?" asked Tom.

He was in the stern. I didn't turn around.

"I came back from the shitter, and you were acting weird," he said. "Like something happened to John?"

"Well, yeah. I guess…I dreamt that we drowned Pat."

"Ha! Your hidden desire."

"Maybe I'm a psycho."

"You're not mental if your dream means that Pat's not who you want on the next trip."

"That's a relief. Who would be the replacement?"

"Wait a minute," said Tom. "Let's go to the front of that island. Uh, maybe two replacements."

"Two?"

"You want John along–he's plenty reliable. But he himself might opt out. He's not an addict."

Like you?"

"Like us."

*

I was still feeling aftershocks from the dream. And I felt like a sinner when I looked at Red O'Day. Maybe I'd tell John later, and he'd have a laugh. Though things were going well, so maybe I wouldn't.

Basswood Lake's habitat, similar to some lakes we fished in Michigan as kids, was right in our wheelhouse. Tom steered us within casting distance of the partially submerged island with a cluster of reeds on one end, in front of which I tossed a 5 inch gold floating Rapala. As I switched the rod into my left hand in order to reel with my right, the water exploded in the landing spot, and the Rapala disappeared .

By the time I took control and yanked back with the rod, I felt nothing.

"What happened?" said Tom.

"It's gone," I said. "A bust off."

"Northern," said Tom. I've said it before: we'll have to bring steel leaders if we're ever up here again."

Still within range, Tom quietly rested his paddle across the gunwales and reached for his own rod.

When I cranked in what was left of my line, I saw that the terminal end curled, which told me it wasn't a northern's sharp teeth that had severed the line, but that my clinch knot had somehow come undone. Or was poorly tied so that the torque from the fish strike pried the Rapala loose.

"Fish!" said Tom. "Did you see that?" He was standing in the canoe, something we didn't dare when we started out, but which by now was second nature. I followed the arc of his rod to the line and down into the water where it was zinging away to the left of the reeds. And then came the snarl of his drag from the strain of a strong fish.

He played it hard and fast, applying sidearm pressure, and grabbed the fish by the lower jaw when he saw it was a bass.

"A largemouth!" I said, as he held it up.

"It's got the gaping mouth," said Tom, his chest heaving after the fight. "But look at the bronze color. It's a huge smallmouth. Should I keep it?"

"You can," I said.

"Na, we'll take a picture," he said, sitting down. "We'll be in town tonight."

After I waved Pat and John over, Tom held up the fish.

"Jee-sus!" said John. "Bigger than Pat's."

"Mine was longer," said Pat. "That, though I admit, is probably heavier. Girthier. More solid."

"Take a picture?" said Tom.

"I'm out of film," said Pat.

"Kee-ryest! The biggest smallmouth I'll probably ever catch."

He lifted it over the side of the canoe and placed it in the water. Still holding its jaw. We watched, mesmerized, as he moved it back and forth, back and forth, passing water through its gills, making sure of its revival before letting go. Probably holding it longer than was needed, though none of us seemed to mind, its black back shining in the sun. And then Tom's hand bumped up above the water, and the thing of beauty swam away.

24.

On the south side of the next cluster of islands, we saw several buildings along shore: cabins, sheds, docks.

Two weeks in the bush, I felt funny about rejoining the world: washing, getting dressed, putting on deodorant. Relieved in many ways for the ending, as everything I needed to catch up on back home started clustering in my head. But already missing the beguiling world of woods and water and quietude which we left, and longing to be folded back in again, though not wanting to actively return. If that makes any sense.

I wasn't sure which of two channels to follow, though the others seemed to know to take the first right turn into a narrow bay of Fall Lake where I was able to make out a pier in the farthest corner. As if to underscore their certainty, nobody said a word: long pulls of the paddle, the canoes skimming hard.

A dark haired kid our age with a red headband was smoking

on the pier, the Canadian Waters van parked up on the hill. Improbably, we must be right on time.

"Are you the Walsh party?"

"It was no party, pal," said John, holding his paddle above the water as the canoe coasted in.

"No?" said the kid.

"Nah, it was great," said Tom. "We're just really glad to see you. Gotta another one of those?"

As soon as the canoes hit the sand, Tom and John bounded up onto the dock, huddling around the kid who held out his pack of Winstons. Tom leaned in for a light and took a long drag, as John cupped his hands around the kid's lighter to fire up his.

I didn't plan on starting up again, but I gave in as soon as I joined them. The four of us smoked on the wooden dock while Tom summarized our adventures. I thought how the kid must have heard all of this a million times in his capacity as a pack mule for the outfitters. But Tom was dramatizing highlights of our saga as episodes you didn't want to miss, and the kid seemed genuinely interested.

Pat stood in the sand by the canoes, inventorying the contents of all his pockets, a slight smile when he looked over. "All you reformed smokers," said Pat. "Not two minutes back in the world, and you revert to evil ways."

For a brief moment, I saw us through Pat's eyes. How we were unformed, unreliable, irresponsible, all due to age. How he used it, believed it, to excuse himself. How he didn't know us, or we, him, in spite of a two week cram course in character.

We transferred all the gear to the van. The driver asked us to turn the canoes over since he didn't have the trailer and would have to pick them up the next day.

It was a short ride, but we managed to have another cigarette on the way. The first Winston tasted good, the second not so much, and I already made a mental note about quitting again, once I got settled back home.

We drove into an alley behind the CW warehouse, where we

emptied our personal gear from the Duluth packs and stuffed it back in our suitcases which we found in a storage room.

CW wasn't yet closed, so we walked through the salesroom and out the front door to wait for Pat, who had gone into the manager's office.

John went to the cafe down the block, and he brought back three packs of Winstons for himself and Tom and the kid, and a flip top box of Marlboros for me. I told him I'd pay him when Pat emerged from the office with the refund.

We were all lit up again, when Pat joined us outside, celebration on his face.

"A full refund for the last three days!" said Pat. "The whole rate, not just food. This is why I'm a repeat customer."

I waited for him to take out his wallet. Instead, he said we had to check in at the motel we had reserved for the night and to use the outdoor sauna before we went out for supper. He said the sauna would leech out all the dirt and insect bites from living outdoors for two weeks.

But after we checked in and parked our suitcases, it was nearly seven, and we decided we'd better eat before everything closed.

We headed for the same supper club we visited at the start of the trip, but apparently it was closed on Sundays; so we hurried back to the cafe where John bought the cigarettes. It, too, was ready to close, but the waitress who was also the owner with her husband, the chef, said she would take our orders.

It was a country cafe that didn't serve liquor, so we three ordered cheeseburgers, fries, and a cup of split pea soup, and Pat had the meatloaf and gravy special with string beans and an iced tea.

When the waitress brought the check, I announced I was out of money, as a reminder to Pat to fork over some of the refund. Instead, he picked up the check and said dinner was "compliments of Canadian Waters."

25.

A sauna was something foreign to me, and I would have not tolerated it by myself because of the claustrophobic atmosphere inside. A fire in a wood stove heated a pile of rocks so that the large thermometer on the wall registered just under 200 degrees.

I had never felt so hot and weak and depleted, and I trusted Pat's assurance that this was a healthful exercise, and that the Swedes lived to be a hundred since they took a sauna every day and then dove into a frozen lake right after, having sawn a hole in the ice ahead of time.

Pat filled a bucket with cold water from the spigot inside the building and poured it over the rocks, filling the wooden shack with steam and surprisingly breathable air. The super heated moisture did not feel especially good, but I accepted that it was healthful and tried to feel its penetration.

We were in our swim trunks, and John went down to the floor and did twenty push-ups, coughing when he stood back up, then explaining how he read that you get ten times the benefit from exercise when you do it in a sauna. I got on the floor myself and thought about staying there where it was cooler and the air tasted better.

A timer went off which Pat had set for twenty minutes, and the three of us went outside into the night air, Pat saying he wanted to "soak" another five minutes.

A thermometer resembling a clock on the outside wall of the shack showed 55 degrees in Ely, but I still felt hot standing outside in swim trunks, waiting for the sweating to subside.

26.

It was still dark when we woke at the motel the next morning. Pat had not rented a car for the trip home and said we would have to skip breakfast and hurry to the Greyhound station to purchase tickets. He was first line, after which he turned to say that tickets to Chicago were $18.50. Tom and John looked at one another while they dug into their wallets, and I asked Tom if he had enough that he could lend me my fare.

It became clear that Pat was keeping the entire refund from the trip. He was probably entitled. He paid for the rental car, of course, as well as for the two nights in the motel room. While he could argue he owed me nothing, I had paid my share of the total amount to the outfitters. I had expected a portion of the refund, beyond Pat's generosity with the other expenses.
But another part of me knew my calculation was debatable.

Meanwhile, the trip was supposed to be a present for his nephews; and there wasn't any small print attached to the offer, as far as they knew, specifying that they had to fend for themselves once out of Quetico. The animosity that had developed over the past two weeks may have had something to do with Pat cutting them off.

The bus trip would take 12 hours. But after just three hours and one pit stop, I had already resolved that I would never take a Greyhound again.

Initially, I thought the problem was the bus: the straight backed, non adjustable seats; the nauseating diesel fumes; the mandatory stops.

Later, I thought it was annoyance from the other 50 or so people aboard: a crabbing toddler; inane conversations from people who did not know how to whisper; and being stuck in an aisle seat with a man who opted to keep the window shut, despite wearing clothes exuding the stench of b.o. and ass sweat.

Ultimately, I decided it was the psychology of imprisonment; being trapped, with no control or freedom, in the uninvited company of several dozen other unhappy inmates. Cattle in a box car.

While I was certain of my repulsion to Greyhound, I had yet to achieve full grasp of the "vacation" we had just concluded. Quetico was paradisiacal: The woods and waters and deep night sky. Morning woodsmoke. Mournful wail of the loon. Rivers, lakes, swamps, and forests untrammeled. But as powerfully and personally impactful as it all was, I assumed at 18 that it was merely one of an untold number of similar experiences I would be having.

One surprise was that I relished the work involved, the muscle strain, the exhaustion, the pain. I learned, if I didn't already suspect, that our bodies, still growing, ascended to a higher level with each test passed. The same high you get from long distance running or pumping iron.

What I wasn't sure about was group travel—that is, the others in your canoe in a literal journey, or others insinuated into your life. Of course, I was used to John and Tom. Vexations among ourselves weren't that different, though compressed in time, than those we three experienced through our earlier decade of acquaintance.

Red O'Day was a unique encounter. We began in admiration of the irresponsible renegade, an anomalous adult still possessed of the attributes we prized, or which we thought we prized: namely, his independent thinking that flouted our parents' ideals of a steady job, a weekly schedule, a nuclear family, and a secure future. Unlike them, but like us, he believed life was not a competition of materialistic acquisition, but a series of opportunities for having fun and being awed, especially in the outdoors.

And then, in just several days, we made a 180 degree turn, embracing the perspective of their father and their other uncle in condemnation of many of those attributes.

We became the grownups intolerant of his habits, his absence of consideration, his beatnik beliefs. And not in any objective or detached way. We did, after all, discuss murder.

And just as I was wondering whether it was Pat, representing the adult world that J.D. Salinger's Holden Caulfield and now we three perceived as disappointment and betrayal, or just our youthful and naive selves, having been beguiled by adventure, but then growing up after an toilsome journey in a canoe–just as I was pondering all that, I started to feel hypocritical.

Did the test in Quetico expose a flawed adult in Red O'Day, or the flaws in us?

Had I been as blind to the realities of human behavior, as I was to the Northern Lights.

I was just starting college. Just starting to drive. Not yet started to date.

Forgiving myself for having no answers, I fell asleep on the bus.

Epilog

No relief from Greyhound's unending agony till the bus's front doors snapped open, and I felt Canal Street's concrete beneath my feet.

Nearly 8pm, it was still light in downtown Chicago, and Tom's father's station wagon was parked and waiting at the curb.

Their sister Nancy, the oldest in the family, was running toward us. She hugged her brothers and her uncle and would have hugged me, too, had I not shied away. She was 21 and pretty, and I was musty from forced proximity to my inmate on the prison bus.

"You guys are so brown," she said.

"Living outside for two weeks," said Tom.

"And you didn't even scratch each other's eyes out on the bus," she said.

When Tom phoned home to give our ETA, he must have hinted at some of the strife over the preceding days. But we were all smiles as we walked to the car to the sound of a taxi horn blaring, a locomotive engine revving, as Quetico felt like a faraway planet.

Mr. Booth rose from the driver's seat to open the trunk for our luggage, and Mrs. Booth rolled down the passenger side window.

"How was it?" she said.

"Trip of a lifetime," said Tom.

"I can't wait to hear everything. But you boys must be starving."

"Not that much," said John. "Uncle Pat bought us dinner at a truck stop in Rockford."

"Chicken pot pies, Veronica, " said Pat. "Remember those? Hadn't had one in a coon's age."

Rockford had been our last stop, and Pat had taken a seat at the lunch counter. Tom and John and I had stayed back, lingering around the entrance way, browsing maps and postcards on a revolving stand. After Pat walked back over and asked why we weren't eating, Tom held his arms out, palms up, and said we were completely out of money.

"Why didn't you say something?" said Pat, and he bid us to follow him back to the lunch counter so he could pay for our meal.

There were seven of us in Booth 's station wagon for the ride back to Evergreen Park, and Tom did most of the talking about the fishing, wildlife sightings, running out of food, hauling gear and canoes over portages, and traversing the treacherous Agnes with our canoes lashed together. Red O'Day inserted jocular commentary, slipping easily into "wise uncle" mode, gently confiding to his sister about his nephews' insatiable hunger, our moodiness, and our lapses in maturity, by which he was never surprised, he pretended, in consideration of our youth and our nicotine withdrawal.

In Shakespeare's *The Tempest,* the shipwrecked characters reinvent themselves because of different circumstances in a different place.

Back in the real world, or the unreal world, they assumed their original roles.

Did that happen with us?

Though I couldn't see everyone in the dark from my quiet corner in the third row seat of the station wagon, I imagined Tom and John giving meaningful looks to their parents, and that the real story would come out later. But the more they talked, the more I wondered if I had had it all wrong.

*

Things returned to normal back home. John and I went back to work at Jewel where I'd gotten a raise from $1.45 per hour to $1.50.

My sister Rosemary had submitted my paperwork for my first year of college, and I immediately had to retract the promise made to myself to stay off buses. Mercifully, the CTA commute to the local teachers college, including a transfer midway, was only an hour.

I became consumed with college, its freedoms compared to high school, the eccentricities of the professors, and the diversity of the student body in the city.

Quetico was becoming a distant memory. And then a month or so after our trip, Tom invited me and my parents over to see the photographs from our voyage.

Brilliant colors, the luminosity of the lakes under the sun, the boughs of towering spruce trees wind-bent on Agnes's shore–all enhanced by the backlight of Pat's slide projector–produced an ache in my chest, and goosebumps on my arm. As though I were watching a travel ad as a consumer.

Tom and John must have felt the same as they offered additional details to Pat's narration: the bear swimming between islands; the ranger plane we nearly forced into landing; the loons, the lake trout, moose tracks; food packs strung up in the trees; Canadian mosquitoes as big as flies; the ancient compass I found in the sand and eventually showed them; skinny dipping in ice water; the sauna in Ely.

"We have to remember to bring a landing net if we go again," said Tom.

"You say that now," said Pat.

"We would have caught twice as many fish," said Tom.

"I'm not talking about the net. About you saying you'd go again."

"I'd definitely go," said Tom. "Wouldn't you, David? All I could think about all during the bus ride were those fish."

"Yeah," I said. "Especially after seeing these slides. I want to go back *now.*"

"I went over in my mind every fish that we caught," said Tom. "Where we caught them. Why. How deep. Some real bulls we lost."

"What about the rest of the trip?" said Pat. He smiled, shaking his head, addressing our parents. "They were whistling a different tune on the trail. Wishing we had motor boats. Complaining about the distance. Too many portages. Too many different camp sites. Water is too cold. Too much of this. Too little of that."

"We've been through all that," said John. "Every night we were racing to make camp before dark. We all agreed, we would have been better off with a single base camp for 4 or 5 days. More fishing, more exploring, more relaxing."

"What I think happened, Veronica," said Pat, ignoring John, "is that they quit smoking on Day 1 and were unhappy campers till they got back to Ely and could start smoking again."

"Is that true, Tom?" said Mr. Booth. His tight smile indecipherable.

"Well, I'll admit it was a bad time to quit," said Tom. "I think we adjusted, though. I really didn't miss it that much. Till we got back."

Back home, before I went to bed, I pulled out the vouchers, the dehydrated onion paper, and a torn section of cardboard from the beer carton, on which I had written our trip log, and I read it while having my last cigarette of the day.

I expected, of course, it would not be as radiant a record as Pat's slide show. But what I was really looking for was evidence of what had apparently become unmentionable about the trip: the impatience; intolerance; anger. Even the threshold of violence.

Certainly there should have been hints of the vitriol. Subliminal murmurings of our homicidal contemplation. But there was nothing. Nada. No verbal winks. No jokes. No obvious omissions. No prompts for reading between the lines.

The log was filtered. Just as Pat's slide show narration was filtered. And what we told our parents was filtered. And whether the catalyst for filtering was shame, amnesia, denial, delusion, maturity, or some sort of fear, I did not know. But because I wrote it down, I'm able to examine it now with the wisdom of age.

And what I believe is what astute readers already know: We began as brash teens wearing Bowie knives on our belts and harboring a dream to blaze a trail through the dangerous bush country in memorable and heroic fashion. We emerged from the woods as men who had had a taste of fear, hardship, resentment, disgust, loneliness, evil, and awe, and a fourteen day dose of truth about human foibles, limitations, and weaknesses, most notably our own.

It's a familiar story about coming of age during a literal and symbolic journey, with one major difference which I'm now able to explain after the passing of half a century:

In the years following the trip, Red O'Day moved to Texas, and John to Mississippi, after which I lost touch with both.

Tom stayed in the midwest, and I moved to Florida. But the two of us remain connected.

Since 1967, he and I have gone on hundreds of trips together in the outdoors. We've capsized in rivers, been lost in the woods, survived treacherous seas, weathered storms, braved temperatures of twenty-five below, escaped boiling whirlpools in a dam's tailwaters, and floundered our way back to shore in fog or darkness on more nights than I can remember.

We do it for the awe, the peace, the exhilaration, and the inspiration from nature that's optimally derived with one another because of our mutual trust, no matter what confronts us on land or sea.

A trust that could not have been foretold but was long ago forged in Quetico.

***

-His Intimacies with Lake and Stream

In Florida, if you're lucky to be the first who wakes up, you are treated to a private welcoming by the still salt air, the plum-colored light.

My two younger brothers remained asleep in our motel room at Lauderdale-by-the-Sea. No sound from my parents and sisters next door.

We had arrived late the night before, after two endless days and over 1,300 miles on U.S. 41 in my father's green '63 Pontiac station wagon. This was my family's first visit to the Sunshine State — its nickname in white letters on every blue license plate in the motel lot — and it was time to rouse Kenneth, 12, and Pat, 11, to join me for reconnaissance. I was 13 years old.

Palm trees, snowy egrets, pink houses with clay-tile roofs: It was all alien to three boys from Chicago. The focus of our search turned up just a block away. A place to fish: a length of canal with no houses in front, its dark surface boiling with concentric circles and bulges from creatures below.

Suddenly a fish resembling a bowling pin launched a foot into the air before crashing back into the water. We looked at one another open-mouthed and sprinted back to the motel for our rods. After a slight detour to a 7-Eleven, where we bought a box of Mrs. Paul's frozen shrimp for bait, we returned to the canal and set up on the bank. Almost immediately, we caught several fish that looked like bream but hurt to handle, like grabbing a fistful of briars.

When I cranked in one catfish with lethal-looking fins, and Kenneth balked at landing a very unhappy "sea serpent," which we later learned was a skate, we sent Pat to fetch our father for help. Dad was our mentor in all things piscatorial.

And our obsession to fish wherever we traveled was, for better or worse, implanted by the old man.

It was not any plan on his part. A traveling salesman who'd grown up in a city apartment, Charlie McGrath never even held a rod till he met my mother in 1939 and accepted an offer he could hardly refuse from her father, Joe Cichoszewski, to soak some earthworms off a muddy creek bank for bullheads and sunfish near their country cabin in Beaverville, Illinois.

He liked it well enough that the two went again, dropping baited hooks over the seawall on Chicago's lakefront, Dad going so far as to propose marriage to my mother — though he swore that the jumbo perch he and Joe caught, so big they resembled lunker bass, had not figured in his decision.

Not long after the wedding, the fish and fun came to an abrupt halt when Dad left town to serve as an anti-aircraft artillery officer in World War II. When after four years he finally came home, he had to find work, along with a place where my mother and he could raise children — eight of them, eventually.

But Dad never forgot the pleasures of fishing. When he finally earned enough money working for his uncle at Consolidated Tile, he rented a housekeeping cabin on a lake up north in summer, for the two weeks of annual vacation from the company.

That first summer at a lakeside resort in Spooner, Wisconsin, he taught all of us — my five brothers, two sisters and me — the rudiments of angling. He had rigged fiberglass rods and Sears bait-casting reels for himself and my two older brothers. For the rest of us, he provided cane poles with black, braided line and split shot above a steel leader and J hook, with which we spent hours on the dock snaring bluegill, perch and bullhead.

Every morning at sunrise, he took my two older brothers in the rowboat to a secret spot out on the lake. The early hour, the darkness, the chill — I was considered too young and would have to wait until next year. Which drove me insane.

Mid-morning, I would stand on the dock and peer across the water for their vessel. I tried to imagine what it might be like to fish out of the boat over unfathomable depths. Each night, I would fall asleep and dream of the giant, exotic fish teeming below.

The three finally returned around lunchtime with a stringer of fish that Jimmy needed to hoist with both hands. It included several bass, an alligator-like pike and bluegill five times larger than those we caught off the dock.

The commotion, excitement and Charlie, Jr.'s ceremonial gutting and scaling in the fish-cleaning shed, somehow made me despair about ever ascending to their lofty rank.

Then, after another night of deep-sea dreams, I awakened in the semidarkness, and Dad was standing beside my bed.

"Ready?"

I can still hear his gravelly whisper. And I remember how hard I tried to stifle my shivering as he rowed us out onto the misty lake — Charlie Jr. manning the anchor at the bow, and Jimmy and I sharing the transom seat.

My father had his own way of rowing: first the left oar, then the right, instead of both at once. The squeaking of the oarlocks was rhythmic, like a metronome. And I would have liked for the music to continue the entire breadth of the lake. But when he paused, looked around and whispered for Charlie to drop the anchor, I could sense his intimacy with the lake and the creatures below.

He showed me how to release the Sears clicker while using two fingers to slow the line as the spool unwound — the weighted rig with the succulent bait falling to the bottom.

He explained how I must "see" underwater through my hands and my head: A single tick in the handle might be a cautious bluegill. A series of vibrations, likely a perch going at the red worm like a woodpecker. A jolt was a big fish, a hit-and-run bass, so hang on.

But after all that, at the first bite, I dropped the rod on the floorboards, so startling was the sensation of a live creature agitating from 15 feet down. And I remember my father's deep laugh, after which he picked up my rod and showed me how to take up the slack and reel the fish home.

What I learned that morning, but which I could not articulate at the time, was that our journey in the boat was not just for fishing. It was about the allure of nature and the unknown. The closeness among four "men" sharing a mission. Each individual's discoveries became everyone's. Each accomplishment a matter of pride for all.

Though I could not have known it at the time, the last fishing trip I would take with my father happened one fall when

I was not working because of a teachers strike. When I called and asked if he wanted to join me for a road trip to Wisconsin, he agreed without hesitation, saying it was about time he broke in the new rod and reel he received as a retirement gift from the Calgon Corporation, for which he had been a regional sales manager.

"You take care of the car and gas, and I'll handle food and lodging," he said, trying to make it sound like a fair split. I did not argue.

I did worry, however. Not about money, the stoppage of my paychecks notwithstanding; but about how the two of us would get along. For as we got closer to our departure date, I realized we had not been alone together in years. Certainly, we saw each other plenty: birthdays, barbecues, Sunday visits.

And since childhood, I had become even more immersed in fishing, participating in tournaments and writing stories for outdoor magazines. I built a cabin on a 2,000-acre lake, and he and Mom would drive up in the summer so they could fish with their three grandchildren, the way he did with me.

But the prospect of being his partner around the clock, with no wives or children around, gave me pause. Whether in the car or the boat or the cabin, would we be compatible? Would we have enough to talk about?

Would he tire of my company, or vice versa?

My fears vanished after we walked through the door of a café in Cornell, Wisconsin, when we stopped for breakfast.

We were welcomed by the abrupt hush with which townies often welcome tourists. And I was apprehensive since my father had this big, booming voice to match his frame.

Whereas the café was tiny, crowded with farm antiques in every corner and on wall shelves, and miniature serving tables nearly touching one another. Like a dollhouse.

"Table or booth?" asked the host.

"Wherever all this will fit," said my father, his palms held out.

"Wait till you try to get into the bathroom," said another big man seated across the room, gesturing toward the narrow door. Laughter jingled. Conversations resumed.

My father was no comic, but wherever we went those few days, he managed to make people feel comfortable. Including me. It was with good reason that he was among the top salesmen at his company all those years.

Our first morning, however, was a mistake. I took him muskie fishing on Moose Lake, casting big plugs and spinners almost until noon. A lone, wary fish followed my bucktail but turned away boat-side. My father had tried to remain enthusiastic, but the hours of standing and casting took their toll.

The second morning, we stopped along the county road where a sign said "Nitecrawlers — Self Serve," and left two dollars for one of the plastic tubs we took out of a fridge next to the garage.

I knew of a secret, deep pool where we might catch some walleye. It was drizzling at the boat launch, but Dad said he had a windbreaker with a hood that ought to keep him dry.

After anchoring, we cast slip sinker rigs toward the hole and tightened our lines. The river wasn't more than 50 feet wide, and we sat inside a tunnel of trees, the leaves all scarlet and yellow. We could hear water flowing from rapids around the bend.

My rod shaft banged against the gunnel, and I took up the slack and set the hook: A smallmouth bass, a two-pound jackhammer, surrendered finally to the net.

Before I could remove the hook, my father had one of his own. His fish made a desperate dash beneath the boat. And just as my father guided it into the net, it twisted and splashed him in the chest and face, and his booming laugh echoed through the woods.

The rain picked up, and the bite got stronger. It was like fishing on a near-shore reef when your shrimp never makes it to the bottom.

"Are you cold, Dad?"

The windbreaker was saturated, but my father couldn't stop smiling, his eyes beaming like headlights with each strike. He hastened to extract the hook from each fish so he could hurry his rig back into the hole.

After catching and releasing several dozen hungry, angry smallmouth, we finally headed back to the cabin. I helped Dad out of the boat, and we turned the heater on high for the ride home.

"Boy, that was something," he said, still shivering.

My thoughts as well. For the indescribable "something" included not just the bass feeding frenzy, but what felt like a spell cast by the river: sharing wonder and beauty and the unspoken bond between father and son.

I can still see his eyes. And his pure joy in nature, which, I realized, he had bequeathed to all of us.

He's been gone over two decades. Still, some mornings I lie awake and hear those sounds: The rhythm of the oarlocks, thirsty for oil. The river murmuring. My father's rumbling laughter.

Fishing. And we are together again.

Notre Dame Magazine, July 7, 2021. Cited in THE BEST AMERICAN ESSAYS 2022.

***